# ANALYZING MEDIA MESSAGES

## Using Quantitative Content Analysis in Research

D1125304

**LEA COMMUNICATION SERIES**
Jennings Bryant/Dolf Zillmann, General Editors

Selected titles in Communication Theory and Methodology Subseries
(Jennings Bryant, series advisor) include:

**Berger** • *Planning Strategic Interaction: Attaining Goals Through Communicative Action*

**Dennis/Wartella** • *American Communication Research: The Remembered History*

**Greene** • *Message Production: Advances in Communication Theory*

**Hayes** • *Statistical Methods for Communication Science*

**Heath/Bryant** • *Human Communication Theory and Research: Concepts, Contexts, and Challenges, Second Edition*

**Reese/Gandy/Grant** • *Framing Public Life; Perspectives on Media and Our Understanding of the Social World*

**Salwen/Stacks** • *An Integrated Approach to Communication Theory and Research*

**Potter** • *An Analysis of Thinking and Research About Qualitative Methods*

For a complete list of titles in LEA's Communication Series, please contact Lawrence Erlbaum Associates, Publishers at www.erlbaum.com

# ANALYZING MEDIA MESSAGES

## Using Quantitative Content Analysis in Research

*Second Edition*

**Daniel Riffe**
*Ohio University*

**Stephen Lacy**
*Michigan State University*

**Frederick G. Fico**
*Michigan State University*

 LAWRENCE ERLBAUM ASSOCIATES, PUBLISHERS
2005    Mahwah, New Jersey                              London

Copyright © 2005 by Lawrence Erlbaum Associates, Inc.
All rights reserved. No part of this book may be reproduced in any
form, by photostat, microform, retrieval system, or any other means,
without prior written permission of the publisher.

Lawrence Erlbaum Associates, Inc., Publishers
10 Industrial Avenue
Mahwah, New Jersey  07430
www.erlbaum.com

Cover design by Kathryn Houghtaling Lacey

**Library of Congress Cataloging-in-Publication Data**

Riffe, Daniel
Analyzing media messages : using quantitative content analysis in research /
    Daniel Riffe, Stephen Lacy, Frederick G. Fico. — 2nd ed.

        p.  cm.  —  (LEA communication series)
    Includes bibliographical references and index.
ISBN 0-8058-5297-2 (cloth : alk. paper)
ISBN 0-8058-5298-0 (pbk. : alk. paper)
1. Content  analysis  (Communication).   2.  Mass  media—Research—
    Methodology. 3. Mass media—Statistical methods. I. Lacy, Stephen,
    1948–   II. Fico, Frederick.   III. Title.   IV. LEA's communication
    series.
P93.R54    2005
302.23'01'4—dc22                                               2004060652
                                                                     CIP

Books published by Lawrence Erlbaum Associates are printed on acid-free
paper, and their bindings are chosen for strength and durability.

Printed in the United States of America
10   9   8   7   6   5   4   3   2   1

*Daniel Riffe:*
For Florence, Ted, and Eliza

*Stephen Lacy:*
For I. P. Byrom, N. P. Davis, and A. G. Smith

*Fred Fico:*
For Beverly, Benjamin, and Faith

# Contents

# Preface

We have conducted or supervised hundreds of quantitative content analyses in our combined 60+ years as researchers, examining content ranging from White House coverage, to portrayal of women and minorities in advertising aimed at children, to environmental reporting and controversial issues in local news. The content analyses have included theses and dissertations, class projects, and funded studies and have involved content from sources as varied as newspapers, magazines, broadcast media, and World Wide Web sites. Some of the projects have been descriptive, whereas others have tested directional hypotheses or sought answers to specific research questions. Our inquiries have been framed in theory about processes that affect content and about the effects of content.

If conducting or supervising those content analyses has taught us anything, it is that some problems or issues are common to virtually all quantitative content analyses. Designing a study raises questions about sample size and technique, about measurement and reliability, and about data analysis that need resolving. These are fundamental questions that must be addressed whether the researcher is a student conducting her or his first content analysis or a veteran planning her or his 20th, whether the content being studied is words or images, whether it comes from an online source or a traditional source such as a newspaper, and whether the focus is news or entertainment or advertising.

In preparing this book and updating it for the second edition, we have tried to address these recurring questions that content analysis must address. Our goal was to make content analysis accessible, not arcane, and to produce a comprehensive guide that is also comprehensible. We hoped to accomplish the latter through clear, concrete language and by providing numerous examples—of recent and "classic" studies—to illustrate problems and solutions. We see the book as a primary text for courses in content analysis, a supplemental text for research methods courses, and a useful reference for fellow researchers in mass communication fields, political science, and other social and behavioral sciences.

In this book, we begin with an overview of the field of mass communication research, emphasizing the centrality of content analysis to that field and its applicability in other disciplines. We then develop a formal definition of content analysis, examining its terms to introduce important principles in measurement, data analysis, and inference. In chapter 3 (this volume), we describe the steps involved in designing a study, concluding with a series of questions that provide a model for conducting quantitative content analysis. With the stage set by those introductory chapters, in the remaining six we explore research issues in greater depth. These include measurement, or finding appropriate units of content and developing rules for assigning those units to categories; sampling, or selecting from all possible content only as much as is needed; reliability, or ensuring that individuals applying the study's coding rules obtain the same results; data analysis, or applying appropriate statistical techniques; validity, or the theoretical and practical significance of the study's findings; and technology, or the use of computers in content analysis.

We owe thanks to many for making this book possible: our friends at Lawrence Erlbaum Associates, Inc. who have worked patiently with us on the first and second editions of the book; teachers who taught us content analysis—Donald L. Shaw, Eugene F. Shaw, Wayne Danielson, James Tankard, G. Cleveland Wilhoit, and David Weaver—colleagues who provided suggestions on improving the book; and our students who taught us the most about teaching content analysis. Finally, our deepest appreciation goes to our families who often wonder whether we do anything but content analysis.

*—Daniel Riffe*
*—Stephen Lacey*
*—Frederick G. Fico*

# 1

# *Introduction*

Consider the rich diversity of focus of the following studies, all of them examples of quantitative content analysis across a five-decade period:

• In the late 1940s, researchers examined change in the international political system by looking at 60 years of editorials in five prestige world newspapers. Lasswell et al. found two concurrent trends in the editorials' language—reflecting increasing nationalism and growth of proletarian doctrines—that seemed to support their hypothesis that international social revolution had been brewing for some time (Lasswell, Lerner, & de sola Pool, 1952).

• Examining the first 5 hr of breaking news coverage on CNN, ABC, CBS, and NBC, researchers showed how the September 11 terrorism attack so jolted journalists that they abandoned traditional roles and standards, reporting personal thoughts and rumors and using anonymous sources (Reynolds & Barnett, 2003).

• Since 1997, the Project for Excellence in Journalism, a research organization underwritten by the Pew Charitable Trusts, has carried out a number of major studies of news coverage exploring the impact of ownership type on local television news as well as coverage of the war in Iraq and the war on terrorism, to name a few (see http://www.journalism.org/resources/research/reports). Similarly, "public," "civic," or "citizen-based" journalism has as its goal the revitalization of civic life; a number of studies have examined how efforts are manifested in print and broadcast news coverage (Massey & Haas, 2002).

• Analysis of photos of African Americans in *Life, Newsweek,* and *Time* during every 5th year chronicled the growing role of Blacks in all aspects of American society from the early to the late 20th century (Lester & Smith, 1990).

• Analyzing a probability sample of 2,696 U.S. newspaper articles drawn from a population of items identified by relevant key words, a study (Kerr & Moy, 2002) documented a consistent negative portrayal of fundamentalist Christians from 1980 until 2000.

• A study (Riffe, Goldson, Saxton, & Yu, 1989) of characters' roles in television advertising during Saturday morning children's programming reported a female and ethnic presence far smaller than those groups' presence in the real-world population as reflected in census data.

• A team of researchers (Pfau et al., 2004) analyzed whether embedded journalists covered Operation "Iraqi Freedom" more favorably than journalists covering the conflict from a distance and whether print coverage of that operation differed from reporting during the 1st days of Operation "Enduring Freedom" and Operation "Desert Storm."

• A Southern daily newspaper publisher, stung by criticisms that his paper was excessively negative in coverage of the African American community, commissioned one of the authors of this text to measure coverage of that segment of the community.

• Using magazine articles cited in *The Reader's Guide to Periodical Literature,* researchers (Simmons & Lowry, 1990) characterized the shifting public image of international terrorism during the 1980 to 1988 period.

• A team of researchers looked at science news in two types of newspapers marking "the end points on the continuum of journalistic responsibility." Surprisingly, tabloid newspapers (*National Inquirer* and *Star*) were "not particularly 'inferior' to more 'respectable' newspapers" (i.e., the *New York Times* and *Philadelphia Inquirer*), in amount of scientific reporting, although prestige papers were more comprehensive and rigorous in science coverage (Evans, Krippendorff, Yoon, Posluszny, & Thomas, 1990, p. 115).

• Finally, the 1995 to 2000 coverage of social issues (pollution, poverty, and incarceration) was content analyzed by Kensicki (2004) for dominant "frames," defined as "persistent patterns of presentation, emphasis, and exclusion" (Gitlin, 1980, p. 7) that make more salient a particular "problem definition, causal interpretation, moral evaluation" and recommendation for solution (Entman, 1993, p. 52). Coverage seldom identified causes or effects for the issues, nor did it often suggest the likelihood that the problems could be solved.

Although these studies differ in purpose (so-called basic research, or applied research, as in the case of the study commissioned by the Southern newspaper publisher), focus, techniques employed, and scientific rigor, they have characterized a variety of applications possible with *quantitative content analysis,* a research method defined in brief as "the systematic assignment of communication content to categories according to rules, and the analysis of relationships involving those categories using statistical methods."

Usually, but not always, content analysis involves drawing representative samples of content, training coders to use the category rules developed to measure or reflect differences in content, and measuring the reliability (agreement or stability over time) of coders in applying the rules. The data collected in a quantitative content analysis are then usually analyzed to describe what are typical patterns or characteristics or to identify important relationships among the content qualities examined. If the categories and rules are conceptually and theoretically sound and are reliably applied, the researcher increases the chance that the study results will be valid (e.g., that the observed patterns are meaningful).

The skeletal definition just presented deliberately lacks any mention of the specific goal of the researcher using quantitative content analysis (e.g., to test a hypothesis about international social revolution or to describe media portrayal of minorities), any specification of appropriate types of communication to be examined (e.g., themes or assertions in prestige newspaper editorials or television commercials), the types of content qualities explored (e.g., placement or length of a news item or presence of a dominant or competing frame), or the types of inferences that will be drawn from the content analysis data (e.g., characterizing change in the global sociopolitical climate across 60 years of international affairs on the basis of language in newspaper editorials, concluding that tokenism is being used in the casting of minority characters in advertising aimed at children, or suggesting that media contribute to public apathy about social problems by failing to suggest causes, effects, or means of resolution).

Such specification of terms is essential to a thorough definition. However, before a more comprehensive definition of this versatile research method is developed in chapter 2 (this volume), in this chapter, we first offer a brief overview of the role of content analysis in mass communication research followed by examples of how content analysis has been used in other fields and disciplines.

## MASS COMMUNICATION RESEARCH

Whereas scholars may approach mass communication messages from perspectives some associate with the humanities (e.g., as literature or art), many others employ a social science approach based in empirical observation and measurement. What that means typically is that these researchers identify questions or problems (either derived from the scholarly literature or occurring in applied mass communication), identify concepts that "in theory" may be involved or at work, and propose possible explanations or relationships among concepts. Implausible explanations are discarded, and viable ones tested empirically, with theoretical concepts now measured in concrete, observable terms.

If members of an ethnic minority, for example, voice concern that they are underrepresented in news media content (in terms of their census numbers), a researcher may propose that racism is at work or that members of the ethnic minority are underrepresented in those occupational groups that serve more often as news sources in the news. Each of these interpretations or explanations involves different concepts that can be "operationalized" into measurement procedures, and each can be tested empirically, as researchers did in the content analyses highlighted previously.

Put another way, explanations for problems or questions for such researchers are sought and derived through direct and objective observation and measurement rather than through one's reasoning, intuition, faith, ideology, or conviction. In short, these mass communication researchers employ what is traditionally referred to as the scientific method. The centuries-old distinction between *idealism* (an approach that argues that the mind and its ideas are "the ultimate source and criteria of knowledge") and *empiricism* (an approach that argues that observation and experimentation yield knowledge) continues to hold the attention of those interested in *epistemology* or the study of knowledge (Vogt, 1999, pp. 96, 136).

Another important distinction involves reductionism and holism. Much of mass communication social science adheres implicitly to a *reductionist* view—the argument that understanding comes through reducing a phenomenon to smaller, more basic, individual parts (Vogt, 1999, p. 238)—rather than *holism,* an assumption that wholes can be more than or different from the sum of their individual parts (Vogt,

1999, p. 132). "Quite literally," wrote Tichenor (1981), "the whole is seen as greater than the sum of its parts" (p. 23) from the holistic perspective so that, for example, collectivities like communities have properties or characteristics that are more than the aggregate of individuals within them. Although the reductionism–holism debate most often involves the place of individual people in larger social systems, it might as easily address the distinction between individual communication messages or message parts, and "the media," the news, and entertainment as institutions.

## CONTENT ANALYSIS AND MASS COMMUNICATION EFFECTS RESEARCH

Although the production of communications among humans is thousands of years old, the scholarly or scientific study of mass communication is fairly new. Historians have traced its beginnings to early work by political scientists concerned with effects of propaganda and other persuasive messages (McLeod, Kosicki, & McLeod, 2002; Severin & Tankard, 1992). In addition to modern scholars in journalism or mass communication, researchers from other disciplines such as sociology and psychology have focused on mass communication processes and effects, enriching and defining mass communication as a field by contributing their own most productive theoretical perspectives and research methods. Regardless of whether they were optimistic, pessimistic, certain, or uncertain about mass communication's effects, researchers have often recognized content analysis as an essential step in understanding those effects.

### Powerful Effects?

One particularly important and durable communication research perspective reflects a behavioral science orientation that grew out of early 20th-century theories that animal and human behaviors could be seen as stimulus–response complexes. Some communication researchers have viewed communication messages and their assumed effects on people's attitudes, beliefs, and behaviors from this same perspective.

Researchers interested in these effects typically have adopted experimentation as their method for testing hypotheses. People serving as experimental participants were assigned to different groups; some were exposed to a stimulus within a treatment (a message), whereas others were not (the control participants). Under tightly controlled conditions, subsequent differences in what was measured (e.g., attitudes about an issue) could be attributed to the exposure–nonexposure difference.

Meanwhile, for most of the first half of the 20th century, there existed a widespread assumption—among scientists and the public—that stimuli such as mass persuasive messages could elicit powerful responses. Why?

Propaganda, as seen during the World Wars, was new and frightening (Lasswell, 1927; Shils & Janowitz, 1948). Reinforcement came in the form of a 10-volume summary of 13 Payne Fund Studies conducted from 1929 to 1932 that showed movies' power "to bring new ideas to children; to influence their attitudes; stimulate their emotions; present moral standards different from those of many adults; disturb sleep; and influence interpretations of the world and day-to-day conduct" (Lowery & DeFleur, 1988, p. 51).

Anecdotal evidence of the impact of Bolshevist or Nazi oratory or, in America, the radio demagoguery of Father Charles E. Coughlin (Stegner, 1949) heightened concern over mass messages and collective behavior. Broadcast media demonstrated a capacity for captivating, mesmerizing, and holding people in rapt attention and for inciting collective panic (Cantril, Gaudet, & Hertzog, 1940). With the rise of commercial advertising and public relations agencies, carefully organized persuasive campaigns used messages that were constructed to make people do what a communicator wanted (Emery & Emery, 1978; McLeod et al., 2002). Communication media were increasingly able to leapfrog official national borders and boundaries and were believed capable of undermining national goals (Altschull, 1984).

These assumptions about powerful media effects were consistent with the early behaviorist tradition and contributed to early models or theories of communication effects that used metaphors such as *hypodermic needle* or *bullet*. In the language of the latter, all one had to do was shoot a persuasive message (a bullet) at the helpless and homogeneous mass audience, and the communicator's desired effects would occur. Some of the data generated in experimental studies of messages and their effects on attitudes were interpreted as supporting these assumptions of powerful effects.

Of course, the assumption that audience members were uniformly helpless and passive was a major one. Methodologists warned of the artificiality of controlled and contrived conditions in laboratory settings and cautioned that experimental attitude-change findings lacked real-world generalizability (Hovland, 1959). Still others have suggested that scientists' concentration on how to best do things to the audience was inappropriate; Bauer (1964) questioned the "moral asymmetry" (p. 322) of such a view of the public.

Nonetheless, content analysis found a legitimate home within the powerful effects perspective because of the implicit causal role for communication content described in the models, tested in the experiments, and ascribed—by the public as well as many scientists and policy-makers—to content, whether the content in question was propaganda, popular comics or films, pornography, political promises, or persuasive advertisements.

In short, communication content was important to study because it was believed to have an effect (Krippendorff, 1980). Scholars have scrutinized content in search of particular variables that, it was assumed, could affect people. One researcher might thus catalog what kinds of suggestions or appeals were used in propaganda, another might describe the status or credibility of sources in persuasive messages, and still another might describe the values reflected in films starring a popular star.

## Limited Effects?

However, the assumption that powerful effects were direct and uniform was eventually challenged as too simplistic and was replaced by more careful specification of other factors that contribute to or mitigate effects (Severin & Tankard, 1992). Experimental findings had suggested that in some cases, mass media messages were effective in changing subjects' knowledge but not targeted attitudes or behaviors. Researchers conducting public opinion surveys brought field observations that ran counter to cause–effect relations found in laboratory settings.

Examination of how people are exposed to messages in the real world and the mixed results on real-world effectiveness of persuasive message bullets have suggested that a more limited effects perspective might be worth exploring (Chaffee & Hochheimer, 1985; Klapper, 1960). Under natural, nonlaboratory field conditions, members of the audience (who, it turned out, were not uniformly helpless or passive, nor, for that matter, very uniform in general) used media and messages for their own individual purposes, chose what parts of messages—if any—to attend, and rejected much that was inconsistent with their existing attitudes, beliefs, and values. Social affiliations such as family and community involvement were important predictors of people's attitudes and behaviors, and networks of personal influence were identified as key factors influencing their decisions.

Real-world (nonlaboratory) audience members had only an opportunity to be exposed to particular media content. They were not forced to attend to the message as were experimental participants. Their decision to accept, adopt, or learn a message was a function of their existing psychological and social characteristics and not necessarily of mere exposure to, perhaps, the manipulated, artificial credibility of a source trying to persuade as part of an experimental treatment.

## Contingency Effects?

Research during the past 35 years suggests that the effects—powerful or limited—of mass media are contingent on a variety of factors and conditions. This contingency effects approach allows theorists to reconcile conflicting conclusions of the powerful and limited effects approaches. Rather than being the result of any single cause (e.g., the message), communication effects reflected a variety of contingent conditions (e.g., whether the message is attended to alone or as part of a group). Of course, some contemporary research on content—particularly that aimed at impressionable children—continues to adhere implicitly to powerful effects assumptions.

However, despite increasing interest in what people do with media messages and how or if they learn from them—rather than a powerful effects focus on what media do to people's attitudes—content analysis remained an important means of categorizing all forms of content. The communication messages that might previously have been analyzed because of their assumed persuasive effects were now important because they could be related to differences in psychological or social gratifications consumers gained from media use (e.g., escape from boredom, sense of being connected to what is going on, or having something to talk about), to differences in cognitive images they developed and retained (e.g., views of appropriate gender roles, of how safe or "mean" the world is, or of the state of the economy), and to different views of what was important on the news media agenda (e.g., what issues in a political campaign were worth thinking about and what attributes of issues were critical).

In short, different theories or hypotheses about varied cognitive (not attitudinal) effects and people's social and psychological uses and gratifications of media and media content were developed that reflected a different view of the audience experience, far different from the "morally asymmetrical" view criticized by Bauer (1964, p. 322). These triggered additional studies aimed at measuring content variables associated with those uses and effects.

For example, content analysts have categorized entertainment content that contained exaggerated ethnic or gender stereotypes to answer questions about how those stereotypes are learned in the public mind (Greenberg & Brand, 1994). They have looked at content of daytime soap operas because of escapism and other gratifications associated with viewing those shows (Perse & Rubin, 1988). They have examined victim gender in "slasher" horror movies because of concern that the violence in such films has a desensitizing effect (Sapolsky, Molitor, & Luque, 2003). Analysts have quantified violent content of television shows because surveys revealed that exposure to television crime and violence was correlated with consumers' views of their own odds of real-world criminal victimization (Gerbner, Gross, Morgan, & Signorielli, 1994). Also, they have analyzed movement of political issues on and off the media's content agenda during political campaigns, assuming that readers can recognize the priorities journalists give issues and issue attributes (by emphasis, placement, and repeated coverage), internalize that agenda, and then use it as a basis for voting decisions (McCombs & Shaw, 1972; McCombs & Reynolds, 2002).

Content analysis remains an important tool for researchers exploring more directly how individual-level cognitive processes and effects relate to message characteristics (Bowers, 1989). For example, Bradac (1989) and others have argued that important differences between one message's effects and another's may be due less to the communicator's or audience member's intent (e.g., to inform or be informed) than to different cognitive or other processes (e.g., enjoyment, entertainment, arousal, mood management, and so on) triggered by message features or structure (Bryant, 1989; Oliver, 2002; Thorson, 1989; Zillmann, 2002). Researchers guided by this individual psychology perspective can use content analysis to examine such features.

## CONTENT ANALYSIS AND THE CONTEXT OF PRODUCTION

Thus far, our discussion of the importance of content analysis has implicitly viewed communication content as an antecedent condition and has presented possible consequences of exposure to content that may range from attitude change (in a powerful effects, attitude-change perspective) to the gratifications people obtain from media use or the cognitive images they learn from it. However, content is itself the consequence of a variety of other antecedent conditions or processes that may have led to or shaped its construction. One classic example is suicide notes. Suicidal people write notes that include clues that experts recognize as links to—and consequences of—their emotional and psychological state (Osgood & Walker, 1959).

Similarly, a newspaper's front page might be examined as a consequence of the news organization's selection from an array of possible stories, or at the individual editor level, one can view that page as reflecting editors' application of what journalists call "news judgment." The content one examines is evidence of those antecedent choices, conditions, or processes (Stempel, 1985). Individual news stories are the consequence of a variety of influences including (but not limited to) a news organization's market (Lacy, 1987, 1988); the resources available for staffing (Fico & Drager, 2001); reporter news judgments and interactions with both purposive and nonpurposive sources (Westley & MacLean, 1957); and decisions about style, structure, emphasis (as in the "framing" process described previously), and language, to name a few. Media sociologists use a metaphor in discussing journalistic routines, practices, and values that is particularly appropriate to this view of content as the consequence of antecedent processes: They speak not of news reporting as mirroring reality but of journalistic practices that constitute *The Manufacture of News* (Cohen & Young, 1973). News content is the product or consequence of those routines, practices, and values (Shoemaker & Reese, 1996) and is constructed by news workers in "The News Factory" (Bantz, McCorkle, & Baade, 1997).

As a consequence of working under the stress of natural disasters (e.g., tornadoes or earthquakes), journalists produce and filter messages in ways that differ from routine news work (Whitney, 1981). Different ownership, management, operating, or competitive situations may also affect news work; news organizations in different competitive situations allocate content differently (Beam, 2003; Lacy, 1992). Similarly, the presence or absence of women in top editorial positions at newspapers influences how female and male reporters are assigned beats (Craft & Wanta, 2004). Under conditions of censorship in authoritarian countries, correspondents gather and report news in ways that enable them to get stories out despite official threats, sanctions, or barriers (Riffe, 1984, 1991).

Of course, many of the symbols that show up in media messages at particular points in time (e.g., allusions to freedom, nationalism, or solidarity during a war effort) are consequences of the dominant culture; communication messages that contain particular images, ideas, or themes reflect the important—and clearly antecedent—values of the culture or its leaders. For example, in 1991, a newspaper reporter examined a radio transcript of Cuban leader Fidel Castro's annual speech to his nation's communist party leaders, concluding that its 27 mentions of "death," "kill," and "die" were evidence of Castro's efforts to create a culture of martyrdom and sacrifice in one of the world's remaining communist states (Harvey, 1991).

Scholars often speak of such evidence as unobtrusive or nonreactive. That is, researchers can examine content after the fact of its production and draw inferences about the conditions of its production without making the communicators self-conscious or reactive to being observed while producing it. As a result, according to Weber (1990), "(T)here is little danger that the act of measurement itself will act as a force for change that confounds the data" (p. 10).

## THE "CENTRALITY" OF CONTENT

So, communication content may be viewed as an end product, the assumed consequence or evidence of antecedent individual, organizational, social, and other contexts. The validity of that assumption depends on how closely the content evidence can be linked empirically (through observation) or theoretically to that context. Also, as just noted, communication content also merits systematic examination because of its assumed role as cause or antecedent of a variety of individual processes, effects, or uses people make of it.

Figure 1.1 is a simple, content-centered model of the communication process summarizing the previous discussion and illustrating why content analysis can be an important tool in theory building about both communication effects and processes. The centrality remains regardless of the importance for theory building that must also be attached to non-content variables such as individual human psychological or social factors and the larger social, cultural, historical, political, or economic context of communication.

However, if the model illustrates graphically the centrality of content, it does not reflect accurately the state of communication research in terms of studies of content production or effects. As Shoemaker and Reese (1990) observed, most content analyses are not linked "in any systematic way to either the forces that created the content or to its effects" (p. 649). As a result, Shoemaker and Reese (1990) concluded, mass communication theory development will remain "stuck on a plateau" (p. 651) until that integration occurs. A 1996 study (Riffe & Freitag, 1997) of 25 years of content analyses published in *Journalism & Mass Communication Quarterly* revealed that 72% of the 486 studies lacked a theoretical framework linking the content studied to either the antecedents or consequences of the content. Trumbo (2004, p. 426) placed the percentage at 73% in his analysis of *Quarterly* content studies during the 1990 to 2000 period. Of course, this lack of theory is not limited to content analyses. Trumbo

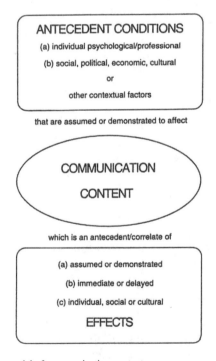

FIG. 1.1.   Centrality model of communication content.

(2004, p. 426) found that 58% of all quantitative studies in eight journals during 1990 to 2000 were "atheoretical." Kamhawi and Weaver (2003) found similar results in 889 studies—employing all methods—in 10 mass communication journals during the 1990s: only 30% involved "specific mention" of theory, and 27% of those mentioning theory were content studies. Not surprisingly, only 46% of the cases examined by Riffe and Freitag (1997) involved development of formal research questions or hypotheses about testable relations among variables. Scientists view such testing as essential to theory building.

Still, research in this field is dynamic, although the scientific goal of prediction, explanation, and control (Reynolds, 1971) of media phenomena may still be decades away. However, quantitative content analysis of media content is key to such a goal. Since initial publication of this book in 1998, some 117 content analysis-related studies have been published in *Journalism & Mass Communication Quarterly*. About 70% have used the kind of quantitative content analysis examined in this book. A fifth of those studies have investigated the effects of content (many, but not all, using experiments) on audience members, and nearly a third probed influences on content, usually news media content.

Nearly two-thirds of the *Journalism & Mass Communication Quarterly* studies since 1998 at least referred to or discussed a theoretical context for their work, a major change since the 1997 Riffe and Freitag review. Many were effects studies that placed the content research into the context of framing, agenda setting, cultivation, and a variety of persuasion theories. Research on content antecedents is still largely atheoretical, though, with some studies using the Shoemaker and Reese (1996) hierarchy of influences approach in the attempt to order, interpret, and interrelate influences on content.

Not surprisingly, considering the journal, nearly three-fourths of the *Journalism & Mass Communication Quarterly* studies since 1998 have focused on the news media, exploring content characteristics in news stories, editorials, advertising and photos, and television. Other studies, however, have explored movies and entertainment programs and increasingly, Web pages and the Internet.

## DESCRIPTION AS A GOAL

Of course, not all individual research projects have theory building as a goal. Even apparently simple descriptive studies of content may be valuable. Indeed, nearly 30% of the content studies in *Journalism & Mass Communication Quarterly* since 1998 have focused exclusively on describing content such as the framing of issues and media portrayals of women, minorities, and those committed to religious faiths. Moreover, recall the example of the content analysis conducted to help the Southern publisher respond to minority reader complaints about negative coverage. That publisher needed an accurate description of his paper's coverage over time to respond to those criticisms and perhaps to change the coverage.

Some descriptive content analyses are "reality checks" whereby portrayal of groups, phenomena, traits, or characteristics are assessed against a standard taken from real life (Wimmer & Dominick, 2003, pp. 142–143). Such comparisons to normative data can, in some instances, serve as an index of media distortion. The study cited (Riffe et al., 1989) earlier comparing census data with female and ethnic minority presence in children's television advertising is an example of this.

Or consider the study by Law and Labre (2002) that analyzed male body images in three popular magazines from 1967 to 1997. Although the study incorporated an implicit time variable as part of its longitudinal design, it was essentially a descriptive study of how male body shapes have become increasingly lean and muscular in visual representations. Law and Labre suggested that male exposure to idealized body images may thus parallel the experience women face with mediated body images.

Moreover, descriptive content analyses sometimes serve as a prelude to other types of research, often in domains not previously explored. The research program (as opposed to a single study) on veiled or anonymous attribution by Culbertson (1975, 1978) and Culbertson and Somerick (1976, 1977) is illustrative.

Reporters sometimes hide the true identity or name of a source behind a veil of anonymity (e.g., "a senior White House official, speaking on condition of anonymity, said today …") to protect the source despite critics' complaint about lack of public accountability for the source. The public became more aware of the practice following revelation of the use of unnamed sources by two *Washington Post* reporters covering the Watergate burglary (Bernstein & Woodward, 1974). In the first phase of the research program, Culbertson (1975, 1978) content analyzed representative newspapers and newsmagazines. Based on the resulting data, which described variables associated with unnamed attribution,

Culbertson and Somerick (1976, 1977) were subsequently able to design experimental treatments (simulated news stories with different levels of attribution specificity) and conduct a field experiment (participants received simulated news stories either with or without veiled attribution) to test the effects of unnamed attribution on readers' views of the believability of the report.

## RESEARCH APPLICATIONS: MAKING THE CONNECTION

As many of the examples previously cited have shown, content analysis is often an end in itself. It is a method used to answer research questions about content. However, it is worth noting that the method also has use in conjunction with other research strategies. In fact, despite Shoemaker and Reese's (1990) complaint about nonintegration of content analysis into studies of effects or media workers, some studies have attempted such a linkage. For example, the Culbertson (1975, 1978) and Culbertson and Somerick (1976, 1977) program integrated content analysis and field experimental techniques. More recently, a body of studies conducted by a variety of researchers has used experiments to test the effects of media frames on audience members, usually fashioning those (manipulated) experimental frames from actual examples used in the mass media (e.g., de Vreese, 2004, p. 39).

McCombs and Shaw (1972) hypothesized an agenda-setting function of mass media coverage of different aspects of a political campaign in which differential media emphasis (in frequency of coverage, length, and placement), over time, communicates to the public a rough ranking (agenda) of what the important issues are. In theory, the media agenda would be recognized, learned, and internalized by the public until the public's priority ranking of issues mirrors the differential emphasis on issues in the media.

McCombs and Shaw (1972) tested the hypothesis with a two-pronged study: In a survey, they asked undecided voters what they thought the most important issues in a campaign were, and they content analyzed campaign coverage in nine state, local, and national media. McCombs and Shaw found a strong, positive correlation between the media agenda and the public agenda, supporting the hypothesized media effect on what issues people think are important.

More recently, Wanta, Golan, and Lee (2004) combined a content analysis of network newscasts with national poll data showing that amount of news coverage of foreign nations is strongly related to public opinion about how important those nations are to U.S. national interests. As in much other research, that finding lends additional support to the "importance" effect described in agenda-setting theory. Wanta et al., also examined the attributes of the foreign nations, specifically how negatively or positively the foreign nations were portrayed. Wanta et al. found a "second-level" agenda-setting effect involving those attributes: The more negative coverage a nation received, the more likely respondents were to think negatively about the nation.

An even larger scale program, the "cultivation" research of Gerbner et al. (1994) brought together the results of survey research and content or "message system" analysis, an approach that looks beyond specific genres or programs to examine the "coherent set of images and messages" (p. 18) common to all television programming. Cultivation researchers asserted that between-program differences notwithstanding, most programming reflects common patterns in "casting, social typing, and the 'fate' of different social types" (Gerbner et al., 1994, p. 25) that cultivate a common perspective among heavy viewers. Among those patterns, for example, are consistent presentation of women in a limited number of activities and roles and virtually inescapable violence. Armed with content analysis data on the nature of television violence and its victims, the researchers asked survey respondents to estimate their own likelihood of criminal victimization. Heavy viewers of television tended to provide estimates closer to the victimization rates found in the "mean world" of television than to real-world rates reported by law enforcement agencies.

These studies involving communication content and survey measures of the (presumed) effect of that content represent important steps in moving beyond merely describing content and assuming effects or surveying attitudes and presuming a causal role for content. Via such an integration, researchers can respond to the challenge posed by Shoemaker and Reese (1990) in their aptly titled article, "Exposure to What? Integrating Media Content and Effects Studies."

However, as impressive as the agenda setting and cultivation approaches are, such methodological integration is rare. Riffe and Freitag (1997) found only 10% of content analyses published in 25 years of *Journalism & Mass Communication Quarterly* involved a second research method, a pattern that has remained largely unchanged since the publication of this book's first edition.

Content analysis has also been used with other methods to explore quite another type of effect. Kerlinger (1973) suggested that content analysis "can be applied to available materials and to *materials especially produced for particular research problems*" (p. 527, italics added). In a classic study of how journalists' views of their audiences affect what they write, de sola Pool and Shulman (1959) asked student reporters to fantasize about receptive or hostile readers and write news stories to be read by those audiences. Content analysis was then used to identify the effect these audience reference groups had on the students' writing and accuracy. Similarly, de Vreese (2004) analyzed "thought lists" written by experimental participants after exposure to newscasts about enlargement of the European Union presented in either a conflict frame or an economic consequences frames. Analysis of the number and nature of the listed thoughts showed that the two frames differed in how they affected participants' thoughts.

Finally, in an example of another type of multimethod study, Riffe, Hedgepeth, and Ziesenis (1992) surveyed newspaper reporters, state press association heads, and journalism educators to identify the most important issues facing the field of journalism. Based on survey responses, they developed a coding scheme and content analyzed leading academic and professional journalism publications to assess which were dealing most with those important issues.

## RESEARCH APPLICATIONS: CONTENT ANALYSIS IN OTHER FIELDS

The examples cited thus far have shown the utility of systematic content analysis, alone or in conjunction with another method, for answering a variety of theoretical and applied questions explored by journalism or mass communication researchers.

It should come as no surprise, however, that scholarly journals include examples of content analysis in academic disciplines as varied as sociology, political science, economics, psychology, and nutrition, to name a few. After all, communication is central to human existence, and the content of communication represents a rich data source whether one focuses on describing images and portrayals because of their assumed effects or examines content as an unobtrusive indicator of antecedent conditions or behaviors.

For example, because messages presumably indicate the psychological state of the communicator, content analysis has a long history of use in psychology, although the degree of quantitativeness has varied. Most sources have dated the earliest use of content analysis by psychologists to the examination by Gordon Allport in the 1940s of more than 300 letters from a woman to her friends. Those *Letters from Jenny* (Allport, 1965) represented a nonreactive measure of the woman's personality for Allport and his associates. The resulting work heralded what Wrightsman (1981) called the "golden age" of personal documents as data in analyzing personality.

More recently, psychologists interested in explanatory style used content analysis of verbatim explanations (CAVE) in examining individuals' routine speaking and writing to see if participants describe themselves as victims and blame others or other forces for events. Early research on explanatory style has used questionnaires to elicit these causal explanations from participants. However, questionnaires have limited use because some participants are "famous, dead, uninterested, hostile, or otherwise unavailable" (Zullow, Oettingen, Peterson, & Seligman, 1988, p. 674). Instead, researchers use explanations recorded in "interviews, letters, diaries, journals, school essays, and newspaper stories, in short, in almost all verbal material that people leave behind" (Zullow et al., 1988, p. 674). For example, Zullow et al. examined President Lyndon Johnson's press conferences during the Vietnam War. Whenever Johnson offered optimistic causal explanations, bold and risky military action followed. Pessimistic explanations predicted passivity on Johnson's part. Analysis of presidential nomination acceptance speeches between 1948 and 1984 showed that nominees who were "pessimistically ruminative" (dwelling on the negative) in causal explanations lost 9 of 10 elections.

Another application of content analysis in psychology involved the celebrated Daniel Schreber case. A British lawyer, Schreber was hospitalized in 1893 for psychosis. His 1903 *Memoirs of My Nervous Illness* (Schreber, 1903/1955) fascinated four generations of psychopathologists seeking to explain Schreber's condition, among them Sigmund Freud (1911). O'Dell and Weideman (1993) used a computer to count words categorized as "bizarre," "clearly psychotic," and "delusional in nature" in *Memoirs of My Nervous Illness*. These were contrasted with word counts from a healthy person's autobiography and with samples Schreber wrote during contrasting episodes of normalcy and acute paranoia. O'Dell and Weideman called the writing in *Memoirs of My Nervous Illness* the most schizophrenic they had ever seen. Despite O'Dell and Weideman's efforts to find allusions to sexual delusions in *Memoirs of My Nervous Illness,* they found little to support Freud's earlier conclusion that Schreber's principal problem was sexual.

Focusing on more obvious sexual content, Duncan (1989) examined 25 years of 158 homosexual pornographic magazines to find changes in homosexual acts depicted and types of models used. The research was patterned on an earlier study (Dietz & Evans, 1982) of the most prevalent sexual fantasies on covers of 1,760 heterosexual pornographic magazines. Both studies had suffered methodological weaknesses because of the sensitive content studied and difficulty of obtaining representative samples. Dietz and Evans resorted to randomly selecting 45 pornography dealers on 42nd Street in New York City, a notorious pornography district.

Psychologists (Malamuth & Spinner, 1980) analyzed 5 years of pictures and cartoons in *Penthouse* and *Playboy* because of concern that the sexual violence suggested in "soft-core" men's erotica contributes—through recurrent themes of domination and assault—to a culture more receptive to violence against women.

Psychologists have also used content analysis for research that did not involve sexual themes. In fact, one team provided a content analysis-based historical overview of psychology as an academic discipline. Ellis, Miller, and Widmayer (1988) examined how research psychologists over the years have addressed recurring questions of evolution and creationism. (Divine fallibility, determinism, selective adaptation, etc. are particularly important issues when one is addressing deviant human behavior.) Ellis et al. examined 90 years of articles noted in *Psychological Index* and *Psychological Abstracts* for references to key words associated with evolution terminology. Ellis et al. acknowledged their study's questionable *external validity* (its generalizability to psychologists whose works were not indexed or abstracted) because most scholarly research is published by a minority of scientists in any discipline.

Content analysis has been used to examine evolution of other academic disciplines. For example, Duncan (1991) used 100 key words to classify content of articles published in two clinical psychology and two health psychology journals to characterize the most important theoretical issues facing both disciplines. Duncan (1991) wondered whether health psychologists and clinical psychologists were studying the same phenomena, whether one of the two areas should rightfully be considered a subspecialty of the other, whether the two share major commonalities, or whether they should be viewed as a hybrid discipline—clinical health psychology. A year earlier, Duncan (1990) used the same techniques to identify differences and overlap health education and health psychology.

An economic historian (Whaples, 1991) collected data on two dozen content and authorship variables for every item published in the first 50 volumes of the *Journal of Economic History,* examining how researchers' focus shifted from one era to another and isolating a particular paradigm change—cliometrics—that swept the profession in the 1960s and 1970s. The same state-of-the-field approach guided a study of more than 2,700 articles published in *The Reading Teacher* during the 1948 to 1991 period (Dillon et al., 1992). Dillon et al., armed with 51 topic categories, examined every issue and classified each article by topic to locate shifts in research and theory about reading. As in Duncan's (1990, 1991) and Whaples' (1991) work, the most frequent topics of research articles were assumed to be the ones most important to the discipline. One cannot help but wonder, however, whether the most frequent topics are the most important or the easiest to examine.

Still, these quantitative histories can help establish the ancestry and evolution of academic disciplines and the points at which new theoretical directions emerge. Also, frankly, they are useful—in terms of salary and promotion—for the researchers identified as key figures in those histories. In journalism and mass communication, for example, Schweitzer (1988) and Greenberg and Schweitzer (1989) have collected authorship data on research articles in mass communication scholarly journals and have identified the most productive scholars and communication schools, much to the delight of those identified.

Less arcane matters are also the focus of content analyses. Sociologists (McLoughlin & Noe, 1988) content analyzed 26 years (936 issues and more than 11,000 articles) of *Harper's, Atlantic Monthly,* and *Reader's Digest* to examine coverage of leisure and recreational activities within a context of changing lifestyles, levels of affluence, and orientation to work and play. Pratt and Pratt (1995) examined food, beverage, and nutrition advertisements in leading consumer magazines with primarily African American (*Ebony* and *Essence*) and non-African American (*Ladies' Home Journal*) readerships to gain "insights into differences in food choices" (p. 12) related to racial differences in obesity rates and "alcohol-related physiologic diseases" (p. 16).

A political scientist (Moen, 1990) explored Ronald Reagan's "rhetorical support" for social issues embraced by the "Christian Right" by categorizing words used in each of his seven State of the Union messages. Moen justified use of content analysis on familiar grounds: Content analysis is nonreactive (i.e., the person being studied is not aware he or she is being studied), allows "access" to inaccessible participants (such as presidents or the late Mr. Schreber), and lends itself to longitudinal—over time—studies.

Writing in *Sex Roles,* Craig (1992) reported an analysis of gender portrayals in 2,209 network television commercials during three parts of the day when audience composition varies: daytime, when women dominate; evening prime time, when audience gender is fairly balanced; and weekend afternoons, when sports programming draws a disproportionate number of male viewers. Riffe, Place, and Mayo (1993) used a similar approach and contrasted sexually suggestive visuals in advertisements aired during Sunday professional football with commercials during evening prime time and afternoon soap opera broadcasts.

Gender roles were also the focus of a study (Lee & Hoon, 1993) of themes emphasized in newspaper article portrayal of male and female corporate managers. In the study, Lee and Hoon (1993) explored contradictions in social reality that "mass media have constructed and shaped over the years" (p. 528): That is, a woman's primary role was to be a mother, but "the economy needed women in other capacities" (p. 538). Male manager portrayals emphasized managerial style, whereas women managers were consistently described in terms of "problems and dilemmas faced by them as managers, wives, and mothers" (p. 534).

Use of systematic content analysis has not been limited to the social or behavioral sciences. Simonton (1990) used computerized content analysis to contrast the style of the (consensually defined) popular and more obscure of Shakespeare's 154 sonnets in terms of whether a sonnet's vocabulary features primitive emotional or sensual meanings or cerebral, abstract, rational, and objective meanings.

## SUMMARY

As it has evolved, the field of communication research has seen a variety of theoretical perspectives that influence how scholars define research questions and the method they use to answer those questions. The focus of their research has often been communication content. Scholars have examined content because it is often assumed to be the cause of particular effects, and it reflects the antecedent context or process of its production. Content analysis has been used in mass communication and in other fields to describe content and to test theory-derived hypotheses. The variety of applications may be limited only by the analyst's imagination, theory, and resources as shown in the 10 specific content analyses described in the introduction to this chapter and the other examples throughout.

# 2

## Defining Content Analysis as a Social Science Tool

In the preceding chapter, we offered a preliminary definition of quantitative content analysis that permitted an overview of the method's importance and utility for a variety of mass communication research applications: The systematic assignment of communication content to categories according to rules and the analysis of relationships involving those categories using statistical methods. A more specific definition derived from previous ones can now be proffered. It is distinguished from earlier definitions by our view of the centrality of communication content. In the complete definition, we address both purpose and procedure of content analysis and discuss its constituent terms.

### ADAPTING A DEFINITION

Stempel (2003) suggested a broad view of content analysis, what he called "a formal system for doing something we all do informally rather frequently—draw conclusions from observations of content" (p. 209). What makes quantitative content analysis more formal than this informal process?

Weber's (1990) definition specifies only that "Content analysis is a research method that uses *a set of procedures* [italics added] to make valid inferences from text" (p. 9). In his first edition, Krippendorff (1980) emphasized reliability and validity: "Content analysis is a research technique for making replicative and valid inferences from *data* [italics added] to their context" (p. 21). The emphasis on data reminds the reader that quantitative content analysis is reductionist, with sampling and operational or measurement procedures that reduce communication phenomena to manageable data (e.g., numbers) from which inferences may be drawn about the phenomena themselves.

Finally, after reviewing six previous definitions, Holsti's (1969) definition is equally inclusive: "Content analysis is any technique for making inferences by objectively and systematically identifying specified characteristics of messages" (p. 14).

Berelson's (1952) often quoted definition—"(C)ontent analysis is a research technique for the objective, systematic, and quantitative description of the manifest content of communication" (p. 18)—includes the important specification of the process as being objective, systematic, and focusing on content's manifest (or denotative or shared) meaning (as opposed to connotative or latent "between-the-lines" meaning).

Kerlinger's (1973) definition, however, reminds researchers that focusing even on manifest content does not free the researcher from a need to explicate carefully the relationship of content to underlying, often abstract theoretical concepts. "Content analysis is a method of studying and analyzing communications in a systematic, objective, and quantitative manner to measure variables. (M)ost content analysis," by contrast, has been used simply "to determine the relative emphasis or frequency of various communication phenomena" (Kerlinger, 1973, p. 525), and not to infer to important theoretical concepts.

Kerlinger (1973) suggested that content analysis is conceptually similar to "pencil-and-paper" scales used to measure attitudes, a parallel consistent with the emphasis we placed in chapter 1 (this volume) on communication content as an unobtrusive or nonreactive indicator. Content analysis, according to Kerlinger (1973), should be treated as "a method of observation" akin to observing people's behavior or "asking them to respond to scales," except that the investigator "asks questions of the communications" (p. 525).

Each of these definitions is useful, sharing emphases on the systematic and objective nature of quantitative content analysis. With the exception of Kerlinger's (1973), however, most forego discussion of the specific goals, purpose, or type of inferences to be drawn from the technique other than to suggest that valid inferences are desirable. Moreover, some of the definitions might apply equally to qualitative content analysis; Stempel's (2003) and Krippendorff's (1980), for example, do not mention quantitative measurement (although each of those researchers has assembled a remarkable record of scholarship using quantitative content analysis).

## CONTENT ANALYSIS DEFINED

Our definition in this volume, by contrast, is informed by a view of the centrality of content to the theoretically significant processes and effects of communication (chap. 1, this volume), and of the utility, power, and precision of quantitative measurement. Quantitative content analysis is the systematic and replicable examination of symbols of communication, which have been assigned numeric values according to valid measurement rules and the analysis of relationships involving those values using statistical methods, to describe the communication, draw inferences about its meaning, or infer from the communication to its context, both of production and consumption.

What do the key terms of this definition mean?

### Systematic

One can speak of a research method as being systematic on several levels. On one hand, most scientists are systematic in their approach to knowledge: The researcher requires generalizable empirical and not just anecdotal evidence. Explanations of phenomena, relationships, assumptions, and presumptions are not accepted uncritically but are subjected to a system of observation and empirical verification. The scientific method is one such system, with its step-by-step protocol of problem identification, hypothesizing of an explanation, and testing of that explanation (McLeod & Tichenor, 2003).

Thus, from a theory-building point of view, systematic research requires identification of key terms or concepts involved in a phenomenon, specification of possible relationships among concepts, and generation of testable hypotheses (*if–then* statements about one variable's influence on another). However, if that process suggests the important role of theory in the research process, recall the use of content analysis for applied or practical problems in which development of theory and testing of hypotheses are not paramount.

Whether testing theory-driven hypotheses or solving practical problems, one may speak of the researcher being systematic on another level in terms of the study's research design: the planning of operational procedures to be employed. The researcher who determines in advance such research design issues as the time frame for a study, what kind of communication constitutes the focus of the study, what the variables are to be, or how precise the measurement must be—who, in effect, lays the ground rules in advance for what qualifies as evidence of sufficient quality that the research question can be answered—is also being systematic. Research design is explored more fully in chapter 3 (this volume).

## Replicable

However, to tie systematic and replicable together in this definition usually suggests issues of reliability, objectivity, and clarity in description of research procedures.

Two defining traits of science are objectivity and reproducibility or replicability. To paraphrase Wimmer and Dominick (2003), a particular scientist's "personal idiosyncrasies and biases" (p. 141), views, and beliefs should not influence either the method or findings of an inquiry. Findings should be objective and not subject to what the researcher believes or hopes the outcome will be. Research definitions and operations that were used must be reported exactly and fully so that readers can understand exactly what was done. That exactness means that other researchers can evaluate the procedure and the findings and, if desired, repeat the operations.

This process of defining concepts in terms of the actual, measured variables is *operationalization*. A quick example is that a student's maturity and self-discipline (both abstract concepts) may be measured or operationally defined in terms of number of classes missed and assignments not completed. Both can be objectively measured and reproduced by another observer.

A researcher interested in a newspaper's commitment to the community might operationalize that concept in terms of how many different bylines appear on stories of local government meetings. This measure is valid because assignment of multiple staffers to such coverage represents a measure of resource or personnel commitment.

In summary, other researchers applying the same system of inquiry, the same research design, and the same operational definitions to the same content should replicate the original findings. Only then can a measure of certainty be obtained; only after repeated replication can a researcher challenge or modify existing theory or explanations for a phenomenon.

Measuring student maturity and discipline by attendance is only one example of an easily reproduced operational definition, albeit a common one (more common than students think). However, consider the systematic and replicable requirements in terms of a protracted example, this one from mass communication research.

Suppose a team of researchers had published a content analysis of the portrayal of minority characters in children's television and reported that the number of those characters was unrepresentative. Obviously, the researchers counted the number of minority characters, an easily replicable operationalization, right?

Consider how many places along the way that the operational procedure used could have influenced what was found and how unclear reporting of that procedure could influence the replicability of the study.

For example, how did the researchers operationally define which characters to count as minority characters? Was the decision based on the assessment of trained coders making judgments with or without referring to a definition or rule based on some specific criterion (e.g., skin color, eye shape, surname, etc.)? Making such judgments without a rule is like asking someone to measure the height of a group of friends but without providing a ruler. Did coders examine content individually, or was the process a consensual one, with two or more coders reaching a decision? Did anybody check the coders to make sure all the coders understood the criterion and applied it the same way in making the character count? Were the individual coders consistent across time, or did their judgments become less certain? Did their counting become less reliable after they became fatigued, consulted with one another, or talked with the senior researcher about the study's objectives?

Television presents both foreground and background characters. Did the definition of minority character take this into account? Did a minority character in the background "weigh" as much as one in the foreground or one in a major or speaking role? Did coders view videotapes in "real time" and estimate the count of minorities in group or crowd scenes, or were they able to freeze scenes and count characters (a process that decreases the chance of missing characters but that is unlike the typical audience viewing experience)?

Did the study focus on children's entertainment programming or commercials? Were the advertisements or programs selected from prime time, afternoons, or Saturday morning? Was a representative sample of commercials or children's programs used?

Finally, how did the researchers conclude the extent of underrepresentation once the data were collected?—by tallying the count to reveal how many entire advertisements or programs had at least one minority character or by using the total count to compare the percentage of total characters that were minority with normative census data (e.g., the percentage of the real population that is minority)? One study (Riffe et al., 1989) of children's Saturday morning television advertising counted characters and found minorities present in proportions comparable to census data (about 15% of all characters were minority) but also found one third of advertisements had at least one minority character, a use of those actors that Riffe et al. (1989) called "a form of tokenism" (p. 136).

The previous example used what at first blush seemed a rather simple form of coding and measurement—counting minority characters—but it demonstrated how difficult it may be to reproduce findings, as required by our definition of quantitative content analysis, without the clear reporting of even such simple operational procedures. What would happen if coders were trying to measure more difficult variables, such as attractiveness, bias, or fairness and balance or were trying to code the deeper meaning of symbols rather than the manifest content?

## Symbols of Communication

This definition also recognizes that the communication suitable for content analysis is as variable as the many purposes and media of communication. All communication uses symbols, whether verbal, textual, or images. The meanings of these symbols vary from person to person and culture to culture by a matter of degrees.

Moreover, the condition under which the symbols of communication were produced is variable in that it may have been natural or manipulated. As Kerlinger (1973) stated, content analysis "can be applied to available materials and to materials especially produced for particular research problems" (p. 527). For example, existing online content or content in archived newspapers, magazines, tapes, and so on may be analyzed, or participants may be placed in experimental situations or conditions, and the content they then produce may be subjected to scrutiny as in the framing and "thought-listing" experiment (de Vreese, 2004) described in chapter 1 (this volume).

However, although the phrase "as variable as the many purposes and media of communication" suggests all-inclusiveness, recall the requirement that content analyses be systematic and replicable and the hope that they be theory driven.

The analyst's decision on what represents appropriate and meaningful communication for content analysis must be based on the research task and specified clearly and without ambiguity. However, even that straightforward requirement is fraught with danger because questions about communication might at once involve questions of medium (if any) of communication (e.g., print vs. broadcast vs. online) or different functions (e.g., entertainment vs. news), to name only two. The issue is compounded further by potential differences in the symbols examined and the units used for coding (e.g., individual qualitative labels, themes, or frames or entire news stories). Although we address this issue of appropriate units and measurement more fully in chapter 4 (this volume), consider for illustrative purposes Berelson's (1954) designation of five key units of analysis that range from the micro (the word) to the macro (the entire item). In between these are themes, individual characters, and measures of space or time (whether minutes of speech or, presumably, airtime).

Appropriate communication content for study might thus be individual words or labels in advertisement copy; phrases or themes in political speeches; paragraphs of space devoted to crime coverage; whole editorials endorsing candidates; or news stories on soft topics, entire front pages, or editions. Within these text units, the focus might be further sharpened to address the presence of particular frames as did Kensicki (2004) in exploring whether news coverage frames social issues as having particular causes, effects, or likelihood of resolution.

Visual communication for study might include photos, graphics, or display advertisements. Examples range from Lester and Smith's (1990) study of 50 years of magazine photos of African Americans to Law and Labre's (2002) development and use of their "male scale" to chronicle changing "sociocultural standards of beauty for males" (p. 697) in men's magazines across the 1967 through 1997 time period.

Although these examples are primarily associated with content analyses of newspapers or magazines, similar content might be the focus in analyses of books, letters, diaries, or other public and private documents. Recall the range of applications of content analysis in chapter 1 (this volume).

Broadcast or film content analyses might involve entire newscasts or individual stories or reports, individual camera shots or scenes, particular sequences of scenes (e.g., in a dramatic program, only the time when the protagonist is on screen with the antagonist), or entire dramatic episodes. Local public access broadcasting represents a source of diverse messages, often far less constrained by advertising pressures than network content. The definition of communication content could be extended to include rock song lyrics or music videos, graffiti, or even gravestones (tombstone inscriptions indicate a culture's views about the hereafter, virtue, redemption, etc.). In fact, if transcripts are available, interpersonal exchanges may serve as a text suitable for content analysis. One can easily imagine extending this approach to examination of presidential and other political debates or to phrases and words used in the conversations in a group of people and so on. Additionally, students of nonverbal communication, using film or tape, may record encounters between people and break sequences of physical movements, gestures, and expressions down into units of communication.

Moreover, if the public–private, print–visual, news–advertisement–entertainment dimensions do not suggest a research domain of virtually unlimited possibilities for the content analyst, consider the possibilities if a traditional versus online media dimension is added to the matrix. Many of the same focal points for content analysis as well as new ones may be extended to new media such as the Internet and the Web. For example, colorful on-screen exchanges among Internet chat-room visitors provide research opportunities for content analysts interested in interpersonal communication. Personal Web home pages might be examined to determine what kind of "self" the creator is projecting to the online masses (Dominick, 1999; Papacharissi, 2002). Browsers chancing on web-page advertising for candidates Bill Clinton and Bob Dole during the 1996 presidential campaign encountered new departures in negative advertising. By the 2000 race between Al Gore and George W. Bush, online mudslinging had reached the point that Wicks and Souley (2003) found three fourths of the releases posted on the candidates' sites contained attacks on the opponent. Tremayne (2004) analyzed nearly 1,500 news stories on online news pages of 10 news organizations (representing newspapers, news magazines, and television news programs) posted from 1997 to 2001. Tremayne examined the growth in stories' linkage to other pages within the framework of a "century-long shift toward long journalism, long on interpretation and context, short on new fact" (p. 237) documented earlier by Barnhurst and Mutz (1997).

## Numeric Values or Categories According to Valid Measurement Rules and Statistical Analysis of Relationships

The definition specifies further that measurement is used: Quantitative content analysis involves numeric values assigned to represent measured differences. For example, a simple look at television advertising and inclusion of diverse characters might follow this procedure. First, a commercial receives a case number (001, 002, etc.) differentiating it from all other cases. Another number reflects the network (1 = ABC), whereas a third number specifies a particular program. In the program, yet another number is assigned to indicate the commercial's position (first, second, etc.) in the cycle of commercials. Another number is assigned to reflect the advertised product (1 = breakfast foods, 2 = toys), whereas another indicates the total count of minority characters presented in the commercial. Different numeric values are assigned to differentiate African American characters from Asian, Hispanic, or White characters. Finally, coders might use a 1 (*very negative*) to 5 (*very positive*) rating scale, assigning a value to indicate how positively the character is portrayed.

Of course, a crucial element in assigning these numbers involves the validity of the assignment rules. The rules must assign numbers that accurately represent the content's meaning. If a television character receives a 1 for being portrayed negatively, the character must be portrayed in a way that the great majority of viewers would perceive it to be negative. Creating number assignment rules that are reliable is fairly easy, but difficulty can arise in creating rules that reflect the "true" manifest meaning of the content. Put another way, reliability and validity issues must be addressed with particular care when assignment of a numerical value is not merely based on counting (e.g., how many characters are African American) but on assignment of some sort of score or rating.

Consider, for example, the task facing Law and Labre (2002, p. 702) in developing their "male scale" to study three decades of changing male body images in magazine visuals. Combining two different dimensions (low, medium, and high body fat; and not, somewhat, and very muscular), Law and Labre established eight types of body composition for coders to use ranging from *"low body fat/not muscular"* at one end of the scale to *"high body fat/somewhat muscular."* Thirty-eight cropped photos were then sorted by three judges to identify the best photo to

represent each of the eight types on the scale. With training, coders using the eight-image male scale were able to achieve acceptable levels of
reliability, calculated using a common formula (Holsti, 1969, p. 140;
see also chap. 6, this volume).

The point here is that measures of concepts or variables such as physical attractiveness or—in news content—fairness or balance, traditionally viewed as individually variable ("in the eye of the beholder"), can
be developed empirically and, with enough care, used reliably. The
chapter 6 (this volume) "coding protocol" for studying fairness and balance in newspaper coverage of the 1996 presidential election represents
a similar example of how researchers are able to examine difficult concepts through careful development of measures (Fico & Cote, 1999).

Rather than using the close reading approach of, say, literary criticism and examining a set of units of communication and then offering a
qualitative assessment of what was observed, quantitative content analysis reduces the set of units to numbers that retain important information
about the content units (e.g., how each scores on a variable and is different from others) but are amenable to arithmetical operations that can be
used to summarize or describe the whole set (Riffe, 2003, p. 182). For
example, using the system described earlier for examining diversity in
television advertising, a study might report the average number of African American characters in children's commercials or the percentage of
those characters in a particular age cohort. The numbers assigned to
variables measured in a single unit of communication make it possible
to determine if that unit is equal to other units or if not equal, how
different it is.

Quantification of content units makes it possible to reduce very large
sets of data to manageable form and to characterize the variation in the
data with summary statistics such as percentages, averages, and ranges.
The use of quantitative measures on representative samples of data permits researchers to assess the representativeness of their samples, and
thus use powerful statistical tools to test hypotheses and answer
research questions (see chap. 8, this volume).

## Describing and Inferring

In the previous discussion, we have dealt with the definition's description of quantitative content analysis procedures, but in the second part of
the definition, we specify two research purposes or goals of content

analysis: to describe the communication and to draw inferences about its meaning or infer from the communication its context of production or consumption.

Simple description of content has its place in communication research, as noted earlier. For example, applied content analysis research is often descriptive. Several years ago, one of the authors was commissioned by a Southern daily to examine the paper's treatment of the local African American community. The publisher's goal was to respond to that community's focus group complaints about underrepresentation in the news pages or about excessively negative coverage. The research involved analysis of 6 months of coverage and culminated in a report that indicated what percentage of news stories focused on African Americans and what part of that coverage dealt with bad news. Unfortunately, the publisher was unable—or unwilling—to make use of the clear-cut findings and the author's suggested remedies because featuring more African American news would, he said, anger White readers.

Other applied descriptive content analyses might be conducted to bring a newspaper's coverage in line with reader preferences discovered via readership surveys or focus groups. For example, if readers want more news about Topic X and less of Topic Y, a careful editor might examine the current level of each before reallocating resources. Public relations applications might involve profiling a candidate's image in print or examining the use of press releases. If a particular angle on the releases is ineffective, change may be in order. Agency practitioners might analyze all of a new client's publications or press coverage to evaluate and plan their actions (see Culbertson, 2003).

On the other hand, there are also instances in which description is an essential early phase of a program of research. For example, researchers in mass communication have found it useful, at one point in the early years of their discipline, to provide descriptive profiles of media such as what percentage of space was devoted to local news and what kinds of page layout were used. In a study of 25 years of *Journalism & Mass Communication Quarterly* content analyses, Riffe and Freitag (1997) found that a majority of published studies might qualify as descriptive: 54% involved no formal hypotheses or research questions, and 72% lacked any explicit theoretical underpinning. Kamhawi and Weaver (2003) reported similar data.

Researchers also continue to discover entirely new research domains with previously unexplored messages or content. Anyone who has monitored the evolution of communication technologies or capabilities over the last 25 years has seen new content or content offered in new forms. Rapidly evolving computer online services continue to spawn multiple concerns, legal and otherwise, about message content (Ekstrand, 2002; Morris & Ogan, 1995). Two decades ago, few music videos existed, but concern about their content quickly prompted researchers to describe the extent of the sex-and-violence themes in them (Baxter, DeRiemer, Landini, Leslie, & Singletary, 1985; Vincent, Davis, & Boruszkowski, 1987).

Consider the continuing concern of psychologists, sociologists, and media critics about the content of "sleaze" talk shows and so-called reality programming (and the picture a viewer might develop of the boundaries of acceptable behavior, public exhibitionism, and remediation of psychological, moral, and behavioral disorders); concern and criticism gain momentum when backed with systematic descriptive study of the programs (Greenberg, Sherry, Busselle, Rampoldi-Hnilo, & Smith 1997). Also, four presidential races ago, who among political communication researchers would have thought seriously about examining Larry King's phone-in show as an allegedly "unmediated" link between candidate and electorate without the filtering of journalists? Three presidential races ago, how many experts on negative advertising would have anticipated the extent of attack campaigning on the Web?

Indeed, quantitative descriptive content analysis often represents the earliest study in an area. Recall Culbertson's (1975, 1978) early unnamed attribution studies, a program of research triggered by Watergate-era attention to veiled attribution. The *Washington Post's* reliance on the source identified then only as "Deep Throat" brought attention to veiling, but Culbertson (1975, 1978) systematically examined news content to describe just how prevalent it was.

If early work in new content areas or new technologies is often necessarily descriptive, consider unprecedented events like the September 11, 2001, terrorist attacks or the Oklahoma City bombing. Such events are so far from the routine of daily journalism that the response of news workers and organizations warrants description (Reynolds & Barnett, 2003).

Some descriptive data are involved in the second goal of content analysis specified in the definition: to draw inferences about meaning or infer from the communication to its context, both of production and consumption. In fact, simple descriptive data invite inference testing—that is, conclusions about what was not observed based on what was observed. A simple example is the "why" question raised even in descriptive content analyses. Why does a Southern daily provide so little "good news" of the African American community? Why does one network's nightly newscast mirror the other networks'? Why does so much news from Washington, DC, come from unnamed sources? Why do particular kinds of press releases make it into print, whereas others do not?

As was suggested in chapter 1 (this volume), social scientists using quantitative content analysis techniques generally seek to do more than describe. Content analysts—whether conducting applied or basic research—typically do not collect descriptive data and then ask questions. Instead, they conduct research to answer questions. In the case of basic research, that inquiry is framed within a particular theoretical context. Guided by that context, they select content analysis from a variety of methods or tools that may provide answers to those questions. From their data, they seek to answer theoretically significant questions by inferring the meaning or consequences of exposure to content or inferring what might have contributed to the content's form and meaning.

To draw from content inferences about the consequences of consumption of content or about production of content, the researcher must be guided by theory, for example, theory as outlined in the discussion of media sociology and shifting perspectives on media effects in chapter 1 (this volume). A content analyst who examines television's necessarily superficial and brief coverage of complex economic issues cannot pronounce that level of coverage dysfunctional for society without understanding people's preferences for particular news media or the credibility they ascribe to them. Other factors include the level of attention people bring to those media, their level of involvement or interest in economic news, competing sources of economic news, different viewer lifestyles, media use habits, and the learning processes that enable media coverage to have any effect at all. Likewise, the content analyst who observes regularity or pattern in different news organizations' output discusses that similarity in terms of shared processes of news judgment, reliance on common news sources, or even common ideological perspectives.

These examples of inference drawing suggest the range of appropriate targets of inference, for example, the antecedents or consequences of communication as discussed in chapter 1 (this volume). However, students with a grounding in research design, statistics, or sampling theory will recognize that there are other questions of appropriateness in inference drawing. Conclusions of cause–effect relationships, for example, require particular research designs. Perhaps more basic, statistical inference from a sample to a population requires a particular type of sample (see chap. 5, this volume). Also, use of certain statistical tools for such inference testing assumes that specific measurement requirements have been met (Riffe, 2003, pp. 184–187; Stamm, 2003; Weaver, 2003).

## ISSUES IN CONTENT ANALYSIS AS A RESEARCH TECHNIQUE

What we as the authors of this volume see as the strengths of quantitative content analysis (primarily its emphasis on replicability and quantification) are the focus of some criticisms of the method. Critics of quantitative content analysis have argued that the method puts too much emphasis on comparative frequency of different symbols' appearance. In some instances, they have argued, the presence—or absence—of even a single particularly important symbol may be crucial to a message's impact. Holsti (1969) described this focus on "the appearance or nonappearance of attributes in messages" as "qualitative content analysis" (p. 10) and recommended using both quantitative and qualitative methods "to supplement each other" (p. 11).

However, if the frequency issue is an important one, a more important criticism repeated by Holsti (1969) is the charge that quantification leads to trivialization; critics have suggested that because some researchers "equate content analysis with numerical procedures" (p. 10) problems are selected for research simply because they are quantifiable, with emphasis on "precision at the cost of problem significance" (p. 10). Although this criticism could be dismissed out of hand as circular, the point it raises about focus on trivial issues seems misdirected. Superficiality of research focus is more a reflection of the researchers using content analysis than a weakness of the method. Trivial research is trivial research whether it involves quantitative content analysis, experimental research, or qualitative research.

Another criticism involves the distinction between manifest and latent content. Analysis of manifest content assumes, as it were, that with the message "what you see is what you get." The meaning of the message is its surface meaning. Latent analysis is reading between the lines (Holsti, 1969, p. 12).

Put another way, manifest content involves denotative meaning—the meaning most people share and apply to given symbols. Given that "shared" dimension, to suggest that analysis of manifest content is somehow inappropriate is curious. Latent or connotative meaning, by contrast, is the individual meaning given by individuals to symbols. The semantic implications notwithstanding, this distinction has clear implications for quantitative content analysis, which so often involves multiple coders applying rules to categorize reliably some communication content.

Recall, for example, Kensicki's (2004) content analysis of frames used in covering social issues, introduced in chapter 1 (this volume). Two coders had to agree on how to identify the cause, effect, and responsibility for those issues. Discussing the "lone-scholar" approach of early framing research, on the other hand, Tankard (2001) described it as "an individual researcher working alone, as the expert, to identify the frames in media content" (p. 98). This approach made frame identification "a rather subjective process" (Tankard, 2001, p. 98). Finally, Tankard (2001, p. 98) asked, "Does one reader saying a story is using a *conflict* frame make that really the case?" (italics in original).

The difference between latent and manifest meaning is not always as clear-cut as such discussions indicate. Symbols in any language that is actively being used change in meaning with time. A manifest meaning of a word in 2005 may not have been manifest 100 years before. The word *cool* applied to a film, for example, means to many people that it was a good film, which would make it manifest. This meaning, which can be found in dictionaries, was certainly not manifest in 1850.

In other words, one might suggest that interpretation strategies should recognize and address changes in meaning that may occur. Some content analyses that encompass the "natural history" of an event—its duration from beginning to end—have noted that the public or media discourse may involve an evolution of meaning over time: What is reported initially as a news story of an attack on an embassy, for example, may become a long-running crisis story. Obviously, historical perspective permits different interpretation of the same types of manifest content at different stages of that natural history. Similarly, scholars need to recognize that denotations change, and connotations move to become part of generally accepted meanings (denotations). John F. Kennedy has come to be viewed by many as having been a great president because of his charisma and appeal, but in fact, he was relatively ineffective in terms of one measure of presidential greatness: generating social change through legislation. Lyndon Johnson, on the other hand, was able to pass legislation because of his political power in Congress.

To a degree, the manifest meaning of a symbol reflects the proportion of people using the language who accept a given meaning. This somewhat arbitrary nature of language is made more concrete by the existence of dictionaries that explain and define shared manifest meaning. Researchers need to be careful of the changing nature of symbols when designing content analysis research. Language users share meaning, but they also can have idiosyncratic variations of meanings for common symbols.

How reliable can the data be if the content is analyzed at a level that implicitly involves individual interpretations? We concur with Holsti (1969), who suggested that the requirements of scientific objectivity dictate that coding be restricted to manifest content; the luxury of latent meaning analysis comes at the interpretative stage, not at the point of coding.

Quantitative content analysis deals with manifest content, by definition, and makes no claims beyond that.

## ADVANTAGES OF QUANTITATIVE CONTENT ANALYSIS OF MANIFEST CONTENT

The strengths of quantitative content analysis of manifest content are numerous. First, it is a nonobtrusive, nonreactive measurement technique. The messages are separate and apart from communicators and receivers. Armed with a strong theoretical framework, the researcher can draw conclusions from content evidence without having to gain access to communicators who may be unwilling or unable to be examined directly. As Kerlinger (1973) observed, the investigator using content analysis "asks questions of the communications" (p. 525).

Second, because content often has a life beyond its production and consumption, longitudinal studies are possible using archived materials that may outlive the communicators, their audiences, or the events described in the communication content.

Third, quantification or measurement by coding teams permits reduction to numbers of large amounts of information or data that would be logistically impossible for close qualitative analysis. Properly operationalized and measured, such a process of reduction nonetheless retains meaningful distinctions among data.

Finally, the method is, as shown in chapter 1 (this volume), virtually unlimited in its applicability to a variety of questions important to many disciplines and fields because of the centrality of communication in human affairs.

Researchers should heed Holsti's (1969) advice on when to use content analysis, advice that hearkens back to the criticism that the focus of the method on precision leads to trivial topics: "Given the immense volume and diversity of documentary data, the range of possibilities is limited only by the imagination of those who use such data in their research" (p. 15). Holsti (1969) suggested three "general classes of research problems which may occur in virtually all disciplines and areas of inquiry" (p. 15). Content analysis is useful, or even necessary, when

1. Data accessibility is a problem, and the investigator is limited to using documentary evidence (p. 15).
2. The communicator's "own language" use and structure is critical (e.g., in psychiatric analyses) (p. 17).
3. The volume of material exceeds the investigator's individual capability to examine it (p. 17).

## SUMMARY

If Holsti's (1969) advice on when to use content analysis is instructive, it is also limited. Like so many of the definitions explored early in this chapter, its focus is primarily on the attractiveness and utility of content as a data source. Recall, however, the model in chapter 1 (this volume) on the centrality of communication content. Given that centrality, both as an indicator of antecedent processes or effects and consequences, content analysis is indeed necessary and not just for the three reasons cited by Holsti.

Content analysis is crucial to any theory dealing with the impact or antecedents of content. It is not essential to every study conducted, but in the long run, one cannot study mass communication without studying content. Absent knowledge of the relevant content, all questions about the processes generating that content or the effects that content produces are meaningless.

# 3

# Designing a Content Analysis

Application of any research method—survey, experiment, content analysis, or the like—to analyze a phenomenon can be viewed as consisting of three phases or stages: conceptualization, planning or research design of the inquiry, and data collection and analysis. These three phases are comparable to stages a property owner might go through in having a structure built.

First, there is the property owner's vision of what the structure will look like and how it will function parallel to the conceptualization phase in terms of whether the building desired is to be a home, a strip mall, an office building, an apartment complex, and so on. This vision includes general ideas about features dictated by the form and function of the building. For example, how many stories will be involved? How many entrances will there be? Will storage space be needed? Obviously, answers to these questions will differ if the structure is to be a home, a strip mall, an office building, or an apartment complex.

Once this general vision is communicated to the architect by the property owner, a far more detailed operational planning process occurs analogous to the research design stage when the architect draws a blueprint of the structure. The architect must determine how the building can best be designed to achieve the property owner's functional goals as well as those general notions the property owner has of some of the desired features.

Clearly, the architect cannot work at the same level of abstraction as the property owner ("I want a lot of open space on the first floor"). Instead, the building designer must consider an array of factors ranging from aesthetics (appearance) to resource efficiency (both in terms of building materials used and the building's use of energy), the property owner's budget, the strength needed for load-bearing walls to provide that desired open space, the available—and affordable—materials that may be used, space, zoning and building code restrictions, the proposed time schedule for completing the project, and seasonal weather conditions that can affect that schedule, to name but a few. Guided by knowledge and experience in dealing with all these and other concerns, the architect produces precise and detailed operational instructions including blueprints of exactly "what goes where" in what sequence, the materials to be used, their dimensions, thickness, clearances, and so on. The architect brings the property owner's vision of the building down to earth in terms of what operations the carpenters, bricklayers, plumbers, electricians, and other building crew members can actually perform, what various building materials are capable of doing, what building codes require, and what the property owner can afford.

Finally, the builder is prepared to execute the plan. Armed with the architect's detailed operational plan and blueprints, the contractors, carpenters, electricians, plumbers, masons, roofers, painters, and other construction workers carry the project to completion.

Obviously, all three parts of the process are essential. Without the property owner's vision, the architect has no focus, direction, or purpose. One cannot imagine a property owner granting permission nor an architect agreeing to "just build something."

Without the architect's precise plan, the vision remains abstract, and the work crew cannot begin. If the crew improvises without a plan, the building that results is unlikely to be what the property owner envisioned.

Also, without workers trained to carry out the plan reliably, the building remains only a vision, albeit a carefully blueprinted one. Whether it would perform successfully the function envisioned for it in the form provided by the architect would never be known.

## CONCEPTUALIZATION, PURPOSE, AND RESEARCH DESIGN IN CONTENT ANALYSIS

The construction analogy involved, at the conceptualization stage, an abstract view of the function or purpose of the building that guided the architect's design phase. Was it to be a dwelling, a strip mall, or an office building? Quantitative content analysis research involves a similar marriage between conceptualization and research design.

Here, however, conceptualization of the study's purpose involves addressing a number of issues as shown in Fig. 3.1. What question is the research supposed to answer? Is a formal hypothesis involved? Is the purpose of the study description or testing relationships among variables? Will the researcher be exploring whether variables are associated with one another, or might the relation be a cause–effect one? Finally, what is the focus of the study in terms of the definition of content analysis and the content centrality model from chapter 1 (this volume)? Is it to describe messages, to infer about messages' meaning, or to infer from the message to the context of its production or consumption?

In other words, defining and describing the purpose of a content analysis study is a substantial task, but as in the construction analogy, it is a critically important one if the study is to achieve its goals.

Why? The answer is simple: The researcher cannot design a study that permits achieving those goals without addressing these questions of purpose. The answer to each of these questions affects the design of the study. Different purposes require different research designs. A content analysis designed to describe messages, for example, may require little more than counting. An analysis designed to test whether incumbent elected officials are treated differently than challengers requires, at minimum, the collection of content data on both types of officials.

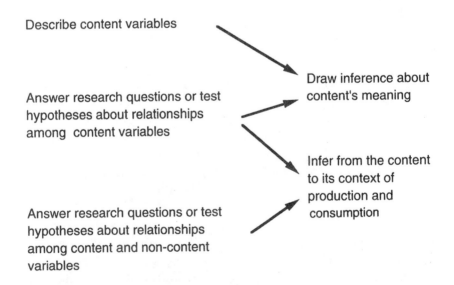

FIG. 3.1.   Purposes of content analysis that guide research design.

It is not our intent in this book to suggest problems or issues for researchers to examine or to direct research focus. It is, however, our goal in this book to provide guidance in using content analysis. The relationship of conceptualization or an abstract vision of a study to the concrete and precise research design of that study—analogous to the architect's work—is the focus of this chapter. We discuss the importance of research design and offer a general model of content analysis as a method, a model that incorporates the ideas of conceptualization and planning.

## Research Hypotheses and Research Questions

Careful thinking about a problem or issue and review of previous related research is absolutely vital to successful research design. Reviewing previous research provides guidance on what variables to examine and on how—or how not—to collect data to measure them. Most important, earlier research provides direction for thinking that can help the researcher formulate specific hypotheses or research questions that focus further the plan for data collection and analysis, that is, the research design.

A *hypothesis* is an explicit statement predicting that a state or level of one variable is associated with a state in another variable. Sometimes taking the form of conditional statements ("if X, then Y"), hypotheses in quantitative content analysis may be as simple as these:

1. Prestige newspapers will present both sides of local controversies more often than will large-circulation newspapers.
2. Prestige newspapers will present more balanced accounts of local controversies than will large-circulation newspapers (Lacy, Fico, & Simon, 1991, p. 366).

Note that both hypotheses identify specific variable levels that can be measured (prestige vs. large-circulation newspapers and balance or imbalance in coverage; the hypotheses implicitly suggest a third condition or variable—controversy—that will be made constant for the study).

Research questions may be slightly more tentative and less focused in that the researchers are unable or unwilling to predict possible outcomes. Typically, however, the research question is also guided by previous research. For example, Riffe, Aust, and Lacy (1993) demonstrated how newspaper publication cycles (larger Wednesday issues, smaller

Saturday issues, etc.) affected the content in daily newspapers and the effectiveness of particular types of samples. Subsequently, Lacy, Robinson, and Riffe (1995) asked whether similar cycles affected the content of weeklies. Previous research had provided no solid basis for prediction or formal hypotheses, so Lacy et al.'s 1995 study research question was simply, "Are there publication cycles that affect weeklies' content?"

Although research questions may be less focused than formal hypotheses because they do not predict an outcome, they are absolutely rigid compared to studies that lack the guidance of either, in some cases disparaged as "fishing expeditions." Imagine beginning an inquiry without knowing what question you are trying to answer, where to look, or what potential evidence to use in answering the question might look like.

Quantitative content analysis is most efficient when explicit hypotheses or research questions are posed. Describing the value of such explicitness, McCombs (1972) argued that a hypothesis (or, presumably, research question) "gives guidance to the observer trying to understand the complexities of reality. Those who start out to look at everything in general and nothing in particular seldom find anything at all" (p. 5).

Hypotheses or research questions mean research designs can focus on collecting only relevant data, sparing unnecessary effort that may yield unreliable or invalid results. They also provide guidance on how to recognize and categorize that data and what level of measurement to use. For example, if a hypothesis specifies a particular variable relationship or effect, then the data should be collected in a way that gives that effect a chance to emerge.

Finally, an explicit hypothesis or research question permits the researcher to visualize what kind of data analysis (e.g., comparisons of proportions or averages) will address the hypothesis or research question. Riffe (2003, pp. 184–188) called this "preplanning" essential to effective data analysis. This kind of visualization before the study is undertaken feeds back into decisions about what content to examine, the level at which it should be measured, and the best analysis technique to be employed. Knowing what is needed before data are collected and analyzed makes for a smoother, more efficient analysis and, most important, one that does not have to be redone.

If hypotheses or research questions permit well-focused research design, it is also true that the purpose of research design is to ensure that the research question is answered and the hypothesis tested. We return to this point again.

## Causation, Correlation, and Design

First, though, in this discussion of research design, we need to address whether the study's purpose is to demonstrate correlation or causation and the three conditions necessary for demonstrating causation. Even though content analysis is seldom used to test directly a hypothesized cause–effect relationship among variables (it is, however, useful for inferring such relationships), understanding these three necessary conditions improves the researcher's ability to design research that answers research questions or permits hypothesis testing.

*Correlation* between two variables means that one is associated with the other. That means that when one attribute or quality is observed in a unit of study, the other is observed as well (e.g., greater length in a political campaign story is associated with a more balanced distribution of paragraphs between the opponents, or in a survey, higher annual income is generally associated with years of education). Across all units of study, one might say that high levels of one variable are associated with high levels of the other if the correlation is positive (e.g., longer stories use more direct quotes), or if the correlation is negative, high levels of one may be associated with low levels of the other (e.g., television advertisements with more actors have fewer minority actors in speaking roles).

Additionally, although some observers may assume that one variable causes the other—its correlate—to change, the change may be coincidental. Indeed, a third variable may be the cause of change in both of the first two variables like a puppeteer working two hand puppets. Consider this simplistic example: A Saturday edition of a paper carries less news, including city and county government news, than other weekday editions. On might argue that public officials and other newsmakers work less hard on Fridays and thus make less news copy for Saturdays. In fact, of course, advertisers purchase less advertising space for Saturday papers, creating a smaller space for news content. The point here, for our discussion of research design, is simply that two variables can be associated (day of the work week and amount of government news coverage), but another variable (day of the advertising week) can be behind what was observed.

A *causal relationship,* on the other hand, is a special kind of correlation or association in which the researcher has demonstrated that one variable is indeed the cause of the other. The distinction between correlation and causation has implications for research design. Some content analyses seek to uncover what variables are correlated with—accompany—another variable of interest without specifying causes and effects. Others may seek to demonstrate what causes the variable of interest to change.

One condition necessary for demonstration of a causal relationship is time order. Quite simply, the alleged or hypothesized cause should precede the effect. Suppose a researcher wanted to examine the impact of a new integrated software and computing system blamed by newspaper staffers for increased typographical or other errors in newspaper content. A poorly designed study suggested, perhaps, by staff happier with the old system might tabulate a measure of current error rate and without measuring the rate before the change, blame errors on the change (see Design A in Fig. 3.2). A better study (Design B) examining the impact of that change would measure number of errors in the content both before (at Time 1 [T1], the first point in time) the change (which occurs at T2) and after the change (at T3). This is a natural before–after design (sometimes described as a pretest and posttest design) with a clear time order.

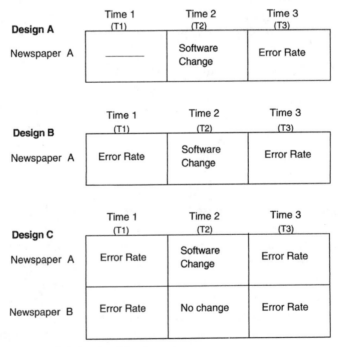

FIG. 3.2.   Research designs involving time order.

It should be clear from our "puppeteer" analogy, however, that some other variable or variables might explain the error difference between T1 and T3.

The second condition necessary for a causal relationship is the very association or correlation we described previously. Variation—different levels or degrees—of the cause must be associated with levels or degrees of the effect. Or, in terms of independent (cause) and dependent (effect) variables, variation in (or levels of) the independent variable must pair with change in the dependent variable. The variables must be correlated; when one observes that values of one change, values of the other must also change. Sometimes, observation of correlations or associations leads people to make (often inappropriate) causal connections every day. One sees two phenomena in the same place or at the same time, intuitively "correlates" them, and labels one the cause of the other. In some instances, in fact, one mistakenly assumes a time order.

Consider the example of the software and computing system change, as described in Design C of Fig. 3.2. If a researcher finds two similar news operations prior to change in the system and software at one of them (T2) and measures their error rates both before (T1) the change and after the change (T3), the study will have ensured the necessary variation on the independent variable (i.e., one operation changed, but the other did not). If the error rates were different after the change, the study will also have found the necessary variation on the dependent variable.

If an investigator looked at two news operations at T3, and one had changed at T2, whereas the *control* or comparison operation did not, and found identical error rates for both, then the study would not have identified the necessary different levels of the effect (errors) paralleling the levels of the cause (the software and system change). It would be inappropriate to infer that the change explained the error rate.

On the other hand, if the investigator looked at two news operations at T3 with identical T2 software and computing systems and found one increased its number of published errors, the study would not have involved the necessary different levels of the cause (viz., a changed system vs. the control unchanged system) that could explain the levels of the effect (increased errors vs. no increase).

These two requirements for inferring causation are fairly straightforward with clear implications for how researchers specify variables and pose research questions or hypotheses and for the design of longitudinal (over time), before–after, or comparative content analyses.

The third requirement for demonstrating a causal relationship, however, may be the most difficult to establish. It involves a type of control slightly different than what has been previously discussed: the control of all rival explanations, of all potential puppeteers to extend the analogy. Answering the question of "what are rival explanations?" clarifies this use of the term *control*. Rival explanations are the full range of potential and possible alternative explanations for what is observed as, apparently, a cause–effect relationship between two variables. If, for example, a move to a new software and computing system at T2 led to heightened anxiety among staffers fearing downsizing, then the increase in errors at T3 might be the product of that anxiety rather than the new system itself. Workers fearing downsizing might even deliberately increase the number of errors. Also, if the two organizations differing in error rate are one small daily and a large metro, can any difference be attributed to software and system changes alone?

Researchers designing content analyses or other studies try to control as many factors as possible that might influence the results. In some studies, that might mean ensuring that a sample of newspapers represents different geographic regions or ownership. Comparisons of newscast content might find researchers ensuring that all networks are included, some days of the week are excluded (for comparability), and that different times of the year are represented proportionately. Some studies deal with rival influences through statistical controls.

It is unlikely, however, that any single study can control or measure every potential important variable. Equally important, few phenomena are themselves the results of single causes. That explains why most scientists are reluctant to close the door on any area of study. It also explains why scientists continue to "tinker" with ideas and explanations, incorporating more variables in their research designs, seeking contingent conditions, and testing refined hypotheses in areas in which the bulk of evidence points in a particular direction.

Of course, tinkering is a rather inelegant phrase to describe the way scientists seek to address the influence of additional variables. More formal terms that we have also used—controls, comparisons, before–after longitudinal designs—are familiar to content analysts. However, whatever the level of formality, the utility of some type of graphic representation or notational system like the one in Fig. 3.2 should be fairly obvious. Sometimes, simply going through the process of graphically identifying elements of a research study can help the researcher avoid pitfalls—and identify rival explanations. Alternative ways of illustrating research designs or of depicting the testing of various research hypotheses and questions—and the types of inferences that can be drawn—have been offered by Holsti (1969, pp. 27–41) and by Stouffer (1977).

To sum up, this discussion of causation provides a useful reminder that explanation—the goal of most science—implicitly involves efforts to associate causes with effects. Yet one of the most frequently heard truisms in research is "correlation is not causation." Many research designs permit demonstration of association or correlation but cannot pinpoint time order or eliminate rival explanations. Also, whether one is an experimentalist examining the effect of exposure to a film on subsequent aggression or a content analyst examining the presence of minority characters in movies before and after the Civil Rights Act, the issues of time order, association or correlation of variables, and elimination of rival explanations are crucial ones. Knowledge of these issues along with careful development of research hypotheses or research questions can aid in the process of research design.

## Research Design

When one speaks of a content analyst's research design, one implicitly assumes the researcher is committed to the careful, systematic approach of the scientific method, has identified a problem presented as either a hypothesis or a research question, and has selected quantitative content analysis as the appropriate research method.

Research design can be as crude as a T1–T2–T3 diagram used to demonstrate time order and between-organization comparisons in Fig. 3.2; as general as an outline of steps to be taken in conducting a particular study (e.g., develop the coding rules, draw a sample of content units, etc.); and as detailed as an operational plan in terms of specific time frame for the study, communication source or medium, units of analysis, set of categories, type and size of sample, plan for assessing reliability, and planned statistical analysis.

For Babbie (1995), Holsti (1969), and Miller (1977), research design has been a plan or outline encompassing all the steps in research ranging from problem identification through interpretation of results. Kerlinger (1973) argued that the "outline of what the investigator will do from writing the hypotheses and their operational implications to the final analysis of the data" (p. 346) is part of research design. Holsti (1969) described research design simply as "a plan for collecting and analyzing data in order to answer the investigator's question" (p. 24). A simple definition, yes, but its emphasis on utilitarianism—"to answer the investigator's question"—is singular and suggests the gold standard for evaluating research design.

## GOOD DESIGN AND BAD DESIGN

How can research be designed to answer a specific question? Holsti (1969) argued that "A good research design *makes explicit and integrates* procedures for selecting a sample of data for analysis, content categories and units to be placed into the categories, comparisons between categories, and the classes of inference which may be drawn from the data" (pp. 24–26). For Wimmer and Dominick (1991), that meant "[t]he ideal design collects a maximum amount of information with a minimal expenditure of time and resources" (pp. 24–25).

To quote Stouffer (1977), strong design ensures that "evidence is not capable of a dozen alternative interpretations" (p. 27). By careful design, the researcher eliminates many of the troublesome alternative or rival explanations that are possible and "sets up the framework for 'adequate' " testing of relationships "as validly, objectively, accurately, and economically as possible" (Kerlinger, 1973, p. 301).

Thus, the hallmarks of good design, according to Kerlinger (1973), are the extent to which the design enables one to answer the question (posed in the property owner's vision of the building), the extent to which it controls extraneous independent variables, and the extent to which it permits generalizable results.

The emphasis in these definitions on "alternative interpretations" (Stouffer, 1977, p. 27) and "troublesome alternative … explanations" (Kerlinger, 1973, p. 301) reflects far more than intolerance for ambiguity. It captures the essence of what makes good, valid research design.

Imagine that somewhere among all the communication messages ever created by all communicators there are message characteristics or variables that would enable a researcher to answer a particular research question. Unfortunately, that same set of messages also contains information irrelevant to the researcher, the answers to countless other questions, and even answers that can distort the answer the researcher seeks. A good research design is an operational plan that permits the researcher to locate precisely the data that permit the question to be answered.

## Some Examples

To demonstrate how research design is the specific combination of procedures and conditions that permit answering the research question, consider the following protracted example based loosely on research questions explored in a pilot study (Riffe & Johnson, 1995).

Ronald Reagan was labeled early in his presidential administration as "the great communicator," a title that some say spoke less to the amount or quality of his communication than to the degree of control exercised over the White House's linkage to the public (Hanson, 1983; Peterzell, 1982). Coming on the heels of the openness of the Jimmy Carter White House, Reagan information management strategy was no doubt a shock to journalists in Washington. However, other than making White House correspondents uncomfortable, did those strategies really have any impact on the amount or quality of communication from the president to the public?

How might a researcher answer that research question? Clearly, systematic content analysis of news coverage would be an appropriate alternative to journalists' anecdotal complaints or the student's own pro- or anti-Reagan sentiments. However, what specific combination of procedures and conditions would permit answering the research question?

One approach might be to draw a representative sample of news stories about the White House published in the *Washington Post* during the Reagan presidency and examine the topics or news events being reported, the role of official spokespersons in presenting the day's "party line," the frequency of stories leaked anonymously (by fearful staffers) to the *Post,* and so on.

However, is the *Post* representative of all newspapers? Perhaps the study should include other national newspapers of record, such as the *New York Times*. What about the wire services that carry more raw copy than is selected for display in either paper? To test whether White House information management efforts affected television news (with its larger audience), perhaps the study should also examine archived tapes from the major network nightly news programs. However, what about then-upstart CNN?

Should the researcher look at coverage across all 8 years of both terms of the Reagan presidency to gauge how effective overall the White

House was at "clamping the lid down" and promoting the Reagan message of the day? Or would it be more appropriate to use a design that establishes a baseline for comparison by examining the earliest days of the administration, when information management strategies were being formulated and initiated, and contrasting that honeymoon period with sampled coverage from much later, after the full game plan had been put in place?

However, if the researcher is indeed testing whether the Reagan White House was a tighter ship than previous administrations, would not the research design then have to be a longitudinal one including data collected over time from several previous administrations rather than relying on anecdotal reports or conventional wisdom about previous administrations?

Was the Reagan offensive a one-time change in press and White House relations, or should the researcher extend the longitudinal design even further, also examining coverage during subsequent administrations to see whether, as critics feared (Peterzell, 1982), the success of the great communicator changed forever the nature of that relationship?

Content analysis is the appropriate research method for answering the research question; the research design is what some might call a "nuts-and-bolts" blueprint for the execution of a specific content analysis to ensure that the specific research hypothesis or questions about relationships of specific variables are tested effectively.

## ELEMENTS OF RESEARCH DESIGN

Research design usually addresses questions of the study's time frame and how many data points are used (whether as a specific epoch, such as World War II, or as a period of time for a longitudinal study in which time is itself a variable under study). It also addresses any comparisons that may be involved (e.g., when the news organization itself is a variable, and comparisons are between organizations).

Comparisons may also be between media (contrasting one communicator or one medium with another), within media (comparing among networks or newspapers with one another), longitudinal or across time (within- or between-media but at different points in time), between markets, between nations, and so on. Moreover, as content analysts seek to link their research to other methods and to other data, comparisons may be between content data and survey results (e.g., the agenda-setting studies discussed earlier) or between content data and extramedia data (e.g., comparing minority representation in advertising with normative Census data).

Adding additional newspapers or broadcast coverage in the pilot study of Reagan information management, for example, would represent a variation in research design because it would permit a different type of question to be answered. So too would the changes in the time element (e.g., contrasting the 1st month's honeymoon period with coverage during the later months of the Reagan administration or comparing coverage of Reagan's with the Carter, Clinton, and both George H. Bush' and George W. Bush's administrations) or comparison of results to extramedia indicators of public support for the presidency as in public opinion polls. None of these variations is being labeled as necessarily better or worse than another. Each provides a different kind of answer to the initial research question.

Consider some other examples of how research design elements permit the researcher to answer specific research questions. Examining content before and after a newspaper adopts a new software and computing system is a before-and-after design, obviously permitting one to assess the effect of that change. Analyzing coverage of a country before, during, and after its government has expelled U.S. correspondents represents a longitudinal, almost quasi-experimental design permitting assessment of the chilling effect of that expulsion on coverage (Riffe, 1991).

Contrasting political campaign coverage on television and in major newspapers and three newsmagazines—each of which allegedly reflects a different point on the liberal–conservative political continuum—is a comparative design that permits testing for that alleged bias (Evarts & Stempel, 1974). A study of 1960 presidential convention coverage was designed to examine two issues of the newsmagazines before, between, and after the Democratic and Republican meetings (Westley et al., 1963). Examining 10 consecutive issues of one newsmagazine in each of three presidential administrations was a narrower design, one that precluded between-magazine comparisons but permitted conclusions about the magazines' stereotyping of the presidents (Merrill, 1965).

Several design elements may be brought together in the same study. Examining how those same newsmagazines covered world leaders during times of changing U.S. policy toward those leaders' countries combines both comparative and longitudinal design elements to permit testing whether "press nationalism" (the press rallying around official policy) is mitigated by the magazines' own political leanings (Yu & Riffe, 1989). Examining two prestige papers' international news coverage sampled from each year across a decade of Third-World complaints about international news flow incorporates both a longitudinal and a comparative design, permitting the researcher to answer questions about between-paper differences and trends in coverage over time (Riffe & Shaw, 1982).

Or consider the complex design of Jung's (2002) examination of how two classes of magazines—three news weeklies and three business magazines—covered three media company mergers in 1989, 1995, and 2000. The three mergers involved the parent company of one of the news magazines (*Time*) and one of the business magazines (*Fortune*), enabling Jung to contrast those magazines' coverage of ownership activities with other magazines' coverage of the parent company.

Although testing relationships among variables and comparing among media and over time have been emphasized in these examples of research design, one needs to reemphasize the value and validity of so-called one-shot design studies that might not compare across media or time. These studies are important for many reasons raised earlier: Their focus may be on variable relationships that do not involve time or comparisons, they may be crucial to a new area of inquiry, or the content that is analyzed may be viewed as the consequence of antecedent processes or the cause of other effects. Armstrong (2004), for example, examined 889 news stories, finding male sources and male newsmakers were mentioned more often and placed more prominently than females, although female reporters "were more likely to write about women and showcase women in news coverage" (p. 149).

This emphasis on relationships and answering research questions, however, is a product of years of working with students who sometimes prematurely embrace a particular research method or procedure without thinking through its applicability for answering a specific research question. One author recalls overhearing a student telling a classmate that she had decided to "do content analysis" for her thesis. "Content analysis of what?," the second student asked. The first student's response was "I don't know. Just content analysis."

This is analogous to a child who enjoys pounding things and wants to hammer without thinking about what is being built. Scholars should be architects not hammerers.

Kerlinger (1973) wrote, "Research designs are invented to enable the researcher to answer research questions as validly, objectively, accurately, and economically as possible. Research design sets up the framework for 'adequate' tests of the relations among variables" (p. 301).

## A GENERAL MODEL FOR CONTENT ANALYSIS

Based on this volume's definition of content analysis and the need for careful conceptualization and research design, how should a researcher go about the work of conducting a content analysis? Although we offer a fairly detailed discussion in subsequent chapters on issues related to measurement, sampling, and so on, we are now ready to offer a verbal model of the process of content analysis guided by this definition. We present the model in terms of primary and secondary questions that a researcher might ask or address at different stages, and we organized under larger headings representing the three processes of conceptualization and purpose, design or planning of what will be done to achieve that purpose, and data collection and analysis—the content analysis itself (see Table 3.1).

Although Table 3.1 suggests a linear progression—and certain steps should precede others—the process is viewed as a recursive one in the sense that the analyst must continually refer back to the theory framing the study and must be prepared to refine and redefine when situations dictate.

### TABLE 3.1
### Conducting a Content Analysis

Conceptualization and purpose

    Identify the problem
    Review theory and research
    Pose specific research questions and hypotheses

Design

    Define relevant content
    Specify formal design
    Create dummy tables
    Operationalize (coding protocol and sheets)
    Specify population and sampling plans
    Pretest and establish reliability procedures

Analysis

    Process data (establish reliability and code content)
    Apply statistical procedures
    Interpret and report results

## Conceptualization and Purpose

*What Is the Phenomenon or Event to Be Studied?*    In some models of the research process, this is called problem identification or statement of the research objective. Researchable problems may come from direct observation or may be suggested by previous studies or theory. Most students of journalism or mass communication can, by observing media content and practices, generate hundreds of such problems. One well-known research methods professor routinely sent graduate students to trade publications such as *Editor & Publisher, The Quill,* and *Columbia Journalism Review* to identify researchable problems.

*How Much Is Known About the Phenomenon Already?*    Have any studies of this or related phenomena been conducted already? Is enough known already to enable the researcher to hypothesize and test variable relationships that might be involved, or is the purpose of the study more likely to be exploratory or descriptive?

Beginning researchers and even experienced ones often approach this step in too casual a manner. The result is a review of existing research and theory that excludes knowledge crucial to a proper framing of a problem. For example, a study of the impact of competition on media content should start with a review of general theory about competition and business performance. This requires reading material found in economics as well as material in mass communication research. Just as a builder who overlooks some elements of a project (e.g., soil composition) can produce an unstable structure, a researcher's failure to gain a full understanding of existing knowledge can lead to a weak design and inaccurate analysis of data.

The incomplete review of existing knowledge occurs mostly for four reasons: (a) an overdependence on Web searches or computer indexes that may not be complete (some may not include all relevant journals or all the volumes of those journals), (b) an exclusion of important journals from the review, (c) an unfamiliarity with scholarship from other fields, and (d) an impatience to get on with a project before all relevant materials have been examined.

*What Are the Specific Research Questions or Hypotheses?*    Will the study examine correlations among variables, or will it test causal hypotheses? Will its purposes include inference to the context of message production or consumption?

It is at the conceptualization stage that many studies are doomed to fail simply because the researcher, like the hammerer just described, may not have spent enough time thinking and pondering the existing research. This step includes identification of key theoretical concepts that may be operative and may involve a process of deduction, with the researcher reasoning what might be observed in the content if certain hypothesized relationships exist.

For example, a content analyst might want to explore how effectively government restrictions on press activity in developing countries affect the news that correspondents file from those countries. The reasoning process that would define the concepts of restrictions and impact might go as follows. If restrictions were imposed, what kind of impact might we find in content? Would the topic of stories be affected, as correspondents shy away from sensitive topics that might offend government officials? Would the nature of news sources cited change, as correspondents allow only appropriate sources to hold forth? Would qualitative labels (e.g., "unusual," "bizarre") that reflect a nonnative perspective disappear, as correspondents seek to avoid offending? Would the amount of attribution increase, as correspondents seek to guarantee that potentially offensive content is associated with other sources and not with the reporter?

In sum, conceptualization involves problem identification, examination of relevant literature, a process of deduction, and a clear understanding of the study's purpose. That purpose will guide the research design.

## Design

*What Will Be Needed to Answer the Specific Research Question or Test the Hypothesis?*    Will newspaper content, broadcast videotape, or some other form of communication content be involved? What resources are available and accessible? Most important, what specific units of content will be examined to answer the question?

Another issue that arises during this phase of planning and design has to do with availability of appropriate materials for analysis (e.g., newspapers, tapes, texts, Web pages). Ideally, existing theory and previous research are the researcher's primary sources of direction in designing a study, but logistical—and sometimes disappointingly pedestrian—concerns sometimes enter and affect how, if at all, one can best answer the

research question. Consider how difficult the study of minority characters in television advertising would have been without videocassette re-
corders permitting commercials to be taped and viewed repeatedly or
how the availability of computerized newspaper databases with keyword search capability has resulted in studies in which the unit of analysis is defined as any story containing a desired key word. Also, although
researchers are increasingly interested in examining Web and Internet
communication, concerns about currency (many Web sites are inactive)
and representativeness require creative sampling approaches (see chap.
5, this volume).

To repeat, logistical and availability factors should not be as important in planning as the theoretical merit of the research question itself.
However, it is unfortunately true that not all researchers have unlimited
resources or access to ideal materials for content analysis. The design
phase should, to be realistic, involve some assessment of feasibility and
accessibility of materials. One cannot content analyze the last 40 years
of environmental coverage in the nation's top 15 prestige dailies if the
library has only the local weekly on microfilm.

*What Is the Formal Design of the Study?*      How can the research
question or hypothesis best be tested? Can the study be designed and
conducted in such a way as to assure successful testing of the hypothesis or answering the research question? Will the chosen design generate data that can be used to achieve these goals? Recall an earlier
observation that good research design is the operational plan for the
study that permits—ensures—that the research objective can be
achieved. Recall also that content analysis is the research method, but
the formal research design is the actual plan or blueprint for execution
of the study. It is directed by what occurred in the conceptualization
process, particularly the decision to propose testable hypotheses or
pursue answering a less specific research question. Each of these objectives suggests particular decisions in the study design process such
as a study's time frame (e.g., a before-and-after study of a paper's
move to a *USA Today* style of graphics), how many data points are
used, or any comparisons that may be involved, whether with other media or other sources of data. Many content analysts find it useful at this
point in planning to preplan the data analysis. Developing "dummy tables" (see Table 3.2) that show which variables and combinations will
be examined can help the researcher evaluate whether the study design

will permit testing the hypothesis or answering the research question. Table 3.2 uses simple percentages, but other more sophisticated techniques can also be represented to help in preplanning. This preplanning helps ensure that the researcher generates data that when plugged into the tables will answer the research question. At this point, some researchers realize that their design will not achieve that goal: better now, however, than later.

*How Will Coders Know the Data When They See It?* What units of content (words, square inches, etc.) will be placed in the categories? The analyst must move from the conceptual level to the operational level, describing abstract or theoretical variables in terms of actual measurement procedures that coders can apply. What sorts of operational definitions will be used? What kind of measurement can be achieved (e.g., simple categories such as male or female characters, real numbers such as story length, or ratings for fairness or interest on a scale)?

The heart of a content analysis is the content analysis protocol or codebook that explains how the variables in the study are to be measured and recorded on the coding sheet or other medium. It is simple enough to speak of abstract concepts such as bias or favoritism, but a coder for a newspaper content analysis must know what it looks like in print. In chapter 4 (this volume), we address the question of measurement in greater detail.

*How Much Data Will Be Needed to Test the Hypothesis or Answer the Research Question?* What population of communication content units will be examined? Will sampling from that population be necessary? What kind of sample? How large a sample?

**TABLE 3.2**
**Example of a Dummy Table**

| Character Is | Character Has | |
|---|---|---|
| | Speaking Role | Nonspeaking Role |
| Minority female | ?% | ?% |
| Minority Male | ?% | ?% |
| White female | ?% | ?% |
| White male | ?% | ?% |
| Total | 100% | 100% |

A population of content is simply the entire set of potential newspaper editions, broadcasts, documents, Web pages, and so on within a pertinent time frame (which is, of course, an element of design). When appropriate, researchers use representative subsets or samples of the population rather than examining all the members. However, in some situations, sampling is not appropriate. If the focus is on a particular critical event (e.g., the September 11 terrorist attacks or a major oil spill) within a specified time period, probability sampling might miss key parts of the coverage. Or, if one is working with content that might be important but comparatively scarce—for example, sources cited in early news coverage of AIDS—one would be more successful examining the entire population of AIDS stories. In chapter 5 (this volume), we discuss sampling in more detail.

*How Can the Quality of the Data Be Maximized?*     The operational definitions will need to be pretested and coders will need to be trained in their use. Before and during coding, coder reliability (or agreement in using the procedures) will need testing. In chapter 6 (this volume), we address the logic and techniques of reliability testing.

Actually, this effort to maximize data quality involves several steps. Many researchers pilot test coding instructions during the process of developing them. Then coders who will be applying the rules and using the instructions are trained. A pretest of reliability (how much agreement among the coders is there in applying the rules) may be conducted and the instructions refined further. Once the researcher is satisfied with precoding reliability and data collection begins, several avenues are available for ensuring continued reliability. Some researchers have the coders collect the data and then code a common subset of the data. Some assess between-coder agreement at the beginning, in the middle, and at the end of the collecting phase. Some researchers check each coder against themselves on the same data to ensure that the coder is consistent with them.

Lacy and Riffe (1993) argued that reporting content analysis reliability is a minimum requirement if readers are to assess the validity of the reported research. As Riffe and Freitag (1997) found, however, many content analyses lack this essential information. Riffe and Freitag's study of 25 years of published content analyses in *Journalism & Mass Communication Quarterly* found only 56% of the studies reported intercoder reliability.

## Data Collection and Analysis

*What Kind of Data Analysis Will Be Used?*    Will statistical procedures be necessary? Which ones are appropriate?

Coders apply the analysis rules and supervisors monitor their progress and edit their work. Resourceful content analysts have found ways to ease the processing of data by precoding code sheets with numeric values that are easily transferred to a computer file. Data processing entails examination of the numbers generated by the analysis and application of appropriate statistical tools. In short, this step converts the coders' work into entries for the dummy tables so that the researcher can determine if she or he has indeed achieved the goal of the research.

What statistical tests are appropriate? A number of factors influence the choice of statistical tests including level of measurement and type of sample used. Some content analyses involve procedures of varying complexity that examine and characterize relationships among and between variables. Others report results in the form of simple percentages or averages. Riffe and Freitag (1997) found that approximately 40% of published content analyses in 25 years of *Journalism & Mass Communication Quarterly* used such simple descriptive statistics.

*Has the Research Question Been Answered or the Research Hypothesis Tested Successfully?*    What are the results of the content analysis and any statistical tests? What is the importance or significance of the results?

Interpreting and reporting the results is the final phase. It enables scientists to evaluate and build on the work of others. The actual form of the report depends on the purpose of the study and the appropriate forum (to a publisher, a thesis committee, the readers of a trade publication, colleagues in the academic community, etc.).

The importance of a research finding, however, is not necessarily a function of how widely it is disseminated. Admittedly, powerful statistical procedures will demonstrate the presence of variable relationships, either through descriptive statistics of a population or inferential statistics when using a randomly selected sample. Also, because associations among variables vary in strength, statistics are available that summarize the degree of these relationships.

However, the importance of the finding is determined by connecting the found relationship with the problem that underlies the research. A relationship can be statistically strong but have little importance for scholarship or society. A fairly strong relationship exists between severity of weather and amount of television watching. People watch television more during winter weather than summer. Is this important? Television networks and advertisers think so, but social scientists may not.

Importance of a research finding cannot be determined statistically. It is determined by the finding's contribution to developing theory and solving problems. Only when the statistical measures of strength of a relationship are put in the context of theory and existing knowledge can importance be evaluated.

## SUMMARY

Content analysis involves conceptualization, design, and execution phases. The research design of a study is its blueprint, the plan specifying how a particular content analysis will be performed to answer a specific research question or test a specific research hypothesis. Design considerations include time, comparisons with other media or data sources, operationalization and measurement decisions, sampling, reliability, and appropriate statistical analysis. Ultimately, good research design can be evaluated in terms of how well it permits answering the research question and fulfilling the study's purpose.

# 4

# *Measurement*

Quantitative research methods use what Babbie (1995) called a variable language, which involves study of variations of attributes among people and people's artifacts. When a concept shows variation, it is called a variable. Variables can be summarized and analyzed quantitatively by assigning numbers to show these variations, and content analysis assigns numbers that show variation in communication content.

Measurement links the conceptualization and analysis steps presented in chapter 3 (this volume). Careful thinking about that process forces a researcher to identify properties of content that represent the theoretical concepts (bias, frames, etc.) that develop through the conceptualization process, to transform them into numbers that can be analyzed statistically.

In more concrete terms, measurement is the reliable and valid process of assigning numbers to units of content. Measurement failure, on the other hand, creates unreliable and invalid data that leads to inaccurate conclusions. *Reliability* requires that different coders applying the same classification rules to the same content will assign the same numbers. *Validity* requires that the assignment of numbers is reliable and that the assignment of numbers accurately represents the abstract concept being studied. As Rapoport (1969) said

> It is easy to construct indices by counting unambiguously recognizable verbal events. It is a different matter to decide whether the indices thus derived represent anything significantly relevant to the subject's mental states. As with all social science measurement, some error will exist, but a carefully constructed measurement procedure that is adjusted with use will give valid and reliable measurement. (p. 23)

However, before assessing reliability or validity and even before developing "a carefully constructed measurement procedure" (Rapoport, 1969, p. 23), researchers must consider the forms of communication under study and select appropriate units of content for study. The type and definition of units are central to generating valid and reliable data.

## CONTENT FORMS

A variety of content forms and combinations of forms can be analyzed. Although chapters 1 and 2 (this volume) have emphasized familiar distinctions among print, broadcast, and online media, a broader classification scheme distinguishes among written, verbal, and visual communication. These three forms are basic and can be found across media.

*Written communication* informs with text, the deliberate presentation of a language using combinations of symbols. The text can be on paper, an electronic screen, or any other type of physical surface. An important characteristic of written communication is that a reader must know the language to understand the communication. Historically, most content analysis articles have involved text because text has been the primary way mass-produced content has been preserved.

A typical example comes from Golan and Wanta (2001) who studied second-level agenda setting in the 2000 New Hampshire primaries by examining election stories in the *Nashua Telegraph,* the *Manchester Union Leader,* and the *Boston Globe.* Golan and Wanta selected all appropriate stories and coded the paragraphs for cognitive and affective variables. The content analysis data were compared with measures of public attitudes collected from polls. Results show that newspapers were more successful in influencing the cognitive perceptions of voters than in changing their affective perceptions.

In another examination of text, Hansen, Ward, Conners, and Neuzil (1994) used content analysis (in conjunction with in-depth interviews) to explore how reporters used electronic information technologies to write stories. Hansen et al. analyzed published stories for types of sources, use of documents, checking of source accuracy, and contextual elements. Hansen et al. (1994) found that despite increased use of electronic news gathering, "reporters rely on the same types of sources representing the same institutional and social power structures as in classic newsmaking studies" (p. 561).

*Verbal communication,* by contrast, is spoken communication, both mediated and nonmediated, intended for aural processing. However, most nonmediated verbal communication is not preserved, and therefore, it is difficult to study. In fact, a similar statement can be made about mediated verbal communication despite the growth of recording technology. For example, the bulk of content broadcast by the thousands of radio stations around the world is not recorded and saved. When such content is preserved, it is often saved as text in transcripts. Note the emphasis on "intended" here and in our discussion of written communication. One distinguishes between written text that is meant or intended to be read and what may be transcriptions of verbal communication meant to be heard.

An example of studying ordinary speech was conducted by Shimanoff (1985) who studied linguistic references to emotive states by having participants tape their conversations during a day. Shimanoff then used transcripts of randomly selected 5-min segments of these conversations to examine emotive states.

Jones (1994) faced the problem of acquiring verbal content from unlicensed or "pirate" radio stations, which are erratic and unpredictable in their broadcasting, to test whether such stations actually provide content that varied greatly from commercial broadcast. Jones' solution was to use logs of broadcasts by interested parties made available through magazines and the Internet. Realizing the potential limits of coding these logs, Jones nonetheless argued convincingly that they were valid; he concluded that most pirate stations do not differ greatly in content from commercial stations.

*Visual communication* involves efforts to communicate through nontext symbols processed with the eyes. Visual communication includes still visuals, such as photographs, and motion visuals, such as film and video. Still visuals are often easier to content analyze than motion because stills freeze the relationship among visual elements. As was observed in discussing the operationalization of "ethnic minority" in the study of television advertising in chapter 2 (this volume), motion visuals often require repeat viewing to identify the elements, symbols, and relationships in the visual space.

Still visuals, however, were analyzed in Leslie's (1995) study of model characteristics in *Ebony* advertising. Focusing on clothing style, facial types, and hairstyles of people pictured in advertisements from the 1950s, 1970s, and 1980s, Leslie (1995) concluded that "while the

Black Revolt of the 1960s 'blackened' *Ebony* ads, the fair-skinned, Eurocentric model had begun to reassert itself as the somatic norm for *Ebony* advertising by the late 1980s" (p. 426).

Similarly, Kurpius (2002) coded videotapes for the race and gender of sources in newscasts that won James K. Batten Civic Journalism Awards. Kurpius' conclusion was that civic journalism stories had more source diversity than did traditional TV newscasts.

In addition to written, verbal, and visual forms, multiform presentations use more than one communication form. Broadcast newscasts, for example, include verbal communication, still visual information, and motion visuals. Foote and Saunders (1990) content analyzed the visual content of 430 stories from the major network newscasts in 1988 for types of visuals. The categories included still visuals—such as maps, photographs, and illustrations—and motion visuals such as video. Not surprisingly, the networks mixed visual communications with combinations of graphics and video or graphics and photographs.

The combination of communication forms will likely expand as people increasingly use multimedia such as the Internet and CDs for information. Some Web sites currently manipulate written, verbal, and visual—both still and motion—presentations. Papacharissi (2002) coded personal Web sites for the presence of graphics, text, and interactivity to see how individuals present themselves online. Papacharissi found that Web page design was influenced by the tools supplied by Web space providers.

## Special Problems Associated with Measuring Nontext Forms

All content analysis projects face common problems such as sampling, reliability, content acquisition, and so on, which are the bases for most of this book. However, projects involving nontext content forms face special problems. Nontext communication adds dimensions that can by comparison cloud the manifest content of communication. For example, spoken or verbal communication depends, like text, on the meaning of words or symbols, but it also involves inflection and tone that affect the meaning applied by receivers. The simple verbal expression "the hamburger tastes good" can be ironic or not if a particular emphasis is added to the words; no such emphasis can easily be inferred from written text unless it is explicitly stated in the text. Inflection and tone can be difficult to interpret and categorize, placing an extra burden on content analysts to develop thorough coding instructions for verbal content.

Similarly, visual communication can create analysis problems because of ambiguities that are not easily resolved from within the message itself. For instance, a text description of someone can easily reveal age with a number: John Smith is 35. A visual representation of that same person becomes much more vague. Olson (1994) found that she could establish reliability for coding character ages in TV soap operas by using wide age ranges (e.g., 20–30 years old, 30–40 years old, etc.). This may not be a problem in some research, but reliability may come at the expense of validity when studying content variables such as the ages of characters in advertising. It is often difficult to differentiate a person who is 16 years old from one who is 18 years old, yet some content analyses would suggest that characters 18 years and older are adults, whereas 17-year-olds qualify as teenagers.

Because of the shared meaning of so many commonly used words, written text may in effect provide within-message cues that can serve to reduce ambiguity. Shared meanings of visual images are less common. Researchers should be cautious and thorough about assigning numbers to symbols whose meanings are to be drawn from visual cues. Consider the task of inferring the socioeconomic status of characters in television programs. Identifying a White, pickup-truck-driving man in his 40s as working class on the basis of clothing—denim jeans, flannel shirts, and a baseball cap—may be more reliable and valid than using the same cues to assign a teenager to that class.

Combinations of communication forms—visual with verbal, for example—can generate coding problems because of between-form ambiguity. That is, multiform communication requires consistency among the forms if accurate communication is to occur. If the visual, text, and verbal forms are inconsistent, the meaning of content becomes ambiguous, and the categorizing of that content becomes more difficult. A television news package might have a text describing a demonstration as not violent, whereas the accompanying video shows people throwing bottles. A researcher can categorize the two forms separately, but it becomes difficult to reconcile and categorize the combined meaning of the two forms.

## MEASURING CONTENT IN UNITS

As described in chapter 1 (this volume), quantitative content analysis takes a reductionist approach. The content under study is divided into smaller elements and then analyzed to draw conclusions about the whole. Therefore, no matter what content form an analyst selects to study, content must be reduced to units to measure it (see Table 4.1). A *unit of content* is a discretely defined element of that content. It can be a word, sentence, paragraph, image, article, television program, or any other description of content based on a definable physical or temporal boundary or symbolic meaning. A minute of television news can be a content unit as can the bias found in a collection of words.

TABLE 4.1
Definitions for Various Types of Units Used in Content Analysis

I. A *unit* of content is a discretely defined element of content. It can be a word, sentence, paragraph, image, article, television program, or any other content elements with a definable physical or temporal boundary. Units of content are used as study units and information units.

II. *Study units* are elements of content that are selected and defined by the content analyst. They include recording, context, sampling, and analysis units.

    A. *Sampling units* are the physical units that will be selected for study from the entire content of interest.

    B. *Recording units* are the elements of content that will be classified in the coding process. Recording units also must have a physical or temporal delineation such as word, article, publication, letter, or speech.

    C. *Context units* are the content elements that should be examined to appropriately assign content to recording units. The context units can be the same as or larger than the recording unit, but they cannot be smaller.

    D. *Analysis unit* is used here to mean the units that are analyzed statistically to test hypotheses or answer research questions.

III. *Information units* are elements specifically related to the meaning and production of content. Content units represent elements defined independently of the study and often by the creator of the content. They are used to operationalize the study units.

    A. *Physical units* are the space and time devoted to content.

    B. *Meaning units* for use in content analysis are syntactical, referential, propositional, and thematic units.

        1. *Syntactical units* occur as discrete units within a language or medium. The simplest unit in language is the word. In addition, sentences, paragraphs, articles, and books are also natural language units.

        2. *Referential units* involve some physical or temporal unit (e.g. event, people, objects, etc.) referred to within content. Some scholars use the term *character units* in place of referential units. Character units involve measuring content about a person to whom the content refers.

        3. *Propositional units* involve placing content into a consistent structure that facilitates analysis of meaning.

        4. *Theme units.* Some scholars have used simpler definitions of theme units. Berelson (1952) said a theme is "an assertion about a subject matter" (p. 18), and Holsti (1969) said a theme "is a single assertion about some subject" (p. 116). For the sake of clarity, the term *subject thematic units* is used for Holsti's and Berelson's (1952) theme, and the term *structural thematic units* is used for Krippendorf's (1980) thematic units.

Two general types of units are relevant to content analysis. *Study units* are the elements of content that are defined by the content analyst in the process of reducing and selecting the material to be studied. If a scholar wants to study the changing content found on an Internet news site during a week, the first step is to reduce and structure the content so it can be selected, analyzed, and recorded. This process must be undertaken before the units can be categorized with a coding protocol. The first step in research design is deciding how content will be divided into study units.

*Information units* are the second type of content units and are specifically related to the meaning and production of content. Information units carry meaning that affects the receiver of the message embedded in the content. They involve meaningful symbols that can be grouped semantically as words, sentences, visual images, or groups in physical units such as time and space. Information units are selected by the content analyst, but they are defined independently of the study, usually by the creator of the content.

Some examples might help explain the two types of units. Law and Labre (2002) studied the images of male bodies in *GQ, Rolling Stone* and *Sports Illustrated* from 1967 to 1997. Law and Labre's study units for sampling included the magazine issues from every 3rd year. From these, Law and Labre identified 8,663 pages with images of men, and 409 of these images fit their definition of body images. All of these were forms of study units that Law and Labre used to get to the content (images) of interest. Law and Labre produced the information unit by concentrating only on the visual portion of the images that included the torso and arms from the neck to waist. These visual units were coded according to eight body types based on body fat and muscular structure. Law and Labre concluded that images of male bodies in these magazines became more lean, muscular, and v shaped during the period studied.

Often information and study units will be equivalent, but they need not be. Terms such as *political activists,* for example, are information units because they have meaning among those who use them whether a content analyst examines them or not. At the same time, terms such as political activists can become study units if the content analyst decides to count the number of times the term appears in newspaper stories about politics and sample a certain number of them.

Jolliffe and Catlett (1994) examined whether having women in editorial positions affected stereotypical treatment of women. Jolliffe and

Catlett's information units were traits and behaviors associated with female characters in nonfiction articles in seven women's magazines. For example, women characters could have traits such as dependent, family servant, and so on. These information units were also used as the study units. Jolliffe and Catlett concluded that having women as editors did not reduce stereotypical portrayals, but positive portrayals did increase.

In a study of advertisements for journalism and mass communication faculty, Stone (1993) examined efforts to increase faculty diversity. One variable was the number of diversity words in the advertisements. These were defined as "words in the advertisement for: (1) Affirmative Action/Equal Opportunity(AA/EO); (2) African American or minority; (3) women; (4) disabled person; and (5) multicultural, specifically distinguishing between African American and other minorities such as Asian, Hispanic, Native American and foreign" (Stone, 1993, p. 195). In Stone's study, the study unit (a word) was the same as the information unit, a word signifying an interest in diversity.

The process of selecting types of information units to use as study units lies at the heart of successful research design. Defining study units involves the practical process of designing a study and developing a protocol. This definition requires selecting from among types of information units, which can be defined in terms of their symbolic and physical qualities.

## Study Units

Study unit identification is the first step in the process of measurement faced by the content analyst. Study units fall into four types: sampling, recording, context, and analysis, and all must be specified for each content analysis.

*Sampling Units.* *Sampling units* are discrete elements of content that will be selected for study from the entire content of interest. The researcher might want to sample from letters written by a person, newspapers, newspaper articles, cable programs, Web URLs, TV news stories, or political speeches. The sampling unit depends on the type of content being studied, and the sampling scheme can be simple or elaborate. For example, the sampling unit in a study (Reid, King, & Kreshel, 1994) of models in cigarette and alcohol advertisements was every half page or larger advertisement from 11 consumer magazines between June 1990 and June 1991. The episode was the sampling unit in a study (Abelman, 1994) of the content in *The 700 Club,* a religious television program. Abelman randomly selected 30 episodes between February and April 1992. In chapter 5 (this volume), we provide detail on how units are sampled.

*Recording Units.* *Recording units* are the elements of content that will be classified in the coding process. Budd, Thorp, and Donohew (1967) called these "coding units." The recording unit is the basic unit in content analysis. They may be equivalent to the sampling units, but they do not have to be. A researcher examining the number of characters in television dramas holding blue-collar jobs could sample television programs and record the number of such characters by network, by night, or even by season.

As Krippendorff (1980) pointed out, it is common for the recording unit to be different from the sampling unit. Prominent literary figures of the 1930s might be sampled and themes in their letters used as recording units. It is often difficult to identify and list all potential recording units. For example, a researcher would find it impossible to list every violent scene in every film. However, such a list is not necessary because sampling can occur in stages. The first sampling unit could be the film, and the second sampling stage would select violent scenes in films. A third sampling unit would be violent acts within violent scenes. The recording units would be individual acts of violence within the films and would be equivalent to the third sampling unit.

Niven (2003) examined newspaper coverage of four U.S. representatives and senators who switched political parties between 1995 and 2001. Niven's sample unit was the newspaper story, and his recording unit was tone of individual paragraphs (positive, negative, and neutral). In her study of sex on soap operas, Olson (1994) used a specific sexual behavior, such as erotic touching and explicit verbal depiction of sexual intercourse, as her recording units. Each such act counted as one unit and was classified under a variety of types of sexual acts. In Jolliffe and Catlett's (1994) study of women editors and stereotypical portrayals, they used the number of traits assigned to women characters as recording units.

*Context Units.* *Context units* are the elements that cue researchers to the context that should be examined in assigning content to categories. If a category is the socioeconomic status of a television character, for instance, the classification of the characters will be based on a character's dress, language skills, friends, and surroundings. These surroundings, characteristics, and behaviors represent the content that provides context for coding.

The context unit can be the same as or larger than the recording unit, but it cannot be smaller. A study examining whether assertions about a candidate are positive or negative (e.g., can or cannot be trusted to fulfill campaign promises) will use the assertion as the recording unit. However, the individual, isolated assertion may or may not be sufficiently meaningful for the researcher to identify whether it is negative or positive. Asserting that a candidate did not fulfill a campaign promise after a previous election would be negative or positive depending on how that promise is presented in the context of the article. In such an example, the researcher must decide whether the paragraph around the assertion, several paragraphs, or the entire article is the appropriate context unit.

In Olson's (1994) study of sex in soap operas, the scene was the context unit for evaluating the nature of a particular sexual behavior. The scene was examined to classify behaviors. A scene could contain more than one behavior or recording unit.

Kurpius and Mendelson (2002) examined the content of the C–SPAN call-in program *Washington Journal.* In an effort to identify how often "new political ideas" were introduced, Kurpius and Mendelson had to develop a context unit. Because the program was treated as a conversation, the entire program was the context unit. If a caller offered new information about a civic issue that had not been mentioned previously on the program, coders categorized it as new.

*Analysis Units.*    Holsti (1969) used analysis unit as a general heading for sampling, recording, and context units because all of these types of units affect the analysis of the data. However, the term *analysis unit* is used here to mean the units that are analyzed statistically to test hypotheses or answer research questions. This more specific definition is used to indicate that the recording units may or may not be the same ones used for analysis.

A study of violence on television might categorize each act by a character as aggressive or not aggressive. The act is the recording unit. The unit of analysis might then become the mean number of acts of aggression in each television program or the percentage of actions in a program that were aggressive. In either case, the unit being analyzed statistically (aggressive acts per program or percentage of acts that are aggressive per program) is not the same as the original recording unit, which was an individual act by a character.

An analysis unit can never be more detailed than a recording unit. Recording units can be combined in a variety of ways by a computer, but the computer cannot break recording units into smaller units than they already are. This maxim is important when a researcher plans to use a variety of measures for analyzing content.

In a study (Lacy & Ramsey, 1994) of advertising content in African American newspapers Lacy and Ramsey used the newspaper as the sampling unit. To determine if a graphic unit was an advertisement, the researchers examined the content within the borders of the graphic, which defined the context unit. The recording units were the number of advertisements per newspaper edition and the square inches of advertising per edition. These two measures also served as analysis units. However, the study included another analysis unit: the percentage of advertisements that fit into specific categories such as local. This analysis unit was calculated by dividing the advertisements in a specific category by the total advertisements in the newspaper.

Most studies end up using more than one type of unit in each of these types. Often more than one sampling, recording, context, or analysis unit is used. An example may clarify the relationship among these study units. Lacy (1987) studied the impact of daily newspaper competition within a city on news and editorial content. The study used two sampling units. First, 114 dailies were randomly selected from a list of U.S. dailies. After the dailies were selected, seven editions were selected from the month of November. The recording units were the individual articles in these newspapers and the square inches devoted to these articles. Each was classified into a number of variables (who wrote it, topic of the article, etc.) based on a reading of the article. Therefore, the context unit also was the article. The analysis used a variety of units. Proportions of *newshole* (total space not devoted to advertising) devoted to a given topic, square inches of space per reporter who was bylined in the editions, square inches of space, and other measures were all included in the analysis.

## Information Units

Study units can be operationalized in a variety of ways, and these involve the use of information units. Smaller units, such as words and shapes, are combined to create larger information units such as photographs, sentences, paragraphs, articles, and publications. Information units are further classified as meaning units and physical units. *Meaning* occurs when a sender or receiver associates a cognitive or affective mental state to symbols used in content. Symbols are discrete units of content that contain meaning for either the sender, the receiver, or both. The word *house* (whether spoken or written) symbolizes a structure in which people live. *Physical units* are the space and time devoted to content. The two are related; generally, the more physical units involved, the more symbols will be present and the more meaning the content is likely to have. A story of 12 column inches probably contains more information and meaning than a 6-in. story. However, the correlation will be less than perfect because all information contains redundancies. Of course, the specific meaning also may vary even if the numbers of physical units are equal because of the different symbols contained in the content.

As noted in chapter 1 (this volume), O'Dell and Weideman (1993) examined language symbols in Schreber's 1903 autobiography, *Memoirs of My Nervous Illness* (1903/1955), which was made famous when Freud (1911) analyzed the book. O'Dell and Weideman used a computer to analyze what they called "psychotic words." These words were both the information unit and the study units. O'Dell and Weiderman (1993) concluded, contrary to Freud, that "sexuality is fairly far down the list, which makes it hard to claim, from our data, that Schreber's principal problem was a sexual one" (p. 124).

Visual images also contain symbols that can be studied. Photographs of dead soldiers can symbolize the horror of war for some but a feeling of victory for others. Grabe (1996) used a "visual dictionary" to analyze the South African Broadcasting Company's coverage of elections. Grabe used shot length, camera angle, camera movement, and editing as ways to detect meaning in the election visuals. Grabe concluded that the National Party received a positive visual bias in its coverage. However, Grabe said she could not infer about the impact of this coverage on the election.

*Types of Physical Units.*    Physical units are item, time, and space measures of content. Measuring text and still visuals involves counting elements, such as number of items (stories, books, etc.), and space units such as square inches and centimeters. Some research has indicated that the two are correlated. Windhauser and Stempel (1979) examined correlations among six measures of local newspaper political coverage (article, space, statement, single issue, multiple issue, and headline). Rank order correlations varied from .692 for headline and multiple issue to .970 for space and article. Windhauser and Stempel concluded that some physical measures might be interchangeable. The type of measure used should be based on the type of information needed in the study, variables being investigated, and the theoretical basis for the study.

Verbal and moving visual communication can also be measured by number of items (e.g., number of times a character appears in a video or number of times a particular word is used to refer to someone), but space has little meaning in such use. Verbal content does not involve space, and the size of space devoted to a visual element depends on the equipment used to display the visual (larger screens have more space than smaller screens). Instead of space, verbal and moving visual communication have time dimensions measured in terms of time devoted to the visual and verbal content. For example, television newscasts can be evaluated by measuring the number of stories that fall into given topics or by the seconds of time given the topic categories. The average length of time given topics is assumed to relate to the depth of coverage. The more time a story consumes, the more information it contains.

Although they are among the most objective units used in content analysis, physical units often are used to infer to the values of the sender and to their impact on the receivers; the higher the number of physical units in a given amount of content, the greater value they will be to senders and the greater the impact on receivers, although the correlation is not perfect. For example, the more space devoted to a topic by a gatekeeper, the more important the topic to the gatekeeper. However, is it also true that the more a television advertisement is repeated, the greater the effects on viewers?

In addition to space, time, or items, physical units can be measured as proportions. Studies have used the percentage of items, space, or time devoted to particular types of content as a measure of value to the sender or impact on the receiver. Newspapers with high proportions of space given to local news indicate the importance of local coverage to the newspaper's staff and possibly to the readers. Matera and Salwen (1996) examined the complexity of questions reporters asked presidential candidates by classifying their levels of complexity (single-barrel, double-barrel, and multibarrel) based on how many different responses were required to answer. Matera and Salwen found that the proportion of complex questions from journalists during debates varied, but no clear longitudinal trend was found.

In sum, because physical units do not represent symbolic meaning, they often are used to infer to allocation decisions about content and the degree of impact on users of content as was suggested in earlier discussion of antecedents and consequences of content in chapter 1 (this volume). The ability to make such inferences is based on two assumptions: First, the allocation of physical units is not random, and these allocations result in identifiable content patterns; second, the greater the content devoted to an issue, subject, or person, the greater will be the total impact on the audience as a group. A newspaper that uses 75% of its news content for stories about the city in which it is located demonstrates a conscious effort to appeal to readers interested in local happenings. At the same time, allocating 75% of space to local coverage has a different impact on the total readership than allocating 50%.

Lacy (1988), for example, found that as competition from all newspapers in a market increased, newshole and the percentage of newshole devoted to news about the home city and county increased. Controlling for other variables, about 14% of variation in newshole was associated with the level of this intercity competition. This finding is consistent with a wide range of anecdotal information about how newspapers try to attract readers and with economic theory.

*Types of Meaning Units.*    Physical information units use standardized measurement units. A square inch, a minute, or a letter have beginning and ending points that all researchers accept. In addition, physical units are independent of symbolic meaning. In fact, if symbolic meaning is involved with a standard physical unit, it is a syntactical unit, which is discussed following. Meaning units, although they may involve physical and temporal qualities, are less standardized. Sources in a news story, for example, will have words attributed to them, but the number of words can vary greatly. It is the meaning of the words or the meaning of using a particular source that is being studied more than the number of words per se.

Krippendorff (1980) suggested four types of symbolic units for use in content analysis: syntactical, referential, propositional, and thematic units. *Syntactical units* occur as discrete units in a language or medium. The simplest syntactical unit in language is the word, but sentences, paragraphs, articles, and books are also syntactical units. Syntactical units in the Bible would be chapters and verses. In plays, they are scenes and acts; in television, the commercials, programs, and scenes within programs are syntax units.

Syntactical units are similar to physical units because they both have definite physical and temporal boundaries. However, they differ in that syntactical units are groupings of symbols (e.g., words, sentences, etc.) that help to communicate meaning. For instance, Lacy (1988) used square inches of newshole in newspapers as a unit of analysis. This is a physical content unit rather than a syntactical unit for two reasons. First, it was arbitrary. Lacy (1988) could have used square centimeters (or any number of physical units) just as easily. Second, the study dealt with allocation of space and not with the meaning of the words in that space.

In contrast, Lacy et al. (1991) used the number of words given a particular side of a controversy to measure balance as units of analysis. Words were syntactical units used because they carry meaning. One could not substitute a physical unit (square inches) for words because the number of words in a square inch varies with typeface and type size.

*Referential units* exist when some physical or temporal unit (e.g., event, people, objects, etc.) is referred to or alluded to within content. The referential unit can be addressed with a variety of symbols, but the particular symbols being used are categorized not as language units but by the object or person to which they refer. Any term referring to Bill Clinton, whether it is "former President Clinton" or "Slick Willy," has the same referential unit. Referential units can be used to measure the meaning attached to a particular person, event, or issue.

Fico, Ku, and Soffin (1994) used source, a referential unit, as a unit of analysis in their study of the Gulf War coverage. Any person who was identified as having provided information was classified as a particular type of source, and this was used to analyze where newspapers got their information about the war.

In an examination of slasher films, Sapolsky et al. (2003) compared violence in such films from the 1990s with those from the 1980s and with action movies from the 1990s. Sapolsky et al. used victims and perpetrators as referential units to define acts of violence. Sapolsky et al. found that 1990s slasher films had more acts of violence than those from the 1980s but that the more recent films rarely mixed scenes of violence and sex.

Holsti (1969) used the term "character units" instead of referential units. Examination of character units involves measuring content about a person to whom the content refers. A study of the meaning of statements about women characters in television situation comedies would involve character or referential units.

Focusing on *propositional units* involves seeing communication content in terms of constituent parts. Such a process in effect places content into a consistent structure that facilitates analysis of meaning. By classifying complex language into simpler propositions, for example, assertions about an object or person can be studied. As noted in chapter 1 (this volume), Zullow et al. (1988) developed the CAVE method to test whether pessimistic explanation style in people's statements could predict depression, achievement, and health. Zullow et al. first examined statements by political leaders and identified propositions within those statements that represented explanation of causes for events. These propositional statements were then rated along 7-point scales (stability vs. instability, globality vs. specificity, and internality vs. externality). The rankings for explanation were used to predict outcomes of events involving the politicians who made the statements.

Husselbee and Elliott (2002) used "statements" as propositional units to study how national and regional newspapers framed hate crimes in Texas and Wyoming. They were guided by a Husselbee and Stempel study (1997) that defined a statement as "a complete thought, which normally means a subject, verb and predicate." (p. 594). A sentence could contain more than one statement.

The *thematic unit* is the fourth unit proposed by Krippendorff (1980), and it relates to how concepts of interest in the content—useful in developing narratives, explanations, or interpretations of content—can be identified structurally. Krippendorff (1980) emphasized that such concepts can have several dimensions embedded in the structure of the content. This content structure can itself be a theme meriting examination.

Other scholars also discussed theme units. Berelson (1952) called a theme "an assertion about a subject matter" (p. 18), whereas Holsti (1969) viewed a theme as "a single assertion about some subject" (p. 116). The singular *an* and *a* in each definition is noteworthy; the advantage of Krippendorff's (1980) approach to thematic units is that they can incorporate nuances particular to the content being studied (i.e., if two or more assertions are required for concluding that a theme exists).

How are these different types of theme analysis applied? Abelman and Neuendorf (1985) classified 5-min segments of religious programming in terms of whether the theme of each was political, social, or religious. This type of study is consistent with the Holsti (1969) and Berelson (1952) use of the term theme. Weiss and Wilson (1996) studied emotional portrayals in family television using a classification system that seems consistent with Krippendorff's (1980) definition. As part of Weiss and Wilson's study, they classified the humorous content of the programs into eight types of humor (sarcasm, repartee, absurd humor, and so on). The classification was based on the structure of the language, interaction among characters, and characters' activities.

The main difference, however, between Krippendorff's (1980) thematic units and Holsti's (1969) and Berelson's (1952) theme units reflects the classification system used for categorizing. The Holsti and Berelson (1952) systems have both emphasized the role of a "subject" in identifying the theme. A subject, such as a trade treaty between the United States and China, is necessary to classify the content properly. The treaty can have a variety of themes associated with it. Krippendorff's (1980) thematic units, however, need not have a subject. The theme is identified more by the structure within the content. Thus, types of humor can become a theme because the content structure, not subject, is used to classify the content. For the sake of clarity, the term *subject thematic units* is used for Holsti's and Berelson's (1952) theme, and the term *structural thematic units* is used for Krippendorff's (1980) thematic units.

Holsti (1969) argued that thematic units may be the most useful to content analysis because they allow the study of values, attitudes, beliefs, and other internal states of the communicator. However, units involving values, attitudes, and beliefs create difficulty in achieving reliability among coders. Thematic units can also create validity problems because clues to internal states of communicators involve more than manifest content.

A particularly promising approach to thematic units developed during the past few decades is the concept of framing (Reese, Gandy, & Grant, 2001). As a term, *framing* has been used widely, and Tankard (2001) identified three common definitions from the academic literature. He suggested the following as a comprehensive definition: "A frame is a central organizing idea for news content that supplies a context and suggests what the issue is through the use of selection, emphasis, exclusion, and elaboration" (Tankard, 2001, pp. 100–101).

Numerous studies, both qualitative and quantitative, have used the concept of framing with a variety of to operationalizations of that concept. For example, Winfield and Friedman (2003) conducted a qualitative analysis of the coverage of candidates' wives during the 2000 election to see how each woman's portrayal fit into four established frames. Andsager (2000) used terms in news stories and interest group news releases to identify 12 frames related to the issue of abortion. Golan and Wanta (2001) looked at how issue and attribute frames were applied to candidates.

Frames as thematic units involve both subject and structure themes. Because frames are applied to people, groups, and issues, they have subjects. Something is framed. Because researchers are looking for commonly used frames that reflect the variables shaping content, analyses should reveal common, typical, or repeated structure. This structure relates to variables such as the news routines, ideology, and economic resources that lead to commonly used frames that are applied consistently across media and across time.

The nature of this structure and the units attached to it continues to develop. Future work should yield a theory or theories relating antecedents to frames in content and the frames to media effects. Because the concept of framing and its empirical application is relatively young, measurement through content analysis continues to evolve. Tankard (2001) offered an excellent discussion and overview of the types of measurements that have been used and the pitfalls that await quantitative content analysis in this area.

Referential, propositional, and thematic (subject and structural) units are similar because they deal with specific semantic elements of messages. Whether one uses referential, propositional, or thematic units depends on what one wants to emphasize. Referential units emphasize the things or people being discussed. Propositional units serve best when the message can be easily restructured to better understand the meaning. Subject thematic units are best when the statements about objects take precedence over the objects themselves. Structural thematic units are useful when the structure of the content is central to defining the meaning in the content.

## Relation Between Content and Study Units

Study units must be defined for every content analysis project. A study of local television news coverage of a station's community would use the newscast (syntactical unit) as the sampling unit, minutes devoted to the city of license (physical and theme units) as the recording units, story (syntactical unit) as the context unit, and percentage of time during newscast (physical unit) as the analysis unit.

The grid in Fig. 4.1 shows how information units can be used to define study units. The information units define the study units. A given study is likely to have more than one type of each of the study units. As discussed in chapter 5 (this volume), some studies require more than one sampling unit. The type of information units used for recording units will be different for different variables. For example, studying the types of sources used in environmental coverage would require two recording units—sources (a referential unit) and the types of environmental coverage (subject thematic unit). In some situations, two forms of information units (symbolic and physical) are combined to create the recording unit (e.g., the square inches of copy devoted to a theme).

Identifying the appropriate information units for defining the various study units is crucial for creating a valid content analysis protocol (i.e., the instructions for coders to use in assigning content to categories). Ultimately, the numbers associated with units of analysis are the values of variables being studied. The process of selecting unit types must reflect

| | | | Sampling Units | Recording Units | Context Units | Analysis Units |
|---|---|---|---|---|---|---|
| Content Units | Physical Units | Space | | | | |
| | | Time | | | | |
| | | Et cetera | | | | |
| | Symbolic Units | Syntactical | | | | |
| | | Propositional | | | | |
| | | Thematic | | | | |
| | | Referential | | | | |

FIG. 4.1.   Information units become the operational definitions for study units.

the nature of the content, theoretical definitions of the variables, and the process of assigning numbers to units we discuss in the next section.

A study conducted by Sumpter and Braddock (2002) illustrates the relation between study units and information units. Sumpter and Braddock examined sources used in stories about the impact of Voter News Service (VNS) exit polls on coverage of the 2000 election. The sampling units were newspaper, broadcast, and wire service stories about VNS. The two recording units and units of analysis were equivalent and were the indirect or direct quotation or quotations attributed to a source and the source's affiliation. The context unit included the quotation itself for the former recording unit, and the context units for affiliation varied from the sentence to the entire story, depending on what was necessary to identify the affiliation. Affiliation was coded as one of 15 descriptions of their role in the story (e.g., Internet news worker, VNS representative) based on the syntactical units journalists use to identify sources' affiliations (e.g., clauses of words). Quotations were operationalized by coding them into 10 themes (information units) that summarized the opinions expressed by the sources. The study units were ways of grouping elements of content so the elements could be selected, categorized, recorded, and analyzed. The information units defined how the recording units would have numbers attached to them.

## CONNECTING UNITS WITH NUMBERS

After the units have been determined, researchers must develop a system for assigning numbers to the units. This involves deciding what level of measurement is appropriate, what types of categories for content will be used, and the rules by which numbers and categories will be connected.

### Levels of Measurement

Content can be assigned numbers that represent one of four levels of measurement: nominal, ordinal, interval, and ratio. These levels concern the type of information the numbers carry, and they are the same levels of measurement used in all social sciences.

*Nominal measures* have numbers assigned to categories of content. If one wants to study which countries are receiving the most coverage in newspaper articles, a researcher would assign each country a number and assign the appropriate number to each article on the basis of the country written about in the story. The numbers used for each story are arbitrary. Germany might be given a 1 and Japan a 2. However, assigning Germany a 10 and Japan 101 would work just as well. The numbers carry no meaning other than connecting the story to a country. Put another way, nominal measures have only the property of equivalency or nonequivalency (if 41 is the code for stories about Ireland, all Irish stories receive the value 41, and no other value is applied to Irish stories).

In a comparison of National Public Radio and Pacifica radio news content (Stavitsky & Gleason, 1994), each source was assigned to one of five subcategories (official, citizen, expert, journalist, and activist/advocate). Each of these was assigned a number for computer entry, but that number was arbitrary because the computer calculated the percentage of sources that fell in each category. In the article, the results were reported by the label of subcategory and not by the assigned number.

Nominal measures can take two different forms. The first treats membership in a collection of subcategories as a variable. Each subcategory in the variable gets a number to designate membership. As the previous example for countries illustrates, Germany would get a 1, Japan a 2, and Brazil a 3. Each is a subcategory of country.

The second form of nominal measure is to treat each subcategory as a variable and assign each case a number that either includes or excludes the case from the variable. Instead of assigning a story a 1 if Germany is covered or a 2 if Japan is covered, each article would get a 1 if Germany is covered and a 0 (zero) if not. Each article also gets a 1 or a 0 for every potential country.

With the one-variable approach, the category has multiple subcategories with one number each. With the multivariable approach, each subcategory becomes a variable with one number for having the variable characteristic and one for not having that characteristic. The multivariable approach allows the same article to be placed into more than one classification. It is particularly useful if a unit needs to be classified into more than one subcategory of a nominal variable. For example, if individual newspaper articles deal with more than one country, the multivariable system might work better.

*Ordinal measures* also place content units into categories, but the categories have an order to them. Each category is greater than or less than all other categories. Arranging categories in order carries more information about the content than just placing units into categories. The ordering of units can be based on any number of characteristics such as time (which article appeared first in a publication), the amount of content that fits a category (publications with more assertions than others), and the order of placement of a unit within a publication (front page placement in newspapers carries more importance than inside placement).

*Interval measures* have the property of order, but the number assignment also assumes that the differences between the numbers are equal. They are called interval measures because each interval is equal to all other intervals. The difference between 2 and 3 is equal to the difference between 3 and 4. The simple process of counting numbers of content units illustrates interval measures. If one wants to study the number of articles in a newsmagazine over time, the researcher could count the articles with headlines published in each issue for a period of time.

*Ratio measures* are similar to interval because the difference between numbers is equal, but ratio data also have a meaningful zero point. Counting the number of words in a magazine has no meaningful zero point because a magazine must have words by definition. However, if one counts the number of active verbs in a magazine, the measure is a ratio. It would be possible (although not likely) for a magazine to be written totally with passive verbs. Because ratio data have a meaningful zero point, researchers can find ratios among the data (e.g., Magazine A has twice as many active verbs as Magazine B).

In some situations, ratio data can be created from a nominal classification system when the ratio of units in one category to all units is calculated. For example, Beam (2003) studied whether content differed between groups of newspapers with strong and weak marketing orientation. Beam classified content units (self-contained units that could be understood independently of other content on the page) into a variety of categories for topic and type of item. Beam then calculated the percentage of content units within the various categories (e.g., content about government or the "public sphere") and compared the percentages for strong market-oriented newspapers with the percentages for weak market-oriented newspapers. This transformation of nominal data to ratio data was used because the number of content units varies from newspaper to newspaper, usually based on circulation size. A ratio measure allows one to compare relative emphasis regardless of number of units.

One advantage to using interval- and ratio-level measures with content analysis is that they allow the use of more sophisticated statistical procedures. These procedures, such as multiple regression, allow researchers to control statistically for the influences of a variety of variables and to isolate the relationships of interest. For example, Lacy (1988) used five market and organizational level variables (e.g., circulation size, number of households, etc.) as control variables to test the hypothesis that intercity competition intensity was related to content variations. Multiple regression allowed the removal of the influence of these control variables from the relationships between intercity competition and content.

## Importance of Measurement Levels

Selecting a measurement level for a category depends on two rules: The measurement level selected should be theoretically appropriate and carry as much information about the variables as possible. *Theoretically appropriate* means the measurement reflects the nature of the content and the particular hypotheses. If a hypothesis states that female writers will use more descriptive adjectives than male writers, content will have to be assigned to a nominal variable called *writer's gender*. The variable of descriptive adjectives could take several forms. One measure would be nominal by categorizing articles by whether they have descriptive adjectives. However, this nominal level fails to incorporate the reality of writing because it treats all articles equally whether they have 1 descriptive adjective or 100. A better measure with more information would be to count the number of descriptive adjectives in each article. This is a ratio level measure that would allow a far more sophisticated statistical procedure.

In fact, the level at which a variable is measured determines what types of statistical procedures can be used because each procedure assumes a level of measurement. Procedures that assume an interval or ratio level are called *parametric procedures,* which require certain population distributions to describe more precisely the population parameters with sample statistics. Nominal- and ordinal-level measures make no such assumptions about the population distribution and are less precise at describing the population of interest. Such nonparametric statistics provide less information about patterns in data sets and are often more difficult to interpret and allow for statistical controls.

## Classification Systems

A *classification system* is a collection of category definitions that assign values to recording units. Each category represents a variable. When values are nominal level, a category will have subcategories. For example, a category that assigns values based on political leaning of content will have subcategories such as liberal, conservative, and neutral. The main category and all subcategories will have definitions to guide assignment of values for the subcategories.

Category definitions can emphasize a variety of content units. Some studies of newspapers have looked at geographic emphasis of the articles, whereas others have assigned numbers that represent an order of importance based on the physical location of articles within the paper. The classification system uses definition categories to turn content into recording units.

Category definitions can be classified in a variety of ways. Deese (1969) provided a six-part typology useful in conceptualizing content analysis categories. These are

1. *Grouping*—Content is placed into groups when the recording units share common attributes. The more shared attributes a group has, the easier to classify the units and the smaller the amount of measurement error. In a study of network news coverage of an environmental controversy, Liebler and Bendix (1996) classified sources in news stories by whether they were in favor of cutting a forest that would endanger the Spotted Owl, against cutting, or neutral.

2. *Class structure*—Class structure is similar to grouping, but the groups have a hierarchical relation, with some classes (or groups) being higher than others. Deese (1969) said, "Abstractly, a categorical structure can be represented as a hierarchically ordered branching tree in which each node represents some set of attributes or markers which characterize all concepts below that node" (p. 45). The Strodthoff, Hawkins, and Schoenfeld (1985) classification system using three levels of abstraction (general, doctrinal, and substantive) for content involved a class structure based on how concrete magazine information was.

3. *Dimensional ordering or scaling*—Some content units can be classified on the basis of a numerical scale. Deese (1969) gave five abstract properties that typically involve scaling: (a) intensity, (b) numerosity, (c) probability, (d) position or length, and (e) time. It is fairly common to find content analyses using one or more of these types of scales.

Washburn (1995) studied the content of radio news broadcasts from three commercial and three nonprofit networks. Included among Washburn's variables were length of broadcast in minutes and seconds, the number of separate news items, and the average time given to news items. Washburn also examined the number of items given to particular topics such as the presidential election, foreign policy, and domestic policy. All of these represent a form of dimensional scaling.

4. *Spatial representation and models*—Language can be thought of as representing a cognitive space or map. The meaning of words and language can be placed in a mental spatial model that allows a person to evaluate objects, issues, and people along continua or dimensions. The analogy of language to spatial mapping can be traced to a number of scholars (Haney, 1973). Osgood, Suci, and Tannenbaum (1957) pioneered using the idea of semantic space to develop the semantic differential for measuring meaning people attach to given concepts.

Spatial models assume content has two or more dimensions that need description. Describing content along these dimensions of meaning is similar to applying a semantic differential through content analysis. A film could be described along 7-point scales as *good–bad, effective–ineffective,* and so on. The use of such models allows content analysts to explore complex meanings attached to symbols.

For example, Douglas and Olson (1995) developed a spatial approach using content in an experimental study. In this study, 308 students saw episodes from 13 television situation comedies and filled out questionnaires about family relationships. Douglas and Olson identified three functions that explained about 84% of the variation in programs. These functions (expressiveness, receptiveness, and task structure) serve as spatial dimensions of content that can differentiate these types of programs based on family relations.

5. *Abstract relations*—Both scales and maps represent effort to make language more concrete. They are practical ways of thinking and measuring abstract concepts. Some of these abstract concepts, such as friendship among TV characters, may not fit maps and scales well. Scales and maps categorize recording units by common characteristics rather than by relations that exist among elements within the recording unit. A classification system can specify and make more concrete these abstract relations expressed in content.

Potter, Vaughan, Warren, and Howley (1995) used the relational dynamics between an aggressive person and the victim to classify aggressive behavior in television content. The sometimes subtle concept of aggression was defined not by behaviors of the aggressor, such as hitting, but by the impact on the victims. Potter et al. thus distinguished between aggression as physical or direct and as symbolic, which included such behavior as coercion, deceit, and malicious remarks.

6. *Binary attribute structure*—In English and related languages, characteristics attributed to a person or thing often have an opposite. Good is the opposite of bad, and bright is the opposite of dark. These binary structures are often found in content, although concepts need not be thought of in these terms. In the field of journalism, reporters are assumed to be either subjective or objective by many readers.

Kenney and Simpson (1993) examined the bias in 1988 presidential campaign photographs in the *Washington Post* and *The Washington Times*. Photographs were classified as either favorable, unfavorable, or neutral toward the Democratic and Republican candidates. Similarly, a study of MTV content by Brown and Campbell (1986) classified content of music videos as prosocial and antisocial.

Deese's (1969) discussion deals with types of classification systems. Within these types, a specific system must be developed by the researcher for categorizing content in a particular study. These classification systems are crucial in determining the validity of a measurement system. The definitions used in a protocol for assigning numbers vary with the type of classification system. The selection of a system should have a theoretical basis. If, for example, a scholar wants to evaluate a way to measure degrees of political bias, a binary attribute classification system makes no sense. A dimensional ordering or a spatial model would be more appropriate.

## Classification Systems Requirements

The process of creating specific coding instructions for content must meet five requirements. Definitions for variables must (a) reflect the purpose of the research, (b) be mutually exclusive, (c) be exhaustive, (d) be independent, and (e) be derived from a single classification principle (Holsti, 1969, pp. 101).

To reflect the purpose of the research, the researcher must adequately define the variables theoretically. Then, the coding instructions must clearly specify how and why content units will be placed in categories for these variables. These instructions provide the operational definition that go with the theoretical definitions of the variables. The operational definition should be a reliable and valid measure of the theoretical concept.

Classification systems must be mutually exclusive when assigning numbers to recording units for a given variable. If magazine articles about environmental issues are being classified as proenvironment and antienvironment, the same article cannot logically be considered to be both. Using statistics to study patterns of content requires that units be unambiguous in their meaning, and assigning more than one number to a recording unit for a given variable creates ambiguity.

Of course it may be that an article contains both proenvironmental and antienvironmental statements. In such cases, the problem is solved by selecting smaller physical units that can be classified in mutually exclusive ways. Instead of selecting the article as the recording unit, statements within the article could become the recording unit. Setting up mutually exclusive categories requires a close examination of the unit categories (symbolic and physical) and the types of units (recording and analysis) being considered.

In addition to mutual exclusion for categories of a variable, classification systems must also be exhaustive. Every relevant recording unit must fit into a subcategory. This requirement is easy to fulfill in areas of content research that have received a great deal of attention. However, in areas that remain relatively unexplored, such as Web content, exhaustive category coding schemes will be more difficult to create. Often, researchers fall back on an "other" category for all the units that do not fit within defined categories. This may even be appropriate if a researcher is interested primarily in one category of content, for example, local news coverage. In such situations, all nonlocal coverage could be grouped together with no loss of important information.

However, the use of other should be undertaken cautiously. The more units that fall within the other category, the less information the researcher has about the content. Extensive pretesting with content similar to that being studied will help create categories that are exhaustive. Researchers can adjust the classification system and fine tune definitions as they pretest.

The requirement of independence in classification requires that placing a recording unit in one category does not influence the placement of the other units, a rule often ignored when ranking of content is involved. Ranking one unit affects all others unless they can be tied. Independence is also an important characteristic for statistical analysis. If recording units are not independent, an inference from a relationship in a sample of content to the population might not be valid. Such a relationship might represent nonindependence of recording units rather than a relationship among variables.

An example can illustrate the point. Suppose a researcher examines two TV situation comedies and two TV dramas for the number of minority characters during a season. Each program has 20 new episodes per year. One system involves assigning ranks based on the number characters who are Black, Hispanic, Native American, or Asian. The program with the most characters during a season is first, the second most is assigned second, and so on. Another system involves calculating the average number of characters per episode. Suppose for the entire season, Comedy A has five minority characters, Comedy B has three, Drama A has four, and Drama B has two.

The ranking system might result in the conclusion that TV comedies provide much more exposure to minority characters during a season because the comedies ranked first and third and the dramas ranked second and fourth. The second system gives an average of .20 minority characters per comedy episode (8 characters divided by 40 episodes) and an average of .15 minority characters per dramatic episode (6 characters divided by 40 episodes). The conclusion based on the second system is that neither program type provides extensive exposure to minority characters.

The first system creates an impression of an important difference because the assignment of rankings is not independent. The assignment of the first 3 ranks determines the fourth. An independent assignment system, such as average number of characters per episode, provides a more valid conclusion of television programming.

Finally, each category should have a single classification principle that separates different levels of analysis. For example, a system for classifying news stories by emphasis could have two dimensions: geographic location (local, national, international) and topic (economic, political, cultural, social). Each of the two dimensions would have a separate rule for classifying units. It would be a violation of the single classification rule to have a classification system that treated local, national, international location, and economic topic as if the four represented a single dimension. A rule that would allow classification in such a scheme mixes geographic and topic cues in the content.

Systems that do not have a single classification principle often also violate the mutually exclusive rule. A classification system that uses local, national, international, and economic would have difficulty categorizing recording units that concern local economic issues.

## Rules of Enumeration

No matter what classification system is used, quantitative content analysis requires rules for connecting recording units with numbers. The numbers will, of course, represent the level of measurement selected by the researcher. The rules may be as simple as applying a 1 to a certain recording unit, say positive stories, and a 0 to other recording units, say negative stories. Enumeration rules for nominal data require arbitrarily picking numbers for the groups. For interval or ratio data, the enumeration rules might be instructions about how to measure a given amount of space or time. For example, rules about measuring length of newspaper articles require a physical description of where to place the ruler.

No matter what the rules are for assigning numbers to content, they must be clear and consistent. The same numbers are applied in the same way to all equivalent recording units. If a scholar studies the percentage of time during a television program devoted to violent acts, the rules of enumeration must clearly identify the point at which the timing of a violent act begins.

The success of enumeration rules affects the reliability as well as the validity of the study. The rules must provide consistent numbering of content.

## MEASUREMENT STEPS

The following five steps summarize the process of measuring content:

1. Develop research hypotheses or questions. Research questions and hypotheses force researchers to identify the variables they want to study. The hypotheses and research questions form the basis of the study. They should be explicitly stated and referred to as the data are analyzed and explained.

2. Examine existing literature that has used the variable or that discusses the measurement of the variable. Social science research

should build on what is already known. This knowledge is best presented in the form of formal theory. However, explicitly presented theory is sometimes absent, so new research is based on existing empirical studies. Occasionally, commentary articles address methodology and measurement issues. Reviewing the existing literature in whatever form is crucial for accurate measurement.

The initial use of the literature is to provide a theoretical definition of the variables being addressed in the research. Theoretical definitions are important for guiding measurement because they play a role in establishing the face validity of a measure. If the measurement of the variable reflects a reasonable representation of the theoretical definition of a variable, the measure can be said to have face validity (see chap. 7, this volume).

3.  Use good previous measures, or if the measurement is not good enough, adjust your measures. Reviewing the literature will provide theoretical definitions of variables and potential operationalization of those variables. However, researchers need to be cautious about using existing measures. They should be used critically. The variable being studied might be slightly different from those in existing literature, and all measures also have error.

If a modified measure is used, the new one should have face validity and be consistent with existing measures. The modification should be aimed at reducing measurement error by making the new measure more consistent with the theoretical definition of the variable being studied.

During this step, the researcher has to decide the appropriate level of measurement for the variables. This level must reflect the theoretical definition. If a new measure is being developed, this new measure should aim at higher levels of measurement when appropriate. Higher level measurements provide more precise tests of hypotheses.

4.  Create coding instructions. Explicit coding instructions require that recording and context units be defined in as much detail as is possible and practical. The more detailed the definitions, the higher the reliability. However, a researcher must be careful not to be so detailed as to make the application of the coding instruction too difficult.

Defining the recording units involves selecting among type of information units, setting up the classification system, and deciding the enumeration rules. All of this must be done and presented in a logical order that will allow a coder to refer to the instructions easily as he or she codes the content being studied.

The coding instructions include any technical information about how the process will work. This would include rules for rounding off numbers and any physical limits used to narrow down the content being studied.

5. Create coding sheets for recording data that will go into a computer. Any quantitative content analysis project of decent size should use a computer for analyzing the data. Computers are faster and make fewer computational mistakes. It is unusual for data to be entered directly from the content into the computer, so most projects require coding sheets. Numbers for the recording units are put on these sheets and then entered into a computer. Although it is possible with laptop computers to go from content to computers, the process might interfere with the flow of coding and could take more time as coders move from content to computer and back.

A variety of coding-sheet formats can be used. The primary criteria are efficiency in data input and keeping cost down. It is important that the coding instructions or protocol and coding sheets can be used easily together. The variables should be arranged and numbered consistently between the two. In chapter 6 (this volume), we go into more detail about coding sheets.

## SUMMARY

Measurement is the process of moving from theoretical definitions of concepts to numerical representations of those concepts as variables. This process is called operationalization. All measures must have face validity, which requires a logical connection between the assignment of numbers to content and the theoretical definitions.

The measurement process involves identifying the appropriate recording units, context units, and analysis units and coming up with classification systems for these units. The classification system uses information units to develop definitions of variables and subcategories for the variables. These variable subcategories must be translated into numbers, which requires the selection of appropriate levels of measurement, a system for classifying content, and rules for applying numbers to the content.

The process is governed by coding instructions and coding sheets. The instructions should allow a variety of coders to assign numbers to content reliably. The sheets should allow efficient and accurate transference of the numbers to a computer.

# 5

# *Sampling*

In chapter 3 (this volume), one of the questions posed in the model of content analysis asked "How much data would be needed to test the hypotheses or answer the research questions?" To begin to answer this question, a distinction must be made between all relevant content and a subset, or sample, of this content. In an ideal world, sampling would not be an issue for social scientists. Researchers would include all relevant content in their studies. A study concerning gender representation on television would examine every program on every channel during all pertinent time periods.

However, social researchers face trade-offs between the ideal and practical limitations of time and money. Examining all relevant content is impractical when thousands or even millions of content units are in the population. In other situations, researchers find content cannot be obtained. These obstacles to conducting a census of all content units require the use of sampling.

A *sample* is a subset of units from the entire population being studied. The usual goal of such samples is to represent the population. When *probability samples* (units are randomly chosen) are selected, scholars can make valid inferences about the population of content under study. The inferences drawn from a probability sample are subject to sampling error, but statistical procedures enable researchers to generate estimates of this sampling error with a given level of probability. If researchers assemble samples in any way other than random sampling (and many do or must), the representativeness of the sample is biased, and sampling error cannot be calculated accurately.

Content sampling follows the same procedural sequence as does survey sampling. In each case, the researcher must define the universe, population, and sampling frame appropriate to the research purpose and design. The *universe* includes all possible units of content being considered. The *population* is composed of all the sampling units to which the study will infer. The *sampling frame* is the actual list of units from which a sample is selected.

An example may help clarify the relationship among these groups. If a researcher were interested in studying the historical accuracy of William Shakespeare's plays, the universe would be all plays written by Shakespeare, published or unpublished. Because Shakespeare might have written some plays that were unpublished and lost over time, the population would be all published plays attributed to Shakespeare. Finally, the sampling frame would be a list of plays available to the researcher. A sample of plays randomly taken from this list would be a sample of the population if the sampling frame and population are the same. If one of the plays had gone out of print and a copy was not available, the population and sampling frame would be different. When an intact set of all units of a population is unavailable, the sampling frame becomes the available content that is sampled and about which inference is made.

The Shakespeare example illustrates a source of possible confusion about sampling and recording units discussed in chapter 4 (this volume). The content one seeks to study is not necessarily the same as the content available for sampling. For example, a content analysis exploring the professional roles of African American characters in television dramas could not reasonably include a list of all the characters before the content is sampled. The population (all African American characters) can be specified, but the sampling frame cannot. This problem may be solved with a technique called *multistage sampling* in which television dramas, which are easily assembled in a sampling frame, are sampled, and then the characters are analyzed as they are encountered. Several types of sampling are available to solve such problems, but selecting among them requires an understanding of the differences between sampling, recording, and analysis units. Confusion over these units can lead to unrepresentative samples.

## SAMPLING TIME PERIODS

Most survey researchers conduct cross-sectional studies. They sample people at one point in time to investigate attitudes and perceptions. Although some content analysts conduct cross-sectional research, they are more likely to study content that appears at more than one point in time. Because communication occurs on an ongoing and often regular basis, it is difficult to understand the forces shaping content and the effects of content without examining content at various times.

When content is available from several time periods, some interesting longitudinal designs are possible. For example, Danielson, Lasorsa, and Im (1992) compared the readability of newspapers and novels from 1885 until 1989. Danielson et al. found that the *New York Times* and *Los Angeles Times* became harder to read, but novels became easier to read during this 104-year period. Such long-term content analysis research designs, discussed in chapter 3 (this volume), require a population and sampling frame that incorporates time as well as content.

The need of content analysis studies to sample units of content (which represent people or media organizations) and time can create confusion as to which population inferences are applicable. For example, in a classic study, Adams (1980) selected 10 television stations in western and central Pennsylvania as a convenience sample of media organizations, but he randomly selected 95 newscasts between August 17 and September 8, 1976. Any generalization from the study can be made only to these 10 stations for the 3 weeks defined by the time sampling frame. The use of random sampling allowed Adams to infer to all 420 early and late evening newscasts during the period.

When researchers infer in content analysis, they should make clear whether the inference concerns content, time, or both. The appropriate dimension of inference (content or time) is based on which was selected with a probability sample.

## SAMPLING TECHNIQUES

At its most basic level, sampling means selecting a group of content units to analyze. Just how this is done affects conclusions that are drawn from analyzing that content. To estimate the sampling error and infer to a large population of content, the sample must be a probability sample. Any estimate of sampling error with a nonprobability sample is meaningless, and inferential statistics have no validity.

Of course, analyzing all content units in a population eliminates sampling error because no such error exists in a census. However, a census of content units requires a great deal of time if the population is large. Researchers face the problem of collecting a sample that will allow valid conclusions about some larger group without taking excessive amounts of time to complete the project. The following sampling techniques help do that.

## Census

A census means every unit in a population is included in the content analysis. McLoughlin and Noe (1988) studied the leisure coverage in *Harper's, Atlantic Monthly,* and *Reader's Digest* from 1960 to 1985 by examining every copy of these three magazines. This involved 936 issues and 11,000 articles. A census provides the most valid discussion of a population because it included all units. However, all studies have limits, either with time period or number of publications involved. In the study just discussed, McLoughlin and Noe could have selected a probability sample for these three magazines to reduce coding time and used that time to expand the number of magazines coded.

A census often makes the most sense for research that examines a particular event or series of events. Jung (2002) wanted to study how *Time* and *Fortune* magazines covered three mergers that involved the parent corporation, Time, Inc. In the study, Jung started by examining all issues from three newsmagazines and three business magazines, including *Time* and *Fortune*, published the month before the merger announcements. All articles and visuals from the 22 issues of these six magazines that included coverage were analyzed. Because of the relatively small population of content dealing with these mergers, a random sample would not have identified all of the stories and would have likely distorted the results.

Deciding between a census and a sample becomes an issue of how best to use coders' time to accomplish the research goals. Whether a census is feasible depends on the resources and goals of individual research projects. The following rule applies: The larger the sample size, the less biased will be the results, but the more resources the project will require.

## Nonprobability Sampling

Despite the limitations of nonprobability samples in generating estimates of sampling error, they are used often. Such samples are appropriate under some conditions but often must be used because an adequate sampling frame is not available. Two nonprobability techniques are commonly used: convenience samples and purposive sampling. In a study by Riffe and Freitag (1997) of content analysis articles in *Journalism & Mass Communication Quarterly* from 1971 to 1995, they found that 68.1% of all articles used purposive samples and 9.7% used convenience samples.

*Convenience Samples.* A convenience sample involves using content because it is available. If all the units in the population being examined are available, the study would be a census, but this is rare. The convenience sample often is used because the content was collected in a way not related to the study's purpose. A library, for example, subscribes to newspapers on the basis of faculty and student requests and not to provide a selection of papers representing some larger population. This means the newspapers in the library were not randomly selected and therefore not statistically representative of any population. One way to think of a convenience sample is that it is a census, but the population is defined by availability rather than research questions. Thus, this population is a biased representation of the universe of units, and that bias is impossible to calculate.

Convenience samples have obvious limitations when used to infer to a larger population, but they can be justified under three conditions. First, the material being studied must be difficult to obtain. For example, a random sample of the magazines published in 1900 cannot be obtained. A sampling frame of such periodicals would be incomplete because a complete list of magazines from that period is unavailable. What is more important, most magazine editions from that period no longer exist. A researcher could, however, acquire lists of magazine collections from libraries around the country and generate a random sample from all the surviving magazine copies from 1900. This, however, would be extremely expensive and time consuming.

Such an example points to a second condition that would justify a convenience sample: Resources limit the ability to generate a random sample of the population. Just how much time and money a researcher should be willing to spend before this condition is satisfied is a question for each researcher to answer. Whatever a scholar's decision, it will eventually be evaluated by journal reviewers.

The third condition justifying convenience sampling is when a researcher is exploring some underresearched but important area. When little is known about a research topic, even a convenience sample becomes worthwhile in generating hypotheses for additional studies. When such exploratory research is undertaken, the topic should be of importance to the scholarly, professional, or policy-making communities. Of course, some areas are under-researched and destined to remain that way because they are neither very interesting nor very important.

Convenience samples play a role when a sampling frame is difficult to create and when important relationships have yet to be tested adequately. For example, the Attorney General's Commission on Pornography in 1986 issued its conclusions about pornography without using quantitative analysis (Duncan, 1989), prompting new research efforts in the area. Some systematic studies of heterosexual pornography were available, but little research examined the commission's conclusions about gay pornography. Duncan (1989) used a convenience sample of 158 gay pornographic magazines from 1960 through 1984. Part of the sample was collected from 1970 to 1984 by purchasing every fifth magazine from adult bookstores in two major cities in the United States. To extend the study backward to 1960, the researcher bought magazines from secondhand sources. Surviving collections of material contain unknowable biases.

Duncan (1989) cautioned, "Generalizations from this convenience sample, must, of course, be made very cautiously" (p. 95). However, Duncan (1989) went on to explain his efforts to reduce and check bias in the sample. Duncan (1989) said: (a) the two cities were in two different regions but contained similar magazines, (b) an informal check in other cities showed that much of the same material was being sold, and (c) mail-order catalogs for gay pornography showed the same material offered in bookstores.

With little research available, such samples provide a starting point for scholarship. However, the researcher should attempt to reduce bias and to justify the use of such limited samples. Convenience samples should never be used purposefully to introduce bias into studies.

*Purposive Samples.*    Purposive sampling uses a nonprobability sample because of the nature of the research project. Studies of particular types of publications or particular times may be of interest because these publications were important or the time played a key role in history. The *New York Times,* the *Wall Street Journal,* the *Christian Science Monitor,* and the *Washington Post* often receive attention in purposive samples of international coverage because they define themselves as national newspapers, and they have international correspondents.

For example, Wells and King (1994) studied prestige newspapers' coverage of foreign affairs issues during the congressional campaigns in 1990. Wells and King examined all issues of the *New York Times*, the *Washington Post*, the *Los Angeles Times*, and the *Chicago Tribune* from October 9 to November 6. Wells and King's explanation for selecting these newspapers is typical of international news studies. Wells and King (1994) wrote, "These newspapers have an international news gathering ability and extensive international/foreign affairs coverage" (p. 654).

Purposive samples differ from convenience samples because purposive samples require specific research justifications other than lack of money and availability. An often used type of purposive sample is consecutive-unit sampling, which involves taking a series of content produced during a certain time. Content analyzing local newscasts during a 2-week period is a consecutive-day sample. Consecutive-day sampling can be important when studying a continuing news or feature story because connected events cannot be examined adequately otherwise. Such samples often are found in studies of elections and continuing controversies.

## Problems With Nonprobability Samples

The main reason nonprobability samples are used is difficulty in collecting content. As a result, the availability of content shapes the nature of the research. The study of local television news provides a good example. Local TV newscasts are rarely available outside the particular market. As a result, the programs must be taped in the area of origin. A study trying to generalize outside a single market might require people around the country to tape newscasts.

However, the problem of taping local news on a national scale can be overcome with adequate funding. For example, the Project for Excellence in Journalism (PEJ, 2002), which is located at Columbia University and sponsored by the Nieman Foundation at Harvard and The Committee of Concerned Journalists, collected national samples of local television news every year from 1998 to 2002. Funded by foundations such as Pew and Knight, PEJ studied the quality of local TV news by selecting markets throughout the United States and balancing them for regional representation. The numbers of markets and stations included each year were the following: 1998, 20 markets and 61 stations; 1999, 19 markets and 59 stations; 2000, 15 markets and 43 stations; 2001, 14 markets and 43 stations; and 2002, 17 markets and 61 stations. During the first 4 years, PEJ approached people, often university professors, in each market to supervise taping. In 2002, PEJ hired a company to tape the programs for them. The reports for the 5 years of content analysis by PEJ can be found at their Web site (Project for Excellence in Journalism, 2002).

An additional problem in taping a probability sample of local TV newscasts is time. Inferring to a year might require asking a person 2,000 miles away to tape news programs on 14 randomly selected days during a year. This is not an easy task. The difficulty of getting tapes from around the country explains why most local TV news studies (e.g., Adams, 1980; Slattery & Hakanen, 1994) have tended to use convenience samples of videotape and scripts furnished by stations. However, some scholars have overcome geographic limitations by finding national purposive samples outside of universities (Carroll, 1989; Harmon, 1989).

The value of research using convenience samples should not be diminished. Science is a cumulative process. Over a period of time, consistent results from a large number of convenience samples suggest important research questions and hypotheses or even generalizations to be checked with probability samples or censuses. A series of replications would either reduce both sampling and measurement error or at least make such error more easily identifiable. Of course, such replication occurs across time, and time itself may "cause" content changes that might be misread as inconsistencies between the studies' findings.

In a strict sense, nonprobability samples are a census of the units being studied. However, they differ from a true census because a true census defines the population along theoretical lines, whereas purposive and convenience samples define the population based on practical considerations.

## Probability Sampling

The core notion of probability sampling is that each member of some population of interest is given an equal chance of being included in the sample. If this is so, characteristics found more frequently in the population—whether of TV dramas, news stories, or poems—also will turn up more frequently in the sample, and less frequent characteristics in the population will turn up less frequently in the sample. This occurs because of the laws of probability.

A simple example can illustrate how this (much more complicated) process works. For example, take a coin. Its population consists of a head and a tail. The chance of getting a head (or a tail) on a single flip is 50%. Flip 100 times and very close to half—but rarely exactly half—of that number will be heads. Flip 1,000 times and the proportion of heads will even more closely approach 50%. Given an infinite number of flips, the "expected value" of the proportion of heads will be 50%. Similarly, the expected value of any variable about people or content being explored will equal the actual population value of that variable if a very large number of relevant people or content is included in the sample.

An extension of this logic would be to take many samples from the same population one at a time. The expected value for each of the sample means would be the population mean, although in reality, the sample means would vary from the population means. However, if an infinite number of samples was taken from a population, the average of all the sample means would equal the population mean. If all the means of all these samples were plotted along a graph, the result would be a distribution of sample means, which is called the *sampling distribution.*

With an infinite number of samples, the sampling distribution of any population will have the characteristics of a normal curve. These characteristics include the mean, median (the middle score in a series arranged from low to high), and mode (the most frequent score value) will be equal; 50% of all the sample means will be on either side of the mean; 68% of all sample means will be within plus or minus 1 standard error (*SE*) of the mean (standard error is an estimate of how much the sample means in a sampling distribution vary from the population mean); and a variety of other characteristics. That any population distribution will take on a normal distribution when an infinite number of samples is taken is called the *central limits theorem.*

Of course, a researcher never draws an infinite number of samples. However, the central limits theorem allows a researcher to estimate the amount of error in a probability sample at a particular level of probability. In other words, what is the chance that a particular sample mean (calculated by the researcher from a random sample) is close to the true population mean in the distribution of infinite (but theoretically "drawable") random samples? This probability can be calculated because the mean of an infinite number of samples (the sampling distribution) will equal the population mean, and the distribution will be normal.

The sampling error for a particular sample, when combined with a sample mean or proportion for that sample, allows a researcher to estimate the population mean or proportion within a given range and with a given level of confidence that the range includes the population value. The best guess at the unknown population mean or proportion is the sample mean or proportion, and the level of sampling error allows a researcher to estimate the amount of error in this guess.

Crucial to understanding inference from a probability sample to a population is sampling error, an indication of the accuracy of the sample. Sampling error for a given sample is represented by standard error. Standard error is calculated differently for estimates and proportions. Standard error of the mean is calculated by using a sample's standard deviation, which is the average that cases in the sample vary from the sample mean. The standard deviation is divided by the square root of the sample size. The equation for standard error of the mean is

$$SE(m) = \frac{SD}{\sqrt{n-1}}$$

in which
$SE(m)$ = standard error of the mean
$SD$ = standard deviation
$n$ = sample size

The standard error of the mean is applied to interval- or ratio-level data. Nominal-level data use a similar equation for standard error of proportions. The equation for standard error of proportions is

$$SE(p) = \sqrt{\frac{p \cdot q}{n}}$$

in which
$SE(p)$ = standard error of proportion
$p$ = the proportion of sample with this characteristic
$q = (1 - p)$
$n$ = sample size

Standard error formulas adjust the sample's standard deviation for the sample size because sample size is one of three factors that affect how good an estimate a sample mean or proportion will be. The sample size is usually the most important. The larger the sample, the better will be the estimate of the population. Very large and very small case values will crop up in any sample. The more cases in a sample, the smaller will be the impact of the large and small values on the mean or proportions in the sample.

The second factor affecting the accuracy of a sample estimate is the variability of case values in the sample. If the case values vary greatly in a sample, the sample will have more error in estimating the population mean or proportion because variability results from the presence of large and small values for cases. Sample size and variability of case values are related because the larger the sample, the more likely case variability will decline.

The third factor affecting accuracy of a sample's estimate of the population is the proportion of the population in the sample. If a high proportion of the population is in the sample, the amount of error will decline because the sample distribution is a better approximation of the population distribution. However, a sample must equal or exceed 20% of the population cases before this factor plays much of a role. In fact, most statistics books ignore the influence of population proportion because surveys—which along with experiments dominate fields such as psychology, sociology, and political science—usually sample from very large populations.

Content analysis researchers should not ignore the impact of the population proportion in a sample because these studies often include fairly high proportions of the population. When the percentage of the population in a sample of content exceeds 20%, a researcher should adjust the sampling error using the finite population correction (fpc). To adjust for a sample that exceeds 20% of the population, the standard error formula is multiplied by the fpc formula, which is

$$fpc = 1 - \left(\frac{n}{N}\right)$$

in which
$fpc$ = finite population correction
$n$ = sample size
$N$ = population size

For further discussion of the fpc, see Moser and Kalton (1972).

Recall that sampling decisions may involve both time and content. A variety of probability sampling techniques—permitting sampling error calculation—are available, and decisions about probability sampling depend on a variety of issues, but virtually every decision involves time and content dimensions. Researchers must decide whether probability sampling is appropriate for both these dimensions and how randomness is to be applied. A probability sample can be taken for both time and content (e.g., a random sample of movies from each of 10 randomly selected years between 1950 and 1980), for just content (e.g., a random sample of all movies released in 1997), for just time (e.g., examine all Paramount movies in 10 years randomly selected from between 1950 and 1980), or for neither (e.g., examine all movies in 1997). In a strict sense, all content involves a time dimension. However, the concept of time sampling used here concerns trend studies over periods longer than a year. A year is used because it represents a natural planning cycle for most media.

All probability sampling aims to produce a sample that is representative of the population. However, the degree of representativeness varies. A representative sample is essential for making valid inference to that population. Sometimes the best probability sample is a simple random sample, whereas at other times, a stratified or systematic sample might work best.

## Simple Random Sample

*Simple random sampling* occurs when all units in the population have an equal chance of being selected. If a researcher wanted to study the gender representation in all feature films produced by the major studios during a given year, random sampling would require a list of all films. The researcher would then determine the number of films in the sample (e.g., 100 out of a population of 375 films). Then, using a computer or random numbers table, the researcher would select 100 numbers between 1 and 375 and locate the appropriate films on the list.

Simple random sampling can occur with two conditions: when units are replaced in the population after they are selected and when they are not replaced. With replacement, a unit could be selected for the sample more than once. Without replacement, each unit can appear only once in a sample. When units are not replaced, every unit does not have an exactly equal chance of being selected. For example, in a population of 100, when the first unit is selected, every unit would have a 1 in 100 chance. On the second draw, each remaining unit would have a 1 in 99 chance. This variation is not a serious problem because even without replacement each potential sample of a given size with no duplication has an equal chance of being selected, even if each unit did not. When populations are quite large, the small variation of probability without replacement has negligible impact on sampling error estimates.

Simple random sampling works well for determining a probability sample. However, it may not be the best sampling technique in all situations. If the population list is particularly long or the population cannot be listed easily, a random sampling technique other than simple random sampling might be in order.

## Systematic Sampling

*Systematic sampling* involves selecting every *n*th unit from a sampling frame. The particular number (*n*) is determined by dividing the sampling frame size by the sample size. If a sample will include 1,000 sentences from a book with 10,000 sentences, the researcher would select every 10th sentence. Taking every *n*th unit becomes a probability sample when the starting point is randomly determined. The researcher could randomly select a number between 1 and 10, which would be the number of the first sentence taken. Every 10th sentence after that would be selected until the complete sample is in hand. Because the starting point is randomly selected, each unit has an equal chance of being selected.

Systematic sampling works well when simple random sampling creates problems. For example, selecting 100 daily newspapers to sample can be done from *Editor & Publisher International Year Book* either by numbering each entry and then randomly selecting 100, or it can be done by dividing the number of total entries—a number available in the front of the book—and then systematically sampling, by 100. Both samples would be equally representative.

However, systematic sampling can generate problems under two conditions. First, it requires a listing of all possible units for sampling. If the sampling frame is incomplete (the entire population is not listed), inference cannot be made to the population. For example, the U.S. dailies listed in the *Editor & Publisher International Year Book* includes all or almost all (depending on the year) of the daily newspapers in the country. Its listing of weekly newspapers, however, is incomplete. So, a sample of weeklies selected from the *Editor & Publisher International Year*

*Book* would not be representative of all U.S. weeklies, but a sample of dailies likely would be.

A second problem is that systematic sampling is subject to *periodicity*, which involves a bias in the arrangement of units in a list (Wimmer & Dominick, 1997). For example, a researcher wants to study the cigarette advertising in consumer magazines, and *Field & Stream* is one of the magazines. If the researcher took four copies per year for 20 years using systematic sampling, a biased sample could result. Assuming a 1 is picked as the random starting point and every fourth copy is selected, the researcher would end up with 20 editions from January, 20 from May, 20 from July, and 20 from December. This creates a problem because January and July are typically smaller editions and excluded from the sample is August, which typically bulges with advertising.

## Stratified Sampling

*Stratified sampling* involves breaking a population into smaller groups and random sampling from within the groups. These groups are homogeneous with respect to some characteristic of importance. If one wanted to study the jingoistic language about the Vietnam War between 1964 and 1974 in speeches made on the Senator floor, the sample could be randomly selected or stratified by year. Stratified random selection would be better because the language likely changed with time. Support for the war was much stronger in 1966 than in 1974. A simple random sample could generate a sample with most of the speeches either at the beginning or end of this period. Using years as strata, however, makes smaller homogeneous groups that would guarantee a more representative sample. The percentage of total speeches that were made in each year would determine the percentage of the sample to come from that year.

Stratified sampling serves two purposes. First, it increases the representativeness of a sample by using knowledge about the distribution of units to avoid the oversampling and undersampling that can occur from simple random sampling. This is *proportionate sampling,* which selects sample sizes from within strata based on the stratum's proportion of the population. A study of online bulletin boards might stratify within topic areas. The percentage of sample messages from a given topic area would represent that topic area's proportion of the entire population. If a bulletin board topic area about movies accounted for 20% of all messages, then 20% of the sample should come from the movie topic. This will make the sample more representative of the entire bulletin board activity.

In addition, stratifying can increase the number of units in a study when those types of units make up a small proportion of the population. This is *disproportionate sampling,* which involves selecting a sample from a stratum that is greater than that stratum's proportion of the population. This procedure allows a large enough sample for comparison. If 5% of the 1,000 participants on the bulletin board are older than 60, and the study concerns the relationship between age and messages, the researcher might want to disproportionately sample from the stratum of participants over 60. If the population has only 50 people within this stratum, a simple random sample of 200 probably would yield only 10 people older than 60 because each person has a 1 in 5 chance of being selected. Disproportionate sampling oversamples particular units to obtain enough cases for a valid analysis. However, it yields a sample that is no longer representative of the entire population because a subset of members is overrepresented in the sample.

Because mass communication media produce content on a regular basis, say every day or every week, stratified sampling can take advantage of known variations within these production cycles. Daily newspapers, for example, vary in size with days of the week because of cyclical variations in advertising. We examine these systematic variations in media in more detail later in the chapter.

Stratified sampling requires adjustments to sampling error estimates. Because sampling comes from homogeneous subgroups, the standard error is reduced. As just mentioned, the standard error of proportion formula for simple random samples is

$$SE(p) = \sqrt{\frac{p \cdot q}{n}}$$

The standard error of proportion for stratified samples equals the sum of the standard errors for all strata (Moser & Kalton, 1972):

$$SE(pst) = \sqrt{\frac{1}{N^2} \sum \frac{N_i^2 p_i q_i}{n_i - 1}}$$

in which

$SE(pst)$ = sampling error of stratified proportions
$N$ = total population
$n_i$ = sample from the $i$th stratum
$N_i$ = population number in the $i$th stratum
$p_i$ = proportion of sample in $i$th stratum with the stratifying characteristic
$q_i = (1 - p_i)$

## Cluster Sampling

Simple random, systematic, and stratified sampling require a list as a sampling frame. This list tells the researcher how many units make up the population and allows the calculation of probabilities. Often with communication research, however, complete lists of units are unavailable. To sample when no list is available, researchers use *cluster sampling,* which is the process of selecting content units from clusters or groups of content.

Mass media products often include clusters of content. For example, each newspaper edition is a cluster of many articles, usually divided into topic clusters such as sports, business, and entertainment. Television news is a cluster of stories. Indexes to the World Wide Web organize content sites by topics and subtopics. Listing all Web sites is impossible. Cluster sampling allows the probability selection of groups and then subgroups from indexes; random sampling within those subgroups would lead to the specific content units.

Cluster sampling can introduce additional sampling error compared to simple random sampling because of intraclass correlation. As the previous newspaper cluster example suggests, content units that cluster together may do so because they are similar in nature. These shared characteristics create a positive correlation among the attributes. Web indexes group Web sites by some common characteristics. By selecting clusters, a researcher is more likely to include units with similar characteristics and exclude units that have different characteristics from units in selected clusters. As a result, the sample, although randomly determined, may not be representative. Interclass correlation can be anticipated, and statistic books (Moser & Kalton, 1972) provide formulas for estimating such biases.

## Multistage Sampling

Multistage sampling is not a form of probability sampling such as simple random, systematic, and stratified sampling techniques. Rather, it is a description of a common practice that may involve one or several of these techniques at different stages. Recall that the simplest form of probability sample would be to list all recording units, randomly select from them, and proceed with the analysis. However, as just noted, most content, especially mediated content, is not that accessible. Often content comes in packages or clusters. Moreover, most content has a time dimension as well. Indeed, Berelson (1952) said mediated content has three different dimensions that must be considered in sampling: titles, issues or dates, and relevant content within the issues. A sampling procedure may be designed that addresses all these dimensions as stages of sampling. At each stage, a random sample must be taken to make inference to the population.

For example, someone studying the content of talk radio would have to randomly select the radio stations, then particular days from which to get content, and then the particular talk programs. Yet another stage might be the particular topics within the radio talk programs. For magazines, the titles, dates, and content within would be the stages. Pure multistage sampling requires random sampling for each stage.

Multistage sampling can also combine a variety of sampling techniques. The techniques should reflect the purpose of the research, with the guiding principle being an effort to produce as representative a sample as possible for inferring to the population.

In a content analysis by Danielson and Adams (1961), they used a sophisticated multistage sampling procedure to study the completeness of campaign coverage available to the average reader during the 1960 presidential campaign. Danielson and Adams selected 90 daily newspapers in a procedure that stratified for type of ownership (group and nongroup), geographic region, and time of publication (a.m. or p.m.). With the exception of a slight oversampling of Southern dailies, the sample's characteristics matched the population's. The sampling of campaign events came from a population of events covered by 12 large daily newspapers from September 1 to November 7, 1960. These 1,033 events were narrowed to 42 by systematic random sampling.

The number of stages in a multistage sampling process is determined by the researcher. The process of sampling weekly newspaper content can have one, two, or three stages of sampling. The first of the three stages would require randomly selecting the newspaper titles from the geographic area under study, say the United States. The second stage involves selecting the dates to be examined. The third requires sampling from within each issue. This process could be reduced to two sampling stages by conducting a census of each of the issues selected. It could be reduced to one stage of probability sampling by examining every story in every edition for a given time period.

Just as cluster and stratified sampling alter the formula for figuring standard error, so does multistage sampling. Multistage sampling introduces sampling error at each stage of sampling, and estimates of error must be adjusted.

## STRATIFIED SAMPLING FOR MEDIA

The question of whether to use simple random sampling or stratified sampling often involves efficiency. Media content produced by commercial enterprises follows cycles. New network television programs usually are produced during the fall, winter, and spring; reruns usually are shown during the summer. Daily newspapers vary in thickness on the basis of advertising, which is determined by the day of the week. Such systematic variations affect content. More news and information run in Sunday newspaper editions than any other day because the newshole is bigger. The newshole is bigger because more advertising is bought in Sunday's paper. If systematic variations in content are known, these variations can be used to select a representative sample more efficiently. These variations allow identification of subsets of more homogeneous content that can be used to select a smaller stratified sample that will be just as representative as a larger simple random sample.

Several studies have looked at stratified sampling in various forms of media to identify the most efficient sample size and technique to infer to

TABLE 5.1
Efficient Stratified Sampling Methods for Inferring to Content

| Type of Content | Nature of Sample |
|---|---|
| Year of daily newspapers | Two constructed weeks from year (randomly selecting two Mondays, two Tuesdays, two Wednesdays, etc.) |
| Year of weekly newspapers | Randomly select one issue from each month in the year |
| Year of evening television network news | Randomly select two days from each month's newscasts during the year |
| Year of news magazines | Randomly select one issue from each month in a year |
| 5 years of consumer magazines | One constructed year (randomly select one issue from each month) |
| 5 years of daily newspapers | Nine constructed weeks (randomly selecting nine Mondays, nine Tuesdays, etc.) |

a particular time period. These studies have often examined types of variables as well (see Table 5.1).

## Daily Newspapers

Because of their traditional dominance as a mass medium, daily newspapers have received more attention in sampling efficiency studies than other forms of media. These studies have concentrated on efficiency of sampling for inference by using the constructed week, which is created by randomly selecting an issue for each day of the week.

An early study of sampling by Mintz (1949) used headlines from 1941 issues of *Pravda*. Mintz used 1 month as a population and drew a variety of sample sizes using a variety of random methods (every third day, whole weeks, etc.). Samples taken every 6th day and every other day (15 days) did not vary significantly from the population mean. However, Mintz's sampling was based on the assumption that number of headlines was not subject to weekday cycles.

Stempel (1952) used number of front-page photographs in a 6-day Wisconsin newspaper in 1951 to study sampling. Stempel (1952) drew 10 samples each of 6, 12, 18, 24, and 48 editions with a random starting point and every $n$th edition. Because of Stempel's (1952) sampling technique, the results were constructed weeks. Stempel (1952) concluded 12 days (two constructed weeks) were sufficient for representing a year's content. Research by Davis and Turner (1951) and Jones and Carter (1959) found results similar to Stempel's (1952). However, in the former case, the population was only 2 months and in the latter only 3 weeks.

Riffe, Aust, et al. (1993) conducted a more thorough replication of Stempel's (1952) work when they used 6 months of local stories in a 39,000-circulation daily. Riffe, Aust, et al. (1993) compared simple random sampling, constructed-week sampling, and consecutive-day sampling for efficiency. Riffe, Aust, et al. (1993) took 20 samples each for each method with 7-, 14-, 21-, and 28-day samples. A sampling technique was sufficient when the percentage of accurate sample means fell within the percentages for 1 and 2 *SE*s found in a normal curve. In other words, if 68% of the 20 sample means fell within plus or minus 1 *SE* of the population mean, and 95% of the sample means fell within plus or minus 2 *SE*s of the mean, a sampling technique was adequate.

It took 28 days of editions for simple random sampling to be adequate, and consecutive-day sampling never adequately represented the population mean. One constructed week adequately predicted the population mean, and two constructed weeks worked even better. Riffe, Aust, et al. (1993) concluded daily stratified sampling was far more efficient than simple random sampling when inferring to a larger population:

> This study found that for a population of six months of editions, one constructed week was as efficient as four, and its estimates exceeded what would be expected based on probability theory. By extension, two constructed weeks would allow reliable estimates of local stories in a year's worth of newspaper entire issues, a conclusion consistent with Stempel's findings on front-page photographs in a six-day-a-week paper. (p. 139)

Taking two constructed weeks of dailies newspapers works well for 1 year, but some researchers are interested in studying content changes across longer time periods. Lacy, Riffe, Stoddard, Martin, and Chang (2000) examined efficiency in selecting a representative sample of daily newspaper content from 5 years of newspaper editions. Perhaps the patterns in newspaper content that make constructed-week sampling more efficient than random sampling might reduce the number of weeks needed for longer periods of time. Lacy et al. (2000) concluded that 9 constructed weeks taken from a 5-year period were as representative as two constructed weeks from each year, provided the variable of interest did not show great variance.

The strategy for sampling editions of daily newspaper over long time periods, such as 100 years, would depend on a variety of factors. If a researcher wants to study newspaper content over 100 years in blocks of 5 years, sampling 9 constructed weeks instead of 10 for each block would reduce the amount of work required for content analysis (90 constructed weeks instead of 100). The best approach for the researcher would be to select the 9 constructed weeks and then examine the variance among the variables. If the coefficients of variation (the standard deviation divided by the mean) for the variables are less than .5, the sample should be representative at the $p < .05$ level. If the coefficients of variation are greater than .5 for one or more variables, an additional constructed week should be sampled.

## Weekly Newspapers

The sparse research on daily newspaper sampling seems extensive compared to research about sampling weekly newspapers. This dearth of sampling research has become noticeable because weeklies have grown in importance during the past three decades, increasing in circulation as dailies have waned.

Lacy et al. (1995) studied sampling of weeklies as an extension of work done about dailies. The main issue was whether stratified sampling would improve sampling efficiency with weeklies as it does with dailies. To explore this issue, Lacy et al. (1995) used two weeklies and five content variables—total stories, total photographs, stories about local government, square inches about local government, and percentage of stories about local government. Lacy et al. (1995) stratified by month and season of the year and compared these results with simple random samples. Lacy et al. (1995) used the same standard for efficient, or adequate, sampling found in Riffe, Aust, et al. (1993). The results indicated stratified sampling has some efficiency compared to random sampling, but the influence of cycles in content is not as strong in weeklies as in dailies.

Lacy et al. (1995) concluded

> Thus, someone interested in studying weekly newspaper content should either randomly select fourteen issues from a year, or pick twelve issues, one from each month. The former is preferable when the results will be used for making risky decisions. Under this condition, precision is important. The latter method will be most useful when decisions are less risky and money and time constraints are of primary consideration. (p. 344).

## Magazines

Magazine sampling studies have addressed efficient sampling for weekly newsmagazines and for monthly consumer magazines. Riffe, Lacy, and Drager's (1996) study of newsmagazines used *Newsweek* to discover whether content cycles might make stratified sampling more efficient. Riffe, Lacy, and Drager found that selecting one issue randomly from each month was the most efficient sampling method for inferring to a year's content. The next most efficient method was simple random selection of 14 issues from a year.

The constructed-year approach, however, carries a warning. Newsmagazines have end of the year roundup editions that differ greatly from the regular issues in several types of variables. Researchers must decide whether or not their projects logically require the inclusion of these roundup editions because their inclusion can drastically alter the population parameters for the year.

Unlike newsmagazines, consumer magazines usually appear monthly, and the best approach to studying a year's content is to examine all issues. However, if a researcher wants to study longer term trends in consumer magazines, stratified sampling might prove more efficient than simple random sampling. Lacy, Riffe, and Randle (1998) used *Field & Stream* and *Good Housekeeping* as examples of consumer magazines and found that a constructed year (1 issue from January, 1 from February, 1 from March, etc.) from a 5-year period produced a representative sample of content for that period. A representative sample with simple random sampling required 20 issues from the 5 years. A longitudinal study of consumer magazines could divide the time period into 5-year subperiods and use constructed years to make valid inferences to the magazines under study.

## Network Television News

Although television content analyses are plentiful, sampling studies to find valid and efficient sampling methods are practically nonexistent. Types of samples found in published research include randomly selecting 1 day from 60 months to construct 12 composite weeks (Weaver, Porter, & Evans, 1984), using the same 2 weeks (March 1–7 and October 1–7) from each year between 1972 and 1987 (Scott & Gobetz, 1992), sampling two constructed weeks per quarter for 9 years (Riffe, Ellis, Rogers, Ommeren, & Woodman, 1986), and using four consecutive weeks per 6-month period (Ramaprasad, 1993).

The variation in types of sampling methods represents particular research questions, but it also reflects the absence of guidance from sampling studies about television news. Riffe, Lacy, Nagovan, and Burkum (1996) began exploration into network news sampling by comparing simple random samples of 25 days, samples of one constructed week per quarter, and 2 days randomly selected from each month. Riffe, Lacy, Nagovan, et al. (1996) used a year's worth of Monday through Friday broadcasts from ABC and CBS as the populations. Five variables (total stories, total international stories, total economic stories, seconds of international stories, and seconds of international news) were examined using 40 samples for each sampling method for each network.

The most efficient form of sampling for network TV news was randomly selecting 2 days from each month for a total of 24 days. It took 35 days with simple random sampling to predict adequately a year's content. Riffe, Lacy, Nagovan, et al. (1996) cautioned that researchers should be aware of extreme variations in particular content categories. In Riffe, Lacy, Nagovan, et al.'s study, for example, total stories showed small variation within and across networks, whereas seconds of economic news varied greatly from day to day for both networks. Riffe, Lacy, Nagovan, et al. (1996) suggested that when the coefficient of variation, which is the standard deviation divided by the mean, for a content category is greater than .5, the researchers should increase the size of the sample through additional random sampling.

## SAMPLING MEDIA IN GENERAL

The series of studies that have examined efficient samples for media suggests the need for additional studies, especially for nonprint media. The weekly and magazine research requires replication, as does the broadcast study. However, media that have not been examined for sampling efficiency include local broadcast news, network entertainment, cable content, consumer magazines, the Internet, and radio. Some of these present more difficulty than others.

Local broadcast news and radio content create difficulties in acquiring the content to study. Unlike newspapers, which are stored on microfilm in libraries, and network news, which is preserved at the Vanderbilt Library archives, extensive collections of radio and local TV news content do not exist. At least with National Public Radio, cable, and network entertainment, a researcher could record with a VCR or tape recorder because the content is available throughout the country. However, local TV news and radio are available for recording in a limited geographic area. Getting a year's worth of content also requires a long-term commitment to collecting content.

## SAMPLING THE INTERNET

The most important mediated communication form of the last 50 years is the Internet. Although the Internet supports a variety of communication forms such as data transfer, e-mail, and voice communication, the World Wide Web has gained most of the attention among scholars. The Web is the consumer portion of the Internet and as such holds the greatest promise of affecting the most people. Scholars have predicted incredible effects of the Internet and Web and have called for increased study of these areas (Tomasello, 2001). However, in a content analysis of scholarly articles between 1994 and 1999, Tomasello (2001) found only 4% of them concerned the Internet, although the number of articles per year has been increasing.

In a discussion of the challenges and opportunities facing research about the Internet, Stempel and Stewart (2000) explained some of the problems with content studies in this area. Stempel and Stewart said a serious problem confronting Internet studies is the absence of sampling frames for populations. To a degree, the Internet is like a city without a telephone book or map to guide people. New houses are being built all the time, and old houses are being deserted with no listing of the changes. Sampling requires creative solutions.

Stempel and Stewart (2000) also warned about using the Internet for accessing content from newspapers and broadcast stations. Stempel and Stewart listed four problems: (a) Internet databases lead to convenience samples rather than representative samples, (b) indexing is not consistent from site to site, (c) files at some sites are missing information such as headlines and placements within broadcasts, and (d) acquiring the content can be expensive, as sites increasingly charge for content.

McMillan (2000) content analyzed 19 research articles and papers that studied Web content and generated a series of recommendations. First, McMillan warned scholars to be aware of how the Web is similar to and not similar to traditional media. Because the Web is interactive and not necessarily linear, researchers must understand that people use the Web differently than they use traditional media. Second, sampling the Web can be very difficult because sampling frames are not readily available, and the content can change quickly. Third, the changing nature of the Web can make coding difficult. Content must either be "captured" in some form and/or sampling must take change into consideration. Fourth, researchers must be aware that the multimedia nature of the Web can affect the various study units (sampling, recording, and context). Fifth, the changing nature of sites can make reliability testing difficult because coders may not be coding identical content.

As with all sampling, the process of sampling online content depends on how the research is conceptualized. A study of representative content on the World Wide Web, for example, presents certain problems, whereas trying to find a representative sample of newspaper home pages would create other problems. Convenience sampling creates fewer problems, but in all cases, researchers must be aware of the time element of changing Web content.

Sampling representative content could use multistage sampling. The first stage would involve identifying all the indexes available such as Yahoo. If these indexes list the number of sites per category, one could estimate the proportion of Web pages that fall into these categories and on a given index. By figuring the proportions for category and index, the researcher could use proportionate sampling of home pages.

This approach presents several problems. First, duplicate listings on indexes would increase the probability of some pages being selected and would result in a biased sample. Such a bias might be overcome by having a very large sample, however. Second, many indexes would likely ignore the smaller individual home pages that make up a large portion of the Web. The sample might be more representative of commercial and organizational sites than individual sites. Third, the content on some pages changes at varying rates. The process is similar to putting personal letters, books, magazines, and newspapers all into the sample population and trying to get a representative sample. The answer might be using categories other than topics to classify Web pages, but such a typology has yet to be developed and accepted.

Asking a research question about specific types of pages—for example, those developed by newspapers—would be easier but still faces the problem of how complete a sampling frame might be. Some sites, such as the *Editor & Publisher Interactive* site, carry extensive list of newspapers' pages, but this list changes often.

Despite the problems of sampling, the number of research articles continues to grow. The authors of the articles solve the sampling issue in a variety of ways. Paul (2001) sampled 64 disaster relief home pages by looking at "a universe of regional, national, and international web sites accessible through search engines and other web sites" (p. 744). Paul stated that this would exclude heavily used local sites. Papacharissi (2002) randomly sampled 250 home pages from four web page hosts and then eliminated commercial and institutional home pages. Wicks and Souley (2003) looked at negative campaigning online during the 2000 presidential campaign. Wicks and Souley visited the Bush and Gore Web sites daily, or more often following high-activity periods such as debates, and downloaded 487 press releases from the final 50 days of the campaign.

The 19 articles analyzed by McMillan (2000) showed a range of sampling frames and techniques. As McMillan suggested, it will take methodological research to establish standard sorts of Internet sampling that will yield valid representative samples. Until that time, researchers are best advised to let their theoretical frameworks, hypotheses, and sampling theory be their guides. A complete explanation in the resulting research article about the sampling method also is advisable for replication purposes.

## SAMPLING INDIVIDUAL COMMUNICATION

Mass communication usually has the sampling advantage of being regular in its creation cycle. Because such communication usually comes from institutions and organizations, records of its creation are often available. More problematic is the study of individual communication such as letters and e-mail. If someone wanted to content analyze the letters written by soldiers during the American Civil War, identifying the sampling frame is a burdensome task, but it is the first step that must be taken. Research about individual communication will be as valid as the list of such communication pieces will be complete.

Of course, researching the communication of particular individuals, such as politicians, writers, and artists, often involves a census of all material available. Trying to research individual communication of non-notable people should involve probability sampling, even if the entire universe cannot be identified. However, just getting such communications is a problem. Often, convenience samples result. For example, Dick (1993) studied the impact of user activity on sustaining online discussion forums. Being unable to sample such forums randomly, Dick used three active forums from the GEnie™ system and came up with 21,584 messages about 920 topics in 53 categories between April 1987 and September 1990. Because Dick was interested in examining relationships and not describing behavior, the set of messages, which was strictly a census, was adequate for his exploratory research.

The scientific method is the solution for the inability to randomly sample. If strong relations of interest exist in larger populations, then they usually will be found consistently even in nonprobability samples. However, accumulated support from convenience samples works best if these samples come from a variety of situations (e.g., the samples are from several locations and time periods).

# SUMMARY

Content analysts have a variety of techniques at their disposal for selecting content. The appropriate one depends on the theoretical issues and practical problems inherent in the research project. If the number of recording units involved is small, a census of all content should be conducted. If the number of units is large, a probability sample is likely to be more appropriate because it allows inference to the population from the sample.

A variety of probability sampling methods are available including simple random, systematic, stratified, cluster, and multistage sampling. The appropriate probability sample also depends on the nature of the research project. However, probability samples are necessary if one hopes to use statistical inference.

Efficient sampling of mass media to infer to a year's content often involves stratified sampling because mass media content varies systematically with time periods. Content analysts need to be aware that sampling may involve probability samples based on time, content, or both.

# 6

## *Reliability*

One of the questions posed in chapter 3 (this volume) was "How can the quality of the data be maximized?" To a considerable extent, the quality of data reflects the reliability of the measurement used. Reliable measurement in content analysis—in any research method—is crucial. If one cannot trust the measures, one cannot trust any analysis that uses those measures.

The core notion of reliability is simple: The measurement instruments applied to observations must be highly consistent over time, place, and circumstance. If one measure changes in something, one must be certain that such changes are in what is being observed and not the result of distortions appearing in one's measuring stick. If, for example, one had to measure day-to-day changes in someone's height, would a metal yardstick or one made of rubber be better? Clearly the rubber yardstick's own length would be more likely to vary with the temperature and humidity of the day the measure was taken and with the measurer's pull on the yardstick. Indeed, a biased measurer might stretch the rubber yardstick. Similarly, if one wanted to measure minority presence in television commercials, as described in chapter 2 (this volume), one would find different results by using an untrained coder's assessment or by using trained coders with explicit coding instructions.

In this chapter, we deal with reliability in content analysis. Specific issues in content analysis reliability involve the definition of concepts and their operationalization in a content analysis protocol, the training of coders in applying those concepts, and mathematical measures of reliability permitting an assessment of how effectively the content analysis protocol and the coders have achieved reliability.

## RELIABILITY: BASIC NOTIONS

*Reliability* in content analysis is defined as agreement among coders about categorizing content. Indeed, content analysis as a research tool is based on the assumption that explicitly defined and accepted concept definitions control assignment of content to particular categories by coders. If the category definitions do not control assignment of content, then human biases may be doing so in unknown and uncontrollable ways. If this is so, findings are likely to be uninterpretable and unreplicable by others. Yet replicability is a defining trait of science, as noted in chapter 2 (this volume). Reliability is thus crucial to content analysis as a scientific method. The problem of assessing reliability comes down ultimately to testing coder agreement to verify the assumption that content coding is determined by the concept definitions.

Achieving reliability in content analysis begins with defining the categories and subcategories that are relevant to the study goals. Coders are then trained to apply those definitions to the content of interest. The process ends with the assessment of reliability through coder reliability tests. Such tests indicate numerically how well the concept definitions have controlled the assignment of content to appropriate analytic categories.

These three steps obviously interrelate, and if any one fails, the overall reliability must suffer. Without clarity and simplicity of concept definition, coders will fail to apply them properly when looking at content. Without coder diligence and discernment in applying the concepts, the reliability assessment will prove inadequate. Without the assessment, an alternate interpretation of any study's findings could be "coder bias." Failure to achieve reliability in a content study means replication by the same or by other researchers will be of dubious value.

## CONCEPT DEFINITIONS
## AND CATEGORY CONSTRUCTION

Reliability in content analysis starts with the category and subcategory definitions and the rules for applying them in a study. These definitions and the rules that operationalize them are specified in a content analysis protocol, a guidebook that answers the chapter 3 (this volume) question "How will coders know the data when they see it?"

## Conceptual and Operational Definitions

In other words, the conceptual and operational definitions specify how
the concepts of interest can be recognized in the content of interest.
Think of it this way: A *concept* is a broad, abstract idea about the way
something is or about the way several things interrelate. Each category
in a content analysis is the operationalized definition of that broader,
more abstract concept. Each subcategory of each content analysis category is an operational definition as well but one subsumed by the
broader operational definition of the category it is part of.

A simple example from one of Fico's (1985) studies makes this process clear. In the study of political visibility of state legislators, the concept of prominence was defined and measured. As an abstract concept,
prominence means something that is first or most important and clearly
distinct from all else in these qualities. In a news story about the legislative process, prominence can be measured (operationalized) in a number
of ways. For example, a political actor's prominence in a story can be
measured in terms of "how high up" the actor's name appears. Or, the actor's prominence can be assessed according to how much story space is
taken up with assertions attributed to the actor. Prominence can even be
assessed by whether the political actor's photo appears, or his or her
name is in a headline, or something he or she said is displayed for emphasis as a "pull quote" outside the body of the story. Fico's (1985)
study operationalized political visibility as the first legislator's name
encountered in the news story (not in the headline or cutline).

Note several things about the concept of prominence and the way it
was applied. Certainly, the concept is much more extensive than the way
it was operationalized. Many concepts have more than one dimension in
their meaning, and almost all have a number of ways in which one or
more of those dimensions of meaning can be measured. For example,
Fico's (1985) study also used the concept of political activity, citing previous research that operationalized that concept as references in the
Congressional directory—essentially a measure of a lawmaker's frequency of congressional addresses. However, the Fico (1985) study
opted for a different operational definition of political activity: the number of bills a lawmaker proposed. Arguably, both—and more—really
make up the various dimensions of political activity.

Certainly it can be argued that the concept of prominence is best
tapped by several measures such as those noted—story position, space,

accompanying photograph—but combined into an overall index. In fact, many concepts are operationalized in just this way. Of course, using several measures of a concept requires making sure that the various components do indeed measure the same thing. For example, story space or number of paragraphs devoted to a politician may not be a good measure of prominence if he or she is not mentioned until the last paragraphs of a story.

## Concept Complexity and Number of Categories

Thus, the more conceptually complex the categories and subcategories, the harder it will be to achieve acceptable reliability for reasons that we explain in the following section. Either more time and effort must be available for a complex analysis, or the analysis itself may have to be less extensive. That is, if the concepts are simple and easy to apply, reliability is more easily achieved, and a content analysis can be more extensive. However, a large number of complex concepts increases the chances that coders will make mistakes, diminishing the reliability of the study.

Reliability also is easier to achieve when a concept is more, rather than less, manifest because coders will more easily recognize the concepts in the content. Recall from chapter 2 (this volume) that something manifest is observable "on its face" and therefore easy to recognize and count. The simpler it is to recognize when the concept exists in the content, the easier it is for the coders to agree and thus the better the chance of achieving reliability in the study. For example, recognizing when the name of a politician appears in a television situation comedy is easier than categorizing the context in which that official is mentioned. Or, if political visibility is operationalized simply as the number of times a legislator's name appears in a sample of news stories, coders will probably easily agree on the counted occurrences of that name. However, categorizing whether the legislator is discussing a specific bill or commenting on some more general political topic may require more complex judgment and thereby affect coder reliability.

Although reliability is easiest to achieve when content is more manifest (e.g., counting names), the most manifest content is not always the most interesting or significant. Therefore, content studies also may attempt to deal with latent content, that is, the meanings embedded in the content interpreted by some observer. In these studies, the application of defined concepts relies on coder interpretation of content meaning. Two problems can ensue, one of which affects the study's reliability. First, agreement among coders on the proper interpretation may be hard to achieve. Beyond within-study reliability, however, a second problem may occur that engages the interpretation of study results. Specifically, even though trained coders may achieve agreement on latent content, it may be unclear whether naive observers of the content (e.g., newspaper readers, soap opera viewers, etc.) experience the meanings defined in the protocol and applied by the researchers. Few viewers of television commercials, for example, repeatedly rewind and review these commercials to describe the relationships among actors. Here, the issue of reliability relates in some sense to the degree to which the study and its operationalizations "matter" in the real world (and therefore to the study's validity, a topic we discuss in chap. 7, this volume).

These issues do not mean that latent content studies should not be done or that they fail to have broader meaning and significance. That depends on the goals of the research. For example, Simon, Fico, and Lacy (1989) studied defamation in stories of local conflict. The definition of defamation came from court decisions: words that tend to harm the reputation of identifiable individuals. Simon et al.'s study further operationalized "per se" defamation that harms reputation on its face, and "per quod" defamation that requires interpretation that harm to reputation has occurred. Obviously, what harms reputation depends on what the reader or viewer of the material brings to it. To call a leader "tough" may be an admirable characterization to some and a disparaging one to others. Furthermore, it is doubtful that many readers of these stories had the concept of defamation in mind as they read (although they may have noted that sources were insulting one another). However, the goal of Simon et al.'s study was to determine when stories might risk angering one crucial population of readers: those sources defamed in the news who might begin a lawsuit.

These concepts of manifest and latent meaning can be thought to exist on a continuum. Some symbols are more manifest than others in that a higher percentage of receivers share a common meaning for those symbols. Few people would disagree on the common, manifest meaning of the word *caravan,* but the word *cool* has seven uses as a verb and two as a noun in a standard dictionary. Likewise, the latent meanings of symbols vary according to how many members of the group using the language share the latent meaning. The latent or symbolic meaning also can change with time, as noted in chapter 2 (this volume). In the 1950s in America, a Cadillac® was considered the ultimate automotive symbol of wealth by the majority of people in the United States. Today, the Cadillac still symbolizes wealth, but it is not the ultimate symbol in everyone's mind. Other cars, such as the Mercedes® and BMW®, have come to symbolize wealth as much or more so than the Cadillac.

The point, however, is that the number of categories requiring complex coder interpretations, whether because of concept complexity or lack of common meaning, should be limited. In an ongoing study, coders may forget the proper interpretation rules for one or more categories. Coding fatigue may set in, eroding the ability of the coder to deal with subsequent material.

The more complex categories there are, the more the coding may have to be controlled by rules of procedure. Before each coding session, instructions should require that coders first review the protocol rules governing the categories. Coding sessions may be restricted to a set amount of content or a set amount of time to reduce the chance that coder fatigue will systematically degrade the coding of content toward the end of the session.

## CONTENT ANALYSIS PROTOCOL

However simple or complex the concepts, the definitions must be articulated clearly and unambiguously. This is done in the content analysis protocol. The protocol's importance cannot be overstated. It is the documentary record that defines the study in general and the coding rules applied to content in particular.

### Purpose of the Protocol

First, the protocol sets down the rules governing the study, rules that bind the researchers in the way they define and measure the content of interest. These rules are invariant across the life of the study. Content coded on Day 1 of a study should be coded in the identical way on Day 100 of the study.

Second, the protocol is the archival record of the study's operations and definitions or how the study was conducted. Therefore, the protocol makes it possible for other researchers to interpret the results and replicate the study. Such replication strengthens the ability of science to build a body of findings and theory illuminating the processes and effects of communication.

The content analysis protocol can be thought of in a more homely way: It is a cookbook. Just as a cookbook specifies ingredients, amounts of ingredients needed, and the procedures for combining and mixing them, the protocol specifies the study's conceptual and operational definitions and the ways they are to be applied. To continue the analogy, if a cookbook is clear, one does not need to be a chef to make a good stew. The same is true for a content analysis protocol. If the concepts and procedures are sufficiently clear and procedures for applying them straightforward, anyone reading the protocol could code the content in the same way as the researchers. If the concepts and procedures are more complex, anyone trained in using the protocol could code the content in the same way as the researchers.

## Protocol Development

Of course, making concepts sufficiently clear and the procedures straightforward may not be such a simple process. Concepts that remain in a researcher's head are not likely to be either very useful or very clear: Memory fails, things that were clear at one time have a way of becoming more obscure, distinctions blur, and so on. Therefore, the researcher writes it down. Although that sounds simple, the act of putting even a simple concept into words is more likely than anything else to illuminate sloppy or incomplete thinking. The attempt to define concepts in words forces more discerning thinking about what the researcher really means and is attempting to get at in a concept.

Furthermore, these written definitions can now be more easily responded to by others with different perspectives and contexts for their thoughts. This dynamic of articulation and response, both within oneself and with others, drives the process that clarifies concepts. The process forces the researcher to formulate concepts in words and sentences that are to others less ambiguous and less subject to alternative interpretations that miss the concept the researcher had in mind.

## Protocol Organization

Because it is the documentary record of the study, care should be taken to organize and present the protocol in a coherent and organized manner.

The document should be sufficiently comprehensive for other researchers to replicate the study without additional information from the researchers. Furthermore, the protocol must be available to any who wish to use it to help interpret, replicate, extend, or critique research governed by the protocol.

A three-part approach works well for protocol organization. The first part is an introduction specifying the goals of the study and generally introducing the major concepts and how they are defined. For example, in a study of fairness and defamation in reporting (Fico & Cote, 1999), the protocol introduction specified the content to be examined (news stories in first and local newspaper sections) and the definitions of defamation, news source, and contention.

The second part specified the procedures governing how the content was to be processed. For example, the protocol directed coders to mark those story paragraphs containing sources in some contention who made attributed statements. The protocol further specified that after one coder had done this, a second coder would review the markings to check the first coder's judgments. Disagreements were resolved by a third, tie-breaker coder. This second part involves identifying content to be coded rather than classifying the content itself. It may not even appear in all protocols. A content analysis of letters exchanged between a writer and an editor might not have this step if all text of all letters is coded.

The third part of the protocol specified each category used in the content analysis. For each category, the overall operational definition was given along with the definitions of the values of each subcategory. These are the actual instructions used by the coders to assign content to particular values of particular categories and subcategories. Obviously, the instructions for some categories will be relatively simple (counting the column inches of quotation or paraphrase attributed to a source) or complex (specifying how the coder can recognize a defamation per se, requiring rules about the kind of source statements meeting appropriate criteria).

How much detail should the category definitions contain?: only as much as necessary. As just noted, the definitions of the concepts and their articulation in the protocol is an interactive process. The protocol itself undergoes change, as coders in their practice sessions attempt to use the definitions, assessing their interim agreement at various stages in the training process. Category definition becomes more coder friendly as examples and exceptions are integrated. Ironically, though, extremes in category definition—too much or too little detail—should be avoided. Definitions that lack detail permit coders too much leeway in interpreting when the categories should be used. Definitions that are excessively detailed may promote coder confusion or may result in coders forgetting particular rules in the process of coding.

The coding instructions shown in Table 6.1 provide an example of the three types of information. It represents one protocol in a series of content analyses conducted by one of the authors into the issues of fairness and balance in newspaper journalism (Fico & Cote, 1999). The introduction provides a brief discussion of the project and an explanation of how content was selected. The procedure section provides the operational definitions of variables and the technical information needed to categorize the content into those variables.

## Coding Sheet

Each category in the content analysis protocol must relate unambiguously to the actual coding sheet used to record the content attributes of each unit of content in the study. This coding sheet has the status of a questionnaire in a random sample survey, and the same rules for clarity of presentation apply. Just as a survey instrument can be respondent friendly, a coding sheet can and should be coder friendly.

Coding sheets can be printed on paper or presented on a computer screen. Each form has advantages and disadvantages. Paper sheets allow flexibility when coding. With paper, a computer need not be available while analyzing content, and the periodic interruption of coding content for keyboarding is avoided. Not having interruptions is especially important when categories are complex and the uninterrupted application of the coding instructions can improve reliability. Paper sheets are useful particularly if a coder is examining content that is physically large, such as a newspaper.

Using paper, however, might add more time to the coding process. Paper coding sheets require the coder to write the value; someone else then must keyboard it into the computer. If large amounts of data are being analyzed, the time increase can be considerable. This double recording on paper and keyboard also increases the chance of transcribing error. On the other hand, having the paper sheets provides a backup for the data should a hard drive crash.

The organization of the coding sheet will, of course, depend on the specific study. However, one important rule applies: The categories on

# TABLE 6.1
## Coding Protocol for Presidential Race, 1996

*Introduction*

This news story protocol is aimed at assessing balance in the coverage of the 1996 presidential election by Michigan newspapers. It examines the coverage given to partisan sources and how this affects coverage balance given various topics. The following four definitions are important in selecting and analyzing the content under study.

*News Story*

An election story focuses on selecting personnel who make public policy. In this study, it is the President of the United States.

News stories are defined as all nonadvertising matter in a news product. In a newspaper, this would usually include all staff-produced news stories found in the first and "local" section, but excluding editorial pages, op ed pages, reader opinions, sports, routine business data, society news, and similar matter. It may include relevant features produces by local staff reporters and syndicated and wire services stories relevant to the issue or election being analyzed.

*Election Issue*

An election issue is a contention by opponents or those speaking on their behalf that may involve public policy issues in the election or more general assertions about themselves or their opponents relative to the election. Public policy issues involve government and by definition are subject to open meeting and public record acts. Other issues may not involve this governmental dimension, although contention is present. Such other issues may include, for example, a candidate's character, credibility, or fitness.

*Source*

A source is a person, or organization, who gives information to news reporters. A partisan source is one whose arguments about a candidate constitutes the information provided news reporters. An expert source is one who does not take a partisan stand on the candidate but has credible knowledge about the probable electoral success of a candidate.

Sources are explicitly identified as such when news reporters quote or paraphrase information from them in stories. The means by which reporters publicly credit a source for story information is called attribution. Such attribution is signaled when a person or organization's name is linked in a story sentence with verbs denoting a person speaking, such as said, claimed, and so forth. Attribution also may be made by verbs denoting a source's state of mind, such as thinks, feels, wants, and so forth. Story information not clearly attributed to a source is assumed to originate from a reporter's direct observations of actions and events.

*Attribution*

How assertions from sources are treated relative to one another is key to assessing news story balance in an election. An assertion is considered to be information from a source relevant to the election appearing in news stories.

The range of assertions on topics relevant to the election is determined by reading all stories on the election. Assertions from contending sources relevant to the election deal with issues or personal qualities of candidates. Assertions from expert sources concern the "course race" aspects of the campaign. Assertions by the reporter or by "third parties" not identified as contenders or experts would not be considered in assessing story balance.

*(continued)*

**TABLE 6.1** (*continued*)

*Procedure*

The following steps should be taken in the content analysis coding described below (v stands for variable): (a) all relevant election stories are read to identify partisan and expert sources, (b) all attributed assertions of those individuals or organizations are marked by one coder and checked by another, and (c) each story is then analyzed for specific characteristics described below.

v1. Story Identification

v2. Story Day (month and day)

v3. Newspaper name/circulation rank

v4. Story prominence

Code these story locations with the associated numbers:

Page one = 2
Section page one = 1
Inside page = 0

v5. Story origin: designated by story byline

1 = newspaper's own reporter
2 = newspaper's state bureau
3 = newspaper's DC bureau

4 = Associated Press (AP)
5 = other bureau or newspaper

v6. Unique AP story:

Code if v5. = 4

1 = story is unique
0 = story is duplicate

v7. Partisan side sourcing

A partisan source is an individual or group that makes attributed assertions supporting or opposing a candidate.

*Attribution*

Attribution to a source is usually made by name. A source initially identified by a label (e.g., a "critic") must be identified somewhere in the story.

An anonymous source can be considered a source provided anonymity is explicitly granted in the story (e.g., "A campaign official who declined to be identified …").

Sources identified as "aides," "advisers," "official," and even as "the campaign" are frequent in election storied and are considered adequate attribution.

*Assertions*

Partisan sources in stories must be linked to assertions by verbs denoting speaking such as said. The link may also be made by verbs denoting state of mind such as feels or believes.

v8. Primary story source

This is the source taking up the most story space.

| | |
|---|---|
| Debate: | Candidate debate comments/interview response. |
| Speech/Rally: | Formal or informal address by candidates/supporters/interview response. |
| Document:. | Comments by poll respondents/partisans |
| Interview: | Interviews independent of just mentioned sources. |
| Other Media Interviews: | Interviews cited in other media. |
| Ad: | Ad information/interview response. |

v9–11. Primary Clinton (Dole, Perot) source

Identify the first source advocating a candidate. If that source is an ad or commercial that uses a person, not the status of that person using the following codes.

v12. Primary story topic

Identify the first topic mentioned by a candidate in the story.

| | |
|---|---|
| 1 = economic: | Job creation, inflation, wages, prices, trade. |
| 2 = social: | Abortion, affirmative action, crime, education, health care, welfare. |
| 3 = ideology: | Liberalism, conservatism, extremism, views over size of government, government activism. |
| 4 = tax/spend: | Taxes and spending, balancing the budget. |
| 5 = personal: | Character issues, corruption, personal morality, trustworthiness, personal qualities. |
| 6 = finance: | Campaign finance issues. |
| 7 = foreign: | Foreign policy issues. |
| 8 = other issues | |
| 9 = horse race: | Commentary on the race. |

v13–15. Source number

Count the number of sources making partisan assertions in support of Clinton, Dole, or Perot.

*(continued)*

## TABLE 6.1 (continued)

v16–18. Column inch number

Each column is standardized as 2 in. in width and .125 in depth for each line.

Count the number of standardized column lines of partisan assertions favoring each candidate. Multiply that by .125 to get total column inches favoring each candidate.

If a partisan assertion of less than a column inch, code the assertion as 1 column inch.

> Partisan assertions are otherwise rounded up or down to the nearest column inch. For example, 1.25 = 1; 2.5 = 3

v19. Inch domination: Does Clinton or Dole have more column inches?

v20. Lead domination: Does Clinton or Dole get lead assertion?

> The lead is the first paragraph in a story.

v21. Graf 2–5 domination: Does Clinton or Dole get graf 2–5 assertion?

v22. Partisan domination.

Count the measures in v19–21 that favor Clinton or Dole.

The candidate who gets the highest score dominates the Partisan Domination measure.

Balance occurs if all three variables are balanced, or if an equal number of measures favor Dole or Clinton.

v23. Imbalance index

Add the total of measures dominated by Clinton, subtract the total of measures dominated by Dole, and them take the absolute value.

v24–v26. Clinton (Dole, Perot) horse race assessment.

If one or more election experts are cited, is that commentary positive, negative, or both toward one or more of the three candidates?

An election expert is one who (a) does NOT take a partisan position on any candidate; and (b) has some recognizable expertise in judging election campaigns, as a pollster, academic, and so forth.

Relevant commentary must focus on one or more of the following:

1. Polling strength/weakness etc.
2. Candidate appeal in appearance, manner, competence.
3. Organization strength or effectiveness.
4. Debate performance.
5. Group support of endorsements.
6. Issue strength or positioning.

the coding sheet should, as much as possible, be ordered to follow the order of variables in the protocol, which in turn follows the flow of the content of interest. The coders should not have to dart back and forth within the content of interest to determine if categories of analysis apply. If, for example, an analysis involves recording whether a contending source has made an assertion in a news story lead, that category should be coded relatively high up on the coding sheet because coders will encounter the lead first. Planning the sheet design along with the protocol requires the researcher to visualize what the process of data collection will be like and how problems can be avoided.

Obviously too, contingent categories that are activated only if particular values of earlier categories are used should be grouped together. For example, coding for speaking or nonspeaking roles for actors who are women and minorities in product commercials is contingent on an earlier coding decision that human (nonanimated) women and minority characters are present.

Coding sheets usually fall into two types: single case and multiple case. The single case coding sheets have one or more pages for each case or recording unit. The analysis of suicide notes for themes might use a "sheet" for each note, with several content categories on the sheet.

Table 6.2 shows the single case coding sheet associated with the coding instructions given in Table 6.1. Each variable (v) and a response number or space is identified with a letter and numbers (v1, v2, etc.) that corresponds with the definition in the coding protocol. Connecting variable locations on the protocol and on the coding sheet reduces time and confusion while coding.

Multicase coding sheets allow an analyst to put more than one case on a page. This form is useful for reducing copying cost and is useful when a larger number of coding units are examined for a limited number of variables. This type of coding sheet often appears as a grid, with the cases placed along the rows and the variables listed in the columns.

Studies that incorporate seconds of video or sound, numbers of items, and space units work well with multicase coding sheets. Under each variable column, the measurement numbers can be listed and totaled at the bottom of the page. This allows for easy summation of several pages. Of course, database computer programs using such grids provide easy summation of data entered directly into the computer.

Figure 6.1 shows an abbreviated multicase coding sheet for a study of monthly consumer magazines. Each row will contain the data for one is-

## TABLE 6.2
## Coding Sheet

*Fairness and Election Coverage: Presidential Race, 1996*

v1. Story identification number                                      _____

v2. Story day (month and date)                                       _____

v3. Newspaper name and circulation rank                              _____

*General Story Characteristics*

v.4. Story prominence (FP = 2; SP1 = 1; Inside = 0)

v5. Story origin

| | |
|---|---|
| 1 = newspaper's own reporter | 2 = newspaper's state bureau |
| 3 = newspaper's D.C. bureau | 4 = AP |
| 5 = other bureau/newspapers | |

_____

v6. AP unique (if v5 = 4)

| | |
|---|---|
| 0 = duplicate story | 1 = unique story, blank = no AP |

_____

v7. Partisan side sourcing effort

| | |
|---|---|
| 1 = only Clinton or Dole | 2 = both Clinton and Dole |
| 3 = only Perot | 4 = Perot and Clinton or Dole |
| 5 = Perot and Clinton and Dole | |

_____

v8. Primary story source

| | |
|---|---|
| 1 = debate | 2 = speech/rally |
| 3 = document | 4 = poll |
| 5 = interview | 6 = other media interview |
| 7 = ad | 8 = other |

_____

v9. Primary Clinton source

| | |
|---|---|
| 1 = candidates | 2 = campaign/party |
| 3 = organizations/groups | 4 = government |
| 5 = citizen | 0 = not applicable |

_____

v10. Primary Dole source

| | |
|---|---|
| 1 = candidates | 2 = campaign/party |
| 3 = organizations/groups | 4 = government |
| 5 = citizen | 0 = not applicable |

_____

v11. Primary Perot source

| | |
|---|---|
| 1 = candidates | 2 = campaign/party |
| 3 = organizations/groups | 4 = government |
| 5 = citizen | 0 = not applicable |

_____

v12. Primary story topic

| | |
|---|---|
| 1 = economic | 2 = social issues |
| 3 = ideological | 4 = tax/spend |
| 5 = personal/character | 6 = campaign finance |
| 7 = foreign policy | 8 = other issues |
| 9 = horse race commentary | |

_Partisan Sources and Space_

| | Clinton | Dole | Perot |
|---|---|---|---|
| Source number | v13. _____ | v14. _____ | v15. _____ |
| Column inch | v16. _____ | v17. _____ | v18. _____ |

_Partisan Dominance (Code Clinton and/or Dole source in story)_

| Clinton/Dole story coverage | Favors Clinton | Favors Dole | Balanced | Not applicable |
|---|---|---|---|---|
| v19. Inch dominance | 1 | 2 | 3 | 0 |
| v20. Lead dominance | 1 | 2 | 3 | 0 |
| v21. Graf 2–5 dominance | 1 | 2 | 3 | 0 |
| v22. Clinton/Dole dominance (see v19–v21) | 1 | 2 | 3 | 0 |

v23. Imbalance index of story
   Absolute value (Clinton v19–v21 score minus Dole v19–v21 score)

_Horse Race Assessment_

| | Positive | Negative | Both | Not applicable |
|---|---|---|---|---|
| v24. About Clinton | | | | |
| v25. About Dole | 1 | 2 | 3 | 0 |
| v26. About Perot | 1 | 2 | 3 | 0 |

_Note._   FP = front page; SP = section page.

sue of the magazine; this example contains data for six cases. Each column holds the numbers for the variable listed. Coders will record the number of photographs in column 4 for the issue listed on the row. For instance, the March issue in 1995 had 45 photographs in the magazine.

Magazine: Good Housekeeping

| ID # | Month | Year | # of Photos | Pages of Food Ads | # of Health Stories | Total space | # of Stories |
|------|-------|------|-------------|-------------------|---------------------|-------------|--------------|
| 01 | 01 | 95 | 42 | 15 | 09 | 102 | 29 |
| 02 | 02 | 95 | 37 | 21 | 10 | 115 | 31 |
| 03 | 03 | 95 | 45 | 32 | 15 | 130 | 35 |
| 04 | 04 | 95 | 31 | 25 | 08 | 090 | 27 |
| 05 | 06 | 95 | 50 | 19 | 12 | 112 | 30 |
| 06 | 01 | 96 | 43 | 19 | 11 | 120 | 25 |
| 07 | 02 | 96 | 45 | 23 | 17 | 145 | 29 |

FIG. 6.1. Coding sheet for monthly consumer magazines.

## CODER TRAINING

One is often warned in life about "going around in a circle," covering the same ground over and over again. However, the process of concept definition, protocol construction, and coder training is just such a circular process. Central to this process—how long it goes on and when it stops—are the coders.

The coders, of course, change as they engage in successive encounters with the content of interest and the way that content is captured by the concepts defined for the study. A content analysis protocol will go through many drafts during pretesting as concepts are refined, measures specified, and procedures for coding worked through.

### Coding Process

This process is both facilitated and made more complex depending on the number of coders. Along with everybody else, researchers carry mental baggage that influences their perception and interpretation of communication content. A single coder may not notice the dimensions of a concept being missed or how a protocol that is perfectly clear to him or her may be opaque to another. Several coders are therefore more likely to hammer out conceptual and operational definitions that are clearer and more explicit.

On the other hand, the disadvantage of collaboration among several coders is that agreement on concepts may be more difficult, or their application may reveal problems that would not occur with fewer or with only one coder. At some point, a concept or its measure may just not be worth further expenditure of time or effort, and recognizing that point may not be easy either.

Category definitions are not very useful if they cannot be applied reliably. Although the protocol may be well organized and clearly and coherently written, a content analysis must still involve systematic training of coders in using it. Again, the analogy to a survey is useful. Survey administrators must be trained in the rhythms of the questionnaire and gain comfort and confidence in reading the questions and recording respondent answers. Coders in a content analysis must grow comfortable and familiar with the definitions of the protocol and how they relate to the content of interest.

The first step in training coders is to familiarize them with the content being analyzed. The aim here is not to precode material, and indeed, content not in the study sample should be used for this familiarization process. The familiarization process is meant to increase the coders' comfort level with the content of interest, to give them an idea of what to expect in the content, and how much energy and attention is needed to comprehend it.

To help minimize coder differences, the study should establish a procedure that coders follow in dealing with the content. For example, that procedure may specify how many pieces of content a coder may deal with in a session or a maximum length of time governing a coding session. The procedure may also specify that each coding session must start with a full reading of the protocol to refresh coder memory of category definitions.

Coders also should familiarize themselves with the content analysis protocol, discussing it among themselves and dealing with problems in applying it to the content being studied. During these discussions, it should become clear whether the coders are approaching the content from similar or different frames of reference. Obviously, differences will need to be addressed because these will almost certainly result in disagreements among coders and poor study reliability.

## Sources of Coder Differences

Differences among coders can have a number of origins. Some are relatively easy to address, such as simple confusions over definitions. Others may be impossible to solve, such as a coder who simply does not follow the procedure specified in the protocol.

*Category Problems.*    Differences over category definitions must be seriously addressed in training sessions. Does disagreement exist because a category is ambiguous or poorly articulated in the protocol? Or is the problem with a coder who just does not understand the concept or the rules for operationalizing it? Obviously, when several coders disagree on a category or interpret it in varying ways, the strong possibility exists that the problem is in the category. A category problem may occur because of fundamental ambiguity or complexity in the category or because the rules assigning content to the category are poorly spelled out in the protocol.

The simplest approach to a such a category problem is to begin by revising its definition to remove the sources of ambiguity or confusion. If this revising fails to remove the source of disagreement, attention must be turned to the fundamental category definition. It may be that an overly complex category can be broken down into several parts that are relatively more simple to handle. For example, the research on defamation required initially that coders identify defamation in general and following that, coding copy as containing defamation per se and defamation per quod. Now defamation per quod is interpreted by courts to mean that the defamation exists in the context of the overall meanings that people might bring to the reading. Coder reliability was poor. However, better reliability was achieved on recognition of defamation in general and defamation per se. The solution was obvious: Given defamation in general, defamation per quod was defined to exist when defamation per se was ruled out. In other words, if all defamation was either per se or per quod, getting a reliable measure of per se was all that was necessary to also define reliably that remaining part of defamatory content that was per quod.

However, researchers may also have to decide if a category must be dropped from the study because coders cannot use it reliably. In another study of how controversy over issues was covered in the news (Fico & Soffin, 1995), the coders attempted to make distinctions between "attack" and "defense" assertions by contenders on these issues. In fact, the content itself proved to so intermix these kinds of assertions that achieving acceptable reliability proved impossible.

*Coder Problems.*    If only one coder is consistently disagreeing with others, the possibility exists that something has prevented that coder from properly applying the definitions. Between-coder reliability measures make it easy to identify problem coders by comparing the agreement of all possible pairs of coders. Attention must then be given to retraining that coder or removing him or her from the study.

There may be several reasons why a coder persistently disagrees with others on application of category definitions. The easiest coder problems to solve involve applications in procedure. Is the coder giving the proper time to the coding? Has the protocol been reviewed as specified in the coding procedures?

More difficult problems involve differences in cultural understanding or frame of reference that may be dividing coders. These differences will be encountered most frequently when coders deal with concepts that are relatively less manifest in content. As just noted, such content requires more coder interpretation about the meaning of content and its application to content categories.

One author recalls working as a student on a content study in a class of students from the United States, Bolivia, Nigeria, France, and South Africa. The study involved applying concepts such as terrorism to a sample of stories about international relations. As might be imagined, what is terrorism from one perspective may well be national liberation from another. Such frame of reference problems are not impossible to overcome, but they will increase the time needed for coder training. Such issues should also signal that the study itself may require more careful definition of its terms in the context of such cultural or social differences.

Peter and Lauf (2002) examined factors affecting intercoder reliability in a study of cross-national content analysis, which was defined as comparing content in different languages from more than one country. Peter and Lauf concluded that some coder characteristics affected intercoder reliability in bilingual content analysis. However, most of their recommendations centered on the failure to check reliability among the people who trained the coders. The conclusion was that cross-country content analysis would be reliable if three conditions are met: "First, the coder trainers agree in their coding with one another; second, the coders within a country group agree with one another, and, third, the coders agree with the coding of their trainers" (Peter & Lauf, 2002, p. 827).

## CODER RELIABILITY ASSESSMENT

### Coder Reliability Tests

Ultimately, however, the process of concept definition and protocol construction must cease. At that point, the researcher must assess the degree to which the content definitions and procedures can be reliably applied. Each variable (content category) in the analysis is tested by looking at how the coders have agreed on using the relevant values of the variable being tested. For example, two coders code 10 newspaper stories dealing with a conflict over abortion. Coding the category of the fairness of stories, as indicated by source citation to both pro-life and pro-choice sides, they compute the percentage of those stories on which they have agreed that the particular story is fair or unfair according to the coding definitions. In a content analysis done by a single coder, the analyst tests the reliability against himself or herself at two points in time—referred to as stability in coding. This tests whether slippage has occurred in the single coder's understanding or application of the protocol definitions.

Mathematical tests of reliability take into account the degree of complexity in coding the variable. Specifically, tests assess the possibility that agreement is the result of chance and not the protocol rules. For example, agreement between coders on a variable with only two values (e.g., something is present or absent) is easiest to achieve because chance alone could produce agreement half of the time. A variable with four to six values will achieve high reliability if the content protocol is actually driving coding decisions (and provided those four to six values are actually used).

Coder training sessions constitute a kind of informal reliability test. However, wishful thinking and post hoc rationalizations of why errors have occurred (e.g., "I made that mistake only because I got interrupted by the phone while coding that story") mean a more formal and rigorous procedure must be applied. In fact, formal coder reliability tests may be conducted during the period of coder training itself as a indicator of when to proceed with the study, as noted in chapter 3 (this volume). Such training tests should not, of course, be conducted with the content being used for the actual study. The reason is that a coder must code independently both of others and of herself or himself. If content is coded several times, prior decisions contaminate subsequent ones. Furthermore, the effect of multiple codings is to inflate the ultimate reliability estimate, thus giving a false confidence in the study's overall reliability.

At some point, the training formally stops, and the actual assessment of achieved reliability must take place. Two issues must be addressed in such an assessment. The first concerns the selection of content that will be used in the reliability assessment. The second concerns the actual statistical reliability tests that will be used.

## Selection of Content for Testing

We advocate random selection of content samples for reliability testing. Other advice has been ambiguous about how much content must be tested and how that content is selected from the larger body of material to be coded. One text (Wimmer & Dominick, 2003) suggests that between 10% and 25% of the body of content should be tested. Others (Kaid & Wadsworth, 1989) suggested that between 5% and 7% of the total is adequate. Earlier works (Cohen, 1960; Scott, 1955) have discussed sampling in the context of their discussions of statistical reliability.

The need for random sampling from the population of content being coded for a reliability test is identical to the need for randomly sampling content from a population of content of interest, as discussed in chapter 5 (this volume). Random sampling, relying on unbiased mathematical principles for selection of observations, accomplishes two things. First, it controls for the inevitable human biases in selection. Second, the procedure produces, with a known possibility of error, a sample that reflects the appropriate proportions of the characteristics of the overall population of content being studied.

Given such a sample, the coder reliability test should then appropriately reflect the full range of potential coding decisions that must be made in the entire body of material. The problem with nonrandom selection of content for reliability testing is the same as the problem with a nonrandom sample of people: Tested material may be atypical of the entire body of content that will be coded. A nonrepresentative sample yields reliability assessments whose relation to the entire body of content is unknown.

Using random selection for content testing also enables researchers to take advantage of sampling theory to answer the question of how much material must be tested. As discussed in chapter 5 (this volume), random sampling entails sampling error at known levels of confidence. For example, if two researchers using randomly sampled content achieve a 90% level of agreement, the actual agreement they would achieve coding all material could vary above and below that figure according to the computed sampling error. That computed sampling error would vary with the size of the sample—the bigger the sample, in general, the smaller the error and therefore the more precise the estimate of agreement. Therefore, if the desired level of agreement is 80%, and the achieved level on a coder reliability test is 90% plus or minus 5 percentage points, the researchers can proceed with confidence that the desired agreement level has been reached or exceeded. However, if the test produced an 84%, the plus or minus 5% sampling error would include a value of 79% that is below the required standard of 80%.

## Selection Procedures

Assuming content for a reliability test will be selected randomly, how many units of content must be selected? Lacy and Riffe (1996) noted that this will depend on several other factors. One is the total number of units to be coded. Another is the desired degree of confidence in the eventual reliability assessment. A third factor is the degree of precision desired in the reliability assessment.

Although each of these three factors is under the control of the researcher, a fourth factor must be assumed on the basis of prior studies, a pretest, or a guess. That is the researcher's estimate of the actual agreement that would have been obtained had all the content of interest been used in the reliability test. For reasons that we explain later, it is our recommendation that the estimate of actual agreement be set 5 percentage points higher than the minimum required reliability for the test. This 5-percentage point buffer will ensure a more rigorous test, that is, the achieved agreement will have to be higher for the reliability test to be judged adequate.

The first object in applying this procedure is to compute the number of content cases required for the reliability test. Researchers surveying a population use the formula for the standard error of proportion to estimate a minimal sample size necessary to infer to that population at a given confidence level. Researchers can use that formula and solve it for a variety of unknown quantities: If they know their obtained sample size and a proportion, they can solve for margin of error within certain confidence intervals; knowing how much error they can tolerate, they can solve for a minimum acceptable sample size, and so on.

A similar procedure is applied here to a population of content. One difference, however, is that a content analysis population is likely to be far smaller than the population of people that is surveyed. This makes it possible to correct for a finite population size when the sample makes up 20% or more of the population. This has the effect of reducing the standard error and giving a more precise estimate of reliability.

The formula for the standard error can be manipulated to solve for the sample size needed to achieve a given level of confidence. This formula is

$$n = \frac{(N-1)(SE)^2 + PQN}{(N-1)(SE)^2 + PQ}$$

in which

$N$ = the population size (number of content units in the study)
$P$ = the population level of agreement
$Q = (1 - P)$
$n$ = the sample size for the reliability check

Solving for $n$ gives the number of content units needed in the reliability check. Note that standard error gives the confidence level desired in the test. This is usually set at the 95% or 99% confidence level (using a one-tailed test because interest is in the portion of the interval that may extend below the acceptable reliability figure).

For the rest of the formula, $N$ is the population size of the content of interest, $P$ is the estimate of agreement in the population, and $Q$ is 1 minus that figure.

Suppose one takes an example in which one assumes an acceptable minimal level of agreement of 85% and $P$ of 90% in a study using 1,000 content units (e.g., newspaper stories). One further assumes a desired confidence level of .05 (i.e., the 95% confidence level). A one-tailed $z$ score—the number of standard errors needed to include 95% of all possible sample means on agreement—is 1.64 (a two-tailed test $z$ score would be 1.96). Because the confidence level is 5% and our desired level of probability is 95%, $SE$ is computed as follows:

$$.05 = 1.64(SE)$$

or

$$SE = .05/1.64 = .03.$$

Using these numbers to determine the test sample size to achieve a minimum 85% reliability agreement and assuming $P$ to equal 90% (5% above our minimum), the results are

$$n = \frac{(999)(.0009) + .09(1000)}{(999)(.0009) + .09}$$

$$n = 92$$

In other words, 92 test units are used (e.g., newspaper stories) for the coder reliability test. If a 90% agreement in coding a variable on those 92 test units is achieved, chances are 95 out of 100 that at least an 85% or better agreement would exist if the entire content population were coded by all coders and reliability measured.

Once the number of test units needed is known, selection of the particular ones for testing can be based on any number of random techniques. For example, if study content has been numerically ordered from 1 to 1,000, a random number program can identify the particular units to be pulled for the test, or a printed table of random numbers can serve as easily.

The procedure just described is also applicable to studies in which coding categories are at interval or ratio scales. The calculation of standard error is the only difference.

If these formulas seem difficult to use, two tables may be useful. Tables 6.3 and 6.4 apply to studies that deal with nominal-level percentage of agreement; Table 6.3 is configured for a 95% confidence level, and Table 6.4 is configured for the more rigorous 99% confidence level. Furthermore, within each table, the number of test cases needed has been configured for 85%, 90%, and 95% estimates of population coding agreement.

For some studies, particularly smaller ones, the selection process for the reliability test just recommended will result in a large proportion of all the cases being used in the test. Regardless, we still recommend that test cases used for coder reliability be randomly selected from the popu-

TABLE 6.3
Content Units Needed for Reliability Test Based on Various Population Sizes,
Three Assumed Levels of Population Intercoder Agreement,
and a 95% Level of Probability

|  | *Assumed Level of Agreement in Population* | | |
|---|---|---|---|
|  | *85%* | *90%* | *95%* |
| Population Size |  |  |  |
| 10,000 | 141 | 100 | 54 |
| 5,000 | 139 | 99 | 54 |
| 1,000 | 125 | 92 | 52 |
| 500 | 111 | 84 | 49 |
| 250 | 91 | 72 | 45 |
| 100 | 59 | 51 | 36 |

**TABLE 6.4**
**Content Units Needed for Reliability Test Based on Various Population Sizes,**
**Three Assumed Levels of Population Intercoder Agreement,**
**and a 99% Level of Probability**

| | Assumed Level of Agreement in Population | | |
|---|---|---|---|
| | *85%* | *90%* | *95%* |
| Population Size | | | |
| 10,000 | 271 | 193 | 104 |
| 5,000 | 263 | 190 | 103 |
| 1,000 | 218 | 165 | 95 |
| 500 | 179 | 142 | 87 |
| 250 | 132 | 111 | 75 |
| 100 | 74 | 67 | 52 |

lation of content of interest. In particular, the reliability tests discussed following that attempt to account for chance in coding decisions must use a sample that reflects the entire population of content to be coded. The level of sampling error for reliability samples should always be reported.

## CATEGORY RELIABILITY TESTS

### Percentage of Agreement

The procedure for selecting content for a coder reliability test works directly into the simplest of coder reliability tests—the percentage of agreement among two or more coders. In the test, coders determine the proportion of correct judgments as a percentage of total judgments made. The acceptable level of agreement necessary will depend on the type of research conducted. However, a minimum level of 80% is usually the standard.

All coding decisions can be reduced to dichotomous decisions for figuring simple agreement. In such cases, each possible pair of coders is compared for agreement or disagreement. For example, if three coders categorize an article, the total number of dichotomous coding decisions will equal three: Coders A and B, Coders B and C, and Coders A and C. Four coders will yield six decisions for comparison (A and B, A and C, A and D, B and C, B and D, and C and D) and so on.

Table 6.5 shows a diagram for evaluating simple agreement for four coders. This layout would be repeated for each variable. The simple agreement for all pairs of coders should be reported for each category in an article. An overall percentage of agreement can also be calculated.

Simple agreement figures may be criticized as possibly overinflating reliability because the chances of accidentally agreeing increase as the number of coders decreases. Two coders have a 50% probability of agreeing by chance, and three coders have a 33.3% probability of agreeing by chance. However, the fact that agreement can take place by chance does not mean it does. It is not automatically true that 50% of the agreements between two coders were due to chance. All agreements could easily be the result of a well-developed protocol. To control for the possibility of chance, at least three formulas are available that take chance into consideration. Content analysis studies should report both a simple agreement figure and one of the statistics mentioned following that take chance into consideration. The simple agreement figures should be placed in an endnote as information for researchers conducting replications. However, the decision as to the reliability of a variable in the protocol should be based on a coefficient that takes chance agreement into consideration.

## Tests for Chance Agreement

Cases for these tests must also be randomly sampled because they require an estimate of the probabilities that particular values of a category

**TABLE 6.5**
**Diagram for Figuring Simple Agreement With Four Coders**

| Name of Category (Variable) | No. Units | Outcome | No. Units | Outcome |
|---|---|---|---|---|
| Coder Pairs | | | | |
| Kate and Faith | 8 | Agree | 2 | Disagree |
| Kate and Ben | 9 | Agree | 1 | Disagree |
| Kate and Laurie | 7 | Agree | 3 | Disagree |
| Faith and Ben | 9 | Agree | 1 | Disagree |
| Faith and Laurie | 6 | Agree | 4 | Disagree |
| Ben and Laurie | 7 | Agree | 3 | Disagree |
| Total | 46 | Agree | 14 | Disagree |

*Note.* Total number of units for each pair of coders = 10.

are present in the population of content. The reliability figures from samples are the best estimates of population reliability figures. However, this will only be the case (at a known sampling error and level of confidence) when data for the reliability test have been randomly selected for the population of study content. Absent random selection of test data, the empirically obtained reliability figures have an unknown relation to the population reliabilities.

A number of reliability tests have been recommended by content analysis texts. One of the most frequently used is Scott's Pi (Scott, 1955), a test that looks at category values and "corrects" for chance agreement in computing a reliability assessment. Scott's Pi computes the agreement expected by chance by looking at the proportion of times particular values of a category are used in a given test and then calculates the chance agreement or expected agreement based on those proportions. This expected agreement is calculated using basic probability theory.

The reason for an assessment tool that corrects for chance is straightforward. Suppose two people are flipping coins, and the object is for both of them on a flip to achieve heads. Each person has a 50% chance of getting a head. However, the probability of both getting a head on the same flip is only 25%, given only four possible outcomes: both flip heads (the desired outcome); both flip tails; one flips heads, whereas the other flips tails; and one flips tails, whereas the other flips heads.

A coin, of course, has only two possible outcomes. Category variables have at least two values and possibly many more. As a result, Scott's Pi looks at the actual usage of every value in the tested variable and uses that distribution to calculate the probability of chance agreement.

Assume that a category variable has four values and that two coders have coded 10 items on content for a total of 20 coding decisions. Value 1 has been used 40% of the time (i.e., 8 of the decisions have been to select Value 1 as the correct coding of the category), Value 2 has been used 30% of the time, and Values 3 and 4 each 15% of the time. The expected value for two coders to use Value 1 by chance alone would be .4 times .4 and similarly with all the other values. Remember, the analogy with the coin flip is exact except that the expected use of a head is .5, whereas the expected use of Value 1 in our example is empirically determined by the coder reliability test to be .4.

Here is where the multiplication rules of probability apply. The probability of using Value 1 on a particular piece of content is .4, but two such events (two coders coding the same variable in the same piece of content) requires .4 to be multiplied by .4. This, of course, makes intuitive sense: A single event is more likely to occur than two such events occurring.

In this example, the expected agreement for the four-value example is .4 times .4, plus .3 times .3, plus .15 times .15, plus .15 times .15. The expected agreement by chance alone would then be .29 or 29%.

The computing formula for the test statistic is only slightly more complex than what has already been worked out. The Scott's Pi formula is

$$Pi = \frac{\% \, OA - \% \, EA}{1 - \% \, EA}$$

in which:

$OA$ = observed agreement

$EA$ = expected agreement

In this figure, $OA$ is the agreement achieved in the test, and $EA$ is the agreement expected by chance, as just illustrated. Note that the expected agreement is subtracted from both the numerator and denominator. In other words, chance is eliminated from both the achieved agreement and the total possible agreement.

To continue with the example, suppose the observed agreement among two coders coding the four-value category for 10 news stories is 90% (they have disagreed only once). In this test, Scott's Pi would be

$$Pi = \frac{.90 - .29}{1 - .29} = \frac{.61}{.71} = .86$$

That .86 can be interpreted as the agreement that has been achieved as a result of the category definitions and their diligent application by coders after a measure of the amount of chance agreement has been removed. Finally, Scott's Pi is similar to a correlation coefficient in that it has an upper limit of 1.0 in the case of perfect agreement and a lower limit of $-1.0$ in the case of perfect disagreement. Figures around 0 indicate that chance is more likely governing coding decisions than the content analysis protocol definitions and their application.

The example cited applies to two coders. If more than two coders are used, the test can be applied to pairs of coders and then averaged across all the tests for the overall average.

The question is often raised about the acceptable level of reliability that a content study should contain. That question can be easily answered if other studies have used identical or similar category definitions. Categories and definitions that have been used extensively should achieve higher levels of reliability if research is to continue to be based on them. Generally acceptable reliability figures will depend on the test used. Research usually reports reliability figures that are .80 or higher. Krippendorff (2004a) suggested that an Alpha of .8 indicates adequate reliability. However, Krippendorff (2004a) added that variables with Alphas as low as .667 could be acceptable for drawing tentative conclusions. The lower coefficient would be appropriate for research that is breaking new ground with concepts that are rich in analytical value. The figures of .8 and .667 also are appropriate for Scott's pi with nominal data and a large sample.

A number of other forms for assessing the impact of chance are available. Cohen (1960) developed Kappa, which has the same formula as Scott's Pi:

$$\text{Kappa} = \frac{P_O - P_e}{1 - P_e}$$

in which:

$P_O$ = observed agreement
$P_e$ = expected agreement

Kappa and Pi differ, however, in the way expected agreement is calculated. Recall that Scott squared the observed proportions used for each value of a category assuming all coders are using those values equally. In other words, if 8 of 20 decisions were to select Value 1 of a category, .4 is squared regardless of whether one of the coders used that value six times and the other only two. However, Kappa is based on the expected agreement on the marginal numbers for a matrix of proportions. The proportion of a particular value of a category used by one coder is multiplied by the proportion of use of that value by the other coder. These proportions are then added for all the values of the category to get the expected agreement.

In the example, one coder has used the value of 1 in 6 of 10 decisions (.6), and the second coder has used the value of 1 in 2 of 10 decisions (.2). Therefore, whereas Pi yielded the expected value of .16 (.4 × .4),

Kappa yields an expected value of .12 (.6 × .2). Kappa will produce somewhat higher reliability figures than Pi, especially when one value of a category is used much more often than others.

The procedure for computing expected value for Kappa also can be carried out using frequencies in categories instead of proportions. When proportions are used, the procedure is the same as calculating expected frequencies for a chi-square statistic. For further explanation of Kappa, see Cohen (1960).

Kappa is used for nominal-level measures, and all disagreements are assumed to be equivalent. However, if disagreements vary in their seriousness (e.g., a psychiatrist reading a patient's diary's content concludes the person has a personality disorder when the person is really psychotic), then a weighted Kappa (Cohen, 1968) has been developed.

Krippendorff (1980) developed a coefficient, Alpha, that is similar to Scott's Pi and Cohen's Kappa. Krippendorff's (1980) Alpha is presented by the equation

$$\text{Alpha} = \frac{D_o}{D_c}$$

in which:

$D_o$ = observed disagreement
$D_c$ = expected disagreement

The process of calculating $D_o$ and $D_c$ depends on the level of measurement (nominal, ordinal, interval, and ratio) used for the content variables. The difference between Alpha and Pi is that Krippendorff's (1980) statistic can be used with nonnominal data. The Alpha also corrects for small samples (Krippendorff, 2004a). When nominal variables with two coders and a large sample are used, Alpha and Pi are equal. For more details about Alpha, see Krippendorff (2004a).

Schutz (1952) took a different approach to controlling for chance agreement. Instead of figuring the impact of chance on agreement after the reliability test, Schutz calculated the level of agreement in the reliability check needed to exceed the minimal level of simple agreement when chance is considered. These necessary levels were calculated for given sample sizes and probability. For example, if a content analysis has 200 recording units in the reliability check and a minimal acceptable level of reliability of .85, the simple agreement must exceed .91 at the .05 level of probability and .93 at the .01 level of probability.

A suggestion by Lombard, Snyder-Duch, and Bracken (2002) that Kappa could be considered for used as a reliability coefficient that controls for chance resulted in a reply by Krippendorff (2004b) that echoed arguments in Krippendorff's (2004a) book that Kappa was not appropriate. Krippendorff (2004b) stated that an agreement coefficient can be an adequate measure of reliability under three conditions. First, content to be checked for reliability requires two or more coders working independently applying the same instructions to the same content. Second, a coefficient treats coders as interchangeable and presumes nothing about the content other than it is separated into units that can be classified. Third, a reliability coefficient must control for agreement due to chance. Krippendorff (2004b) followed this statement with a review of standard reliability coefficients.

Krippendorff (2004b) pointed out that most coefficients have similar numerators that subtract observed agreement from 1. However, they vary as to how the denominator (expected agreement) is calculated. Scott's Pi and Krippendorff's (2004a) Alpha are the same except Alpha adjusts the denominator for small sample bias, and Scott's Pi exceeds Alpha by $(1 - pi)/n$. As n increases, the difference approaches zero.

In the article, Krippendorff (2004b) criticizes Cohen's Kappa because expected disagreement is calculated by multiplying the proportion of a category value used by one coder by the proportion for that value used by the other coder. Krippendorff (2004b) said the expected disagreement is based, therefore, on the coders' preferences, which violates the second and third of the three conditions he listed. Krippendorff (2004b) concluded that Scott's Pi is acceptable with nominal data and large samples, although what qualifies as large was not defined. In situations in which data other than nominal are used and the samples are small, Alpha is recommended.

In their reply, Lombard, Snyder-Duch, and Bracken (2004) pointed out that Alpha can be difficult to calculate and called for the development of software that will calculate it for all levels of data. Such a computer program would be extremely useful, but the difficulty in calculating a reliability coefficient is an unacceptable reason for refusing to use it. Readers who want to explore Alpha's calculation should consult Krippendorff (2004a).

## Pearson's Product–Moment Correlation

Pearson's correlation coefficient ($r$) is sometimes used as a check for accuracy of measurement with interval- and ratio-level data. This statistic, which we explain more fully in chapter 8 (this volume), measures the degree to which two variables, or two coders in this case, vary together. Correlation coefficients can be used when coders are measuring space or minutes. With this usage, the coders become the variables, and the recording units are the cases. If, for example, two coders measured the length in seconds of news stories on network evening news devoted to international events, a correlation coefficient would measure how similarly the coders were in their use of high and low scale values to describe the length of those stories relative to one another.

Krippendorff (1980) warned against using correlations for reliability because association is not necessarily the same as agreement. However, this is not a problem if agreement and accuracy of measurement are determined separately. The correlation coefficient is used not to measure category assignment but to measure the consistency of measuring instruments such as clocks and rulers.

## SUMMARY

Conducting and reporting reliability assessments in content analysis are a necessity, not a choice. However, a study (Riffe & Freitag, 1997) of 25 years (from 1971–1995) of content analysis research in *Journalism & Mass Communication Quarterly* indicated that only 56% of such studies have reported that assessment. During this same period, the percentage of content analysis articles in *Journalism & Mass Communication Quarterly* climbed from 6% to nearly 35%, and after 1978, no fewer than 20% of the studies in that journal were content analyses. Yet, even in the most recent years of that period studied, from 1991 to 1995, nearly 29% of content studies failed to report an intercoder reliability assessment.

This situation has hardly improved since then. An unpublished review of 80 quantitative content analysis studies published in *Journalism & Mass Communication Quarterly* since 1998 showed that some 26% failed to conduct or report the results of reliability testing. Only 16% of the studies conducted the reliability testing on randomly selected content, included a test for chance agreement, and reported the reliability figures for all relevant variables—the three reliability requirements emphasized in this book. Only one in three studies randomly selected content for the test. About 46% of the studies used a measure of chance agreement, and only 54% of the studies provided the test results for all variables or at least provided the range of results for the relevant variables.

Moreover, full information on the content analysis should be disclosed or at least made available for other researchers to examine or use. A full report on content analysis reliability would include protocol definitions and procedures. Because space in journals is limited, the protocol should be made available by study authors on request. Furthermore, information on the training of judges, the number of content items tested and how they were selected should be included in footnotes or appendixes to the protocol. At a minimum, the specific coder reliability tests applied and the achieved numeric reliability along with confidence intervals should be included for each variable in the published research.

In applying reliability tests, researchers should randomly select a sufficient number of units for the tests (Lacy & Riffe, 1996), apply and make decisions on whether the variables reach acceptable reliability levels based on coefficients that take chance into consideration, and report simple agreement in an endnote to assist in the replication of the study.

Failure to systematize and report the procedures used as well as to assess and report reliability virtually invalidates whatever usefulness a content study may have for building a coherent body of research. Students must be taught the importance of assessing and reporting content analysis reliability. Journals that publish content studies should insist on such assessments.

# 7

## *Validity*

When we introduced the definition of quantitative content analysis in chapter 1 (this volume), it was noted that if the categories and rules are conceptually and theoretically sound and are reliably applied, the chance increases that the study results will be valid. The focus of chapter 6 (this volume) is on reliability leads easily to one of the possible consequences of reliable measurement: valid measurement. What does the term *valid* mean?

"I'd say that's a valid point," one person might respond to an argument offered by another. In this everyday context, validity can relate in at least two ways to the process of reason by which one knows things with a degree of certainty. First, valid can mean the speaker's argument refers to fact or evidence, for example, that the national debt in 2004 topped $7 trillion. Second, valid can mean the speaker's logic is persuasive. For example, one might judge as nonvalid what a politician says he believes because it is contradicted by his behavior.

On the other hand, the social science notion of validity relates more rigorously to procedures for obtaining information so that appropriate inferences and interpretations may be made. In survey research, such procedures may include random sampling to make valid inferences from characteristics in a sample to characteristics in a population. In an experiment, such procedures may include randomly assigning subjects to create equivalent control and experimental treatment groups, thereby permitting a logical inference that only the treatment variable administered to the experimental group could have caused some effect. Validity in these procedural applications relates to one's confidence in what is known.

However, the notion of validity can also have a social dimension that relates to how such knowledge is understood, valued, or used. In the hypothetical conversation just discussed, two persons communicate knowledge that is meaningful to both. This meaningfulness results from a common language; a common frame of reference for interpreting the concepts being communicated; and a common evaluation of the relevance, importance, or significance of those concepts. In this social dimension of validity as meaning, the broader importance or significance of what has been found can be assessed. For research, the minimum required validation comes from the peer review process in which competent judges pass on the fitness of the research to be part of scientific knowledge. However, research can also be meaningful in the broader social world humans all inhabit.

## CONCEPTUALIZING VALIDITY

How does content analysis relate to these notions of validity? First, content research must satisfy the appropriate criteria for scientific validation. Without that validation, generalization or interpretation of findings would be difficult or impossible. However, the social significance of a content study will depend on additional factors. These include the pervasiveness and social importance of the content being explored and the relation of the conceptual categories used in the analysis to the broader society.

### Internal and External Validity

One way to think about these kinds of validity issues in content analysis comes from educational research. In their assessment of experimental method in educational research, Campbell and Stanley (1963) made the distinction between an experimental research design's internal and external validity. By internal validity, Campbell and Stanley meant the ability of an experiment to illuminate valid causal relationships. An experiment does this by the use of controls to rule out other possible sources of influence, the rival explanations we mentioned in chapter 3 (this volume). By external validity, Campbell and Stanley meant the broader relevance of an experiment's findings to the vastly more complex and dynamic pattern of causal relations in the world. An experiment may increase external validity by incorporating "naturalistic settings" into the design. This permits assessment of whether causal relations observed in the laboratory are in fact of much importance relative to other influences operating in the world.

These notions of internal and external validity in experimental design also are useful for thinking about content analysis validity. A first and obvious observation is that content analysis, used alone, cannot possess internal, causal validity in the sense that Campbell and Stanley (1963) used. Recall from chapter 3 (this volume) that inferring causal relations requires knowledge of the time order in which cause and effect operate, knowledge of their joint variation, control over the influence of other variables, and a rationale explaining the presumed cause–effect relationship.

However, content analysis can incorporate other research procedures that strengthen the ability to make such causal inferences. For instance, if some content is thought to produce a particular effect on audiences, content analysis could be paired with survey research designs to explore that relationship, as in the agenda-setting and cultivation studies we described in chapter 1 (this volume). We discuss some of these designs in more detail in the following sections.

Content analysis can be a very strong research technique in terms of the external validity or generalizability of research that Campbell and Stanley (1963) discussed. This, of course, will depend on whether a census or appropriate sample of the content has been collected. However, the notion of external validity can also be related to a study's social validity. This social validity will depend on the social significance of the content that content analysis can explore and the degree to which the content analysis categories created by researchers have relevance and meaning beyond an academic audience. We explore some of these issues in the following pages.

Figure 7.1 summarizes several types of validity. Note first that internal validity deals with the design governing data collection and how designs may strengthen causal inference. Data collection also requires assessment of measurement validity consisting of face, concurrent, predictive, and construct validity. Statistical validity is a subset of internal validity. Finally, the external and social validity of a content analysis presupposes the internal validity of measurement and design that makes content analysis a part of scientific method. However, the notion of external and social validity used here goes beyond those qualities to assess the social importance and meaning of the content being explored. The overall validity of a study therefore depends on a number of interrelated factors we discuss in the following section.

## Internal Validity and Design

Content analysis by itself can only illuminate patterns, regularities, or variable relations in some content of interest. Content analysis cannot alone illuminate the antecedent causes producing those patterns in the content, nor can it explain the subsequent effects that content produces in some social system. Of course, the analyst may make logical inferences to antecedent causes or subsequent effects of such content, as we discussed in chapter 1 (this volume), with the model showing the centrality of content to communication processes and effects. Also, certain research designs pairing content analysis with other methods strengthen the ability to infer such causal relationships, thereby enhancing internal validity.

Obviously, research designs that strengthen causal inferences from content analysis must first consider the place of the content in the presumed causal flow. Specifically, content can be seen as the dependent variable of other social processes or as an independent variable influencing those other processes. In either case, control over time is necessary to strengthen causal inference. Furthermore, content cannot logically explain its own antecedents or effects. For this, content analysis is best paired with other research techniques that can explore these types of influence.

*Control in Content Analysis.* Designs that attempt to explain patterns of content must look to information outside the content of interest.

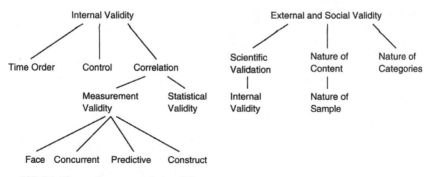

FIG. 7.1. Types of content analysis validity.

This requires a theoretical or hypothesized model including the kinds of factors that may influence content. In other words, this model is assumed to control for other sources of influence by bringing them into the analysis. The model itself is derived from theory, previous research, or hunch. Consider a simple example. A researcher, noting the collapse of communist regimes, predicts rapid growth of new newspaper ventures as alternative political voices seek audiences, even as existing newspapers "open up" to previously taboo topics.

Two problems need to be emphasized. First, however plausible a model may be, there is always something—usually a lot of things—that is left out and that may be crucial. However, the second problem is what makes the first one so interesting: Such a model can always be empirically tested to assess how well it works to explain patterns in content. If it does not work as planned, interesting and engaging work to figure out a better model can be undertaken. Unimportant variables can be dropped from the model and other theoretically interesting ones added. In this example, failure to find new newspapers might simply reflect limited access to printing facilities rather than a lack of dissent. Also, failure to find criticism of former party programs in existing papers may simply indicate residual citizen distrust of journalists who were viewed for years as political party tools.

*Time Order in Content Analysis.* Furthermore, in designing such a model, these presumed influences must incorporate the time element into the design, as we noted in chapter 3 (this volume). Such incorporation may be empirical—data on the presumed cause occurs and is collected and measured before the content it presumably influences. For example, studies have looked at the effects on a newspaper's community coverage after the loss of a city's competing daily or after the takeover of a daily by a group.

Incorporation of the time element may also be assumed from the logic of the design. For example, circulation size and population in a city at one point in time may be measured to help predict and explain newshole at a subsequent point in time. Clearly, the logic here would rule out newshole influencing population or certainly not in the short run, circulation. Similarly, Fico (1984) attempted to account for continuity of story topic and diversity of source use in legislative stories. Incorporated into the design was time variation in type of legislature being covered. In one state, the legislature met only part of the year, and in another, the legislature met during the full year.

Absent an empirical or logical means to incorporate time into the design, post hoc incorporation using other research methods may still help strengthen inference. Obviously, such an analysis has potential flaws, especially if done by researchers attempting to salvage a favored hypothesis. However, even this problem can be minimized by a design that incorporates checks on potential researcher bias.

An example may be illustrative. Fico and Soffin (1994) analyzed the fairness of reporting a local controversy. The controversy involved the effort of people in one neighborhood to secede from the city. All stories dealing with this controversy in the local daily and weekly were analyzed. Following resolution of the controversy 6 months later, researchers interviewed both the primary reporters covering the controversy and the major sources being cited. Both groups were shown the results of the analysis and asked to help explain the patterns found, with particular focus on how particular sources were incorporated into stories. Those perspectives were then taken into account in the explanation of the content.

Obviously, exploring the effects of content is the converse of the situation discussed. Here, time also must be part of the design, but other methods to assess effect are mandatory as well.

As in the case in exploring antecedents of content, the logic of the design may be sufficient for controlling time order. For example, Lacy and Fico (1991) explored the effect of newspaper quality at one point in time on subsequent circulation. Quality was assessed from measures of newspaper content in a national sample of newspapers. Circulation was obtained from national audit figures. Clearly circulation at a subsequent time could not possibly influence the measures of quality at an earlier time.

Other factors possibly influencing effects can also be brought more rigorously under control. As part of a research program on effects of negative political advertising, Garramone (1984, 1985, 1988; Garramone, Atkin, Pinkleton, & Cole, 1990) has used experiments in which groups of participants were exposed to such advertisements and their political reactions recorded. In these cases, the experimenter achieved full internal validity and gained some external validity by using advertisements that were recognizably part of political campaigns familiar to experimental participants. Fico, Richardson, and Edwards (2004) used a controlled experiment to test the effects of balanced and imbalanced stories on reader perception of newspaper credibility. Fico et al's., (2004) experimental treatment, balanced and imbalanced stories on three controversial issues, was designed following content analysis studies that focused on imbalanced story structures and how typically such imbalanced stories occurred in the coverage of controversial issues.

Perhaps the most frequent multimethod example of content analysis research that assesses effect is the agenda-setting research we described in chapter 1 (this volume). This line of research explores whether differences in news attention to various topics at one point in time creates a similar subsequent ordering of importance among news consumers. Of course, the possibilities that the news priorities of consumers really influence the media or that both influence one another must be taken into account in the design.

A technique called *cross-lag correlation* is used to do this. In this technique, both content analysis and survey research are performed at two different points in time. At each point, the media agenda is assessed through content analysis, and the public agenda is measured through a survey. The cross-lag correlation is then computed between the Time 1 media agenda and Time 2 public agenda and between the Time 1 public agenda and the Time 2 media agenda. If the correlation between the Time 1 media agenda and Time 2 public agenda is stronger than the correlation between the Time 1 public agenda and Time 2 media agenda, that must logically be the result of media's having an effect on the public rather than the reverse. Obviously, cross-lagged correlation has methodological limits including other potential variables that may be having an effect but are left out of the analysis. Still, the technique allows for establishing correlation between two variables while controlling for time order in a nonexperimental design.

*Correlation in Content Analysis.*    As Fig. 7.1 showed, the validity of content analysis research can be assessed in terms of requirements for causation we introduced in chapter 3 (this volume): specification of time order, control, and demonstration of joint variation or correlation. This last requirement brings our discussion to the special issue of statistical validity.

We discuss statistics used for analyzing content data in chapter 8 (this volume). These techniques range from simple correlation measures for relating two variables to multivariate techniques that enable the analysis to more fully control and assess the effects of multiple variables. Different statistics have different assumptions that must be considered. The specific techniques that can be employed will also depend on the level at which variables have been measured. Furthermore, if content data have been randomly sampled, tests of statistical significance must be employed for valid inferences to content populations. These issues relate to the statistical validity of the analysis of content. However, underpinning all these analysis techniques are assumptions about the reliability and validity of the measurements or observations of the content that we discuss in the following section.

## THE PROBLEM OF MEASUREMENT RELIABILITY AND VALIDITY

Recall the study that related circulation of a newspaper to measures of its quality (Lacy & Fico, 1991). Those measures included the ratio of newshole to advertising, the number of news services carried, and the amount of local coverage. However, who says measures such as those are good measures of quality? Is quality, like beauty, in the mind of the beholder?

The answer to that second question is, of course, yes: Quality is often in the mind of the beholder. That question also nicely illustrates the validity problem in content analysis measurement. Do the measures used actually capture the concepts that one thinks they do? Also, a related question—which we grapple with in the second part of this chapter—asks whether the concepts used in research matter in the broader world beyond the research community. In other words, how wide is the agreement that the concepts used here are described and measured appropriately?

The answer to that question must be a layered one. Before one can even discuss meaningfully the validity of a measure, one must know that the measure is reliable. Measurement reliability is a necessary but not sufficient condition for measurement validity. Validity of measurement presupposes that a study has achieved reliability, which we discussed earlier in this text. Recall that a reliable measure is consistent across time, place, or circumstance of application, and recall the chapter 6 (this volume) example of the rubber yardstick. Absent reliability of measurement, the truth of research would vary from study to study merely because the measuring stick kept varying in unknown and unpredictable ways.

However, a reliable measure does not necessarily measure what one thinks it does. A measure can be reliable in its application but wrong in what researchers assume it is really measuring. A valid measure is both reliable in its application and valid for what it measures. The types of measurement validity we describe in the following section attempt to establish a measure's truthfulness in capturing some concept.

## TESTS OF MEASUREMENT VALIDITY

The types of validity of particular measures used in a content study relate to the broader research context of which the particular study is a part. Some also describe these as "tests" of validity in the sense that a researcher or critic asks, "Does this measure meet the test of face validity?" Analysts such as Holsti (1969) and Krippendorff (2004a) have discussed validity assessment at length. In particular, Holsti's familiar typology identifies four tests of measurement validity: face, concurrent, predictive, and construct.

### Face Validity

The most common validity test used in content analysis and certainly the minimum one required is face validity. Basically, the researcher asks if a particular measure of a concept makes sense on its face. Examining Civil-Rights-era letters to the editors of Southern newspapers for changing references to literacy tests, poll taxes, integration, and states' rights might, on the face of it, index the changing focus and nature of public debate. In essence, the researcher assumes that the adequacy of a measure is obvious to all and requires little additional explanation. Relying on face validity sometimes can be appropriate when agreement on a measure is high among relevant researchers.

However, assuming face validity of measures is sometimes chancy, especially in broader contexts. One of the authors of this text participated in a study assessing fairness and balance in reporting a state political race (Fico & Cote, 1997). The measure of such fairness and balance—equivalent treatment of the candidates in terms of story space and prominence—was subsequently discussed with seven reporters who wrote the largest number of campaign stories. None agreed with the research definition. That is not to say that either the research definition or the professional definition was wrong per se. However, what seems obvious on its face sometimes is not.

### Concurrent Validity

Even face validity, however, can be strengthened for purposes of inference. One of the best techniques is to correlate the measure used in one study with a similar one used in another study. In effect, the two methods can provide mutual or *concurrent validation*.

In the study of newspaper quality and circulation mentioned previously (Lacy & Fico, 1991), a number of different measures were operationalized into an overall indicator. Those included amount of newshole devoted to local news, number of wire services carried, and proportion of news to advertising copy. These measures were validated by a previous survey of some 700 editors who answered questions about quality in journalism and who rated a number of indicators subsequently used in the content study. Presumably, the researchers reasoned, editors were in a very good position to recognize quality when they see it. Therefore, in addition to the face validity of each measure of the index, the research incorporated a cross-check with a relevant (and large) sample of experts.

## Predictive Validity

A test of *predictive validity* is a test that correlates a measure with some predicted outcome. If the outcome occurs as expected, the validity of the measure is established. The classic example cited by Holsti (1969, p. 144) concerns a study of suicide notes left by real suicides and a companion sample concocted by experimenters. Half the real notes were used to put together a linguistic model predicting suicide. Based on this model, coders successfully classified real and feigned notes, thereby validating the predictive power of the content model. In the newspaper quality study just cited (Lacy & Fico, 1991), theory predicting circulation based on news quality was consistent with empirical results.

## Construct Validity

*Construct validity* involves the relation of an abstract concept to the observable measures that presumably indicate the concept's existence and change. The underlying notion is that a construct exists but is not directly observable except through one or more measures. Therefore, some change in the underlying abstract concept will cause observable change in the measures. Statistical tests of construct validity assess whether the measures relate only to that concept and to no other concept (Hunter & Gerbing, 1982). If construct validity of measures exists, then any change in the measures and the relation of the measures to one another is entirely a function of their relation to the underlying concept. If construct validity does not exist, then measures may change because of their relation to some other, unknown concepts. In other words, construct validity enables the researcher to be confident that when the measures vary, only the concept of interest is actually varying.

Put another way, the issue of construct validity involves whether measures "behave" as theory predicts and only as theory predicts. Wimmer and Dominick (2003) wrote that "construct validity is present if the measurement instrument under consideration does not relate to other variables when there is no theoretic reason to expect such a relationship. Therefore, if an investigator finds a relationship between a measure and other variables that is predicted by theory and fails to find other relationships that are not predicted by theory, there is evidence for construct validity" (p. 60).

More fundamentally, construct validity must exist if a research program in a field such as mass communication is to build a cumulative body of scientific knowledge across a multitude of studies. Common constructs used across studies help bring coherence and a common focus to a body of research. Valid constructs also make for more efficient research, enabling researchers to take the next step in extending or applying theory without needing to duplicate earlier work. The newspaper quality study, for instance, uses the "financial commitment" (Lacy, 1992) construct, which in turn is related to broader economic theory.

## EXTERNAL VALIDITY AND MEANING IN CONTENT ANALYSIS

Research is, of course, symbolic communication. It is also a collective communication among a group of researchers. Isaac Newton summed this up in his often-quoted saying, "If I have seen further it is by standing on the shoulders of giants" (Oxford University, 1979, p. 362). The researcher interacts professionally within a community of scientists. Even more, the researcher is also part of the larger society, interacting with it in a variety of roles such as parent, neighbor, or citizen.

### External Validity and the Scientific Community

The ultimate validity of content analysis derives from its importance to some attentive and competent audience to whom the research is relevant, significant, or meaningful. That audience may be the scientific community of researchers in the relevant field, or it may be the entire citizenry of a nation. The minimum standard of validity-as-meaning is that such research be validated as important by scientific peers. However, a maximum standard could include—and go well beyond—that audience.

The judgment of the scientific community provides the crucial link between the internal and external validity of research. Clearly, research that is flawed because of some aspect of design or measurement cannot be trusted to generate new knowledge. Furthermore, research must link any new knowledge to what is already known as revealed by the work of other researchers. The scientific validation of research is necessary before that research can have any broader meaning or importance. In essence, internal validity is a necessary condition for external validity. The requirements for the scientific validation of research are relatively straightforward. Presumably, the current research grows out of previous work, and the researcher explicitly calls attention to its relevance for developing or modifying theory, replicating findings, extending the research line and filling research gaps, or resolving contradictions in previous studies.

Furthermore, researchers submit their final work to a peer-review process before it is judged suitable for publication and possible influence on other work. In this process, judges unknown to the author review the work of the author who is unknown to them. The judges, usually two or three, apply scientific criteria for validating the research's relevance, design and method, analysis, and inference. Only after this process is the research deemed fit to be presented or published as part of scientific knowledge.

However, the status of any one study as part of scientific knowledge is still tentative until other research provides validation in the scientific community. This validation can take place through direct replication and extension in similar studies as in the example of agenda-setting research. Replication of findings by other studies is important because any one study, through researcher or sampling error, might be wrong. However, if study after study finds similar patterns in replications, the entire weight of the research as a whole strengthens one's confidence in the knowledge that has been found. Recall in chapter 5 (this volume) that it was noted that even data sets drawn consistently from nonprobability samples can be useful if their findings make a cumulative contribution.

Scientific community validation of a study can also happen through the use, modification, or further development of that study's definitions or measures or through more extensive work into an area to which some study has drawn attention. Cultivation research on the social effects of television violence (Gerbner, Signorielli, & Morgan, 1995) is an example of this kind of validation.

## External Validity and Social Validity

The validation of research method and inference is usually determined by the scientific community acting through the peer review and replication process just discussed. This validation is necessary but not sufficient to establish the broader meaning and importance of research to audiences beyond the scientific community.

The external validity of a content analysis beyond the scientific community is strengthened in two ways. These concern the social importance of the content and how it has been collected and the social relevance of the content categories and the way they have been measured and analyzed. In the following sections, we address these issues in the external validity of content studies.

*Nature of the Content.* The external validity of a content analysis can be increased if the content being explored is important. The more pervasive and important the content of interest to audiences, the greater will be the external validity of the analysis exploring that content. One dimension concerns the sheer size of the audience exposed to the content. Much of the research and social attention to television, for example, emerges from the fact that its content is almost universally available and that very large audiences are routinely exposed to its content for many hours on a daily basis.

Another dimension of the importance of the content being analyzed deals with the exposure of some critical audience to its influence. Violence on children's television, to continue the example, is explored because it may have important implications for the social development of a presumably vulnerable and impressionable population.

Finally, content may be important because of some crucial role or function it plays in society. For example, advertising is thought to be crucial to the economic functioning of market societies. Obviously, the effectiveness of advertising in motivating consumers to buy products will affect not only producers and consumers but also the entire fabric of social relations linked in the market. Furthermore, advertising messages can have cultural by-products because of social roles or stereotypes they communicate. Similarly, news coverage of political controversy is examined because it may influence public policy affecting millions. The political ethic of most Western societies is that an informed citizenry, acting through democratic institutions, determines policy choices. Clearly then, the way these choices are presented has the potential to influence the agendas and opinions of these citizens.

Whatever the importance of the content, the external validity of the analysis will also be affected by how that content has been gathered and analyzed for study. Specifically, whether content has been selected through a census or a probability sample will influence what generalizations can be validly made.

A major goal in most research is knowledge about populations, whether they be of people or documents. Knowledge of an unrepresentative sample of content is frequently of limited value for knowing or understanding the population. Probability sampling, however, enables researchers to generalize to the population from which the sample was drawn. Taking a random sample or even a census of the relevant population of content obviously enables the researcher to speak with authority about the characteristics being measured in that population.

Findings from content selected purposively or because of convenience cannot be generalized to wider populations. However, a strong case for the external validity of purposively selected content may be made in specific contexts. For example, the news content of the "prestige" press is clearly atypical of news coverage in general. However, those newspapers influence important policymakers and other news outlets as well and therefore have importance because they are so atypical.

*Nature of the Categories.*   Content analysis creates categories for the study of content. The conceptual and operational definitions of a content category can also influence a study's social validity. Such concepts may be interpretable by only a small body of researchers working in some field or accessible and relevant to far broader audiences. Krippendorff's (1980) "semantical validity" (p. 157) relates to this notion of relevance in content analysis. For Krippendorff (1980), semantical validity "assesses the degree to which a method is sensitive to the symbolic meanings that are relevant within a given context" (p. 157). In particular, Krippendorff (1980) considered a study to be high in semantical validity when the "data language corresponds to that of the source, the receiver or any other context" (p. 157). To what extent, therefore, do content analysis categories have corresponding meanings to audiences beyond the researchers? This question is particularly relevant when content analysis research concerns the creation of content categories that attempt to interpret communication characteristics rather than merely observe and record them.

This distinction is sometimes referred to as the difference between analysis of manifest and latent content. Manifest content, as we discussed earlier in this text, is relatively more easily recognized and counted than latent content: person A's name is in a story, maybe accompanied by a picture; a television show runs $X$ number of commercials; a novel's average sentence length is $X$ number of words. Presumably such manifest qualities of communication are recognizable and meaningful to any person exposed to the content.

The study of manifest content achieves high reliability in counting, but the implicit assumption that what is counted is relevant is seldom addressed. Again, using the research on prominence cited earlier, who, apart from the researcher, considers easily counted name mentions high in a story to be a valid indicator of this concept? A legitimate objection may be that the prominence of a story figure may depend on a variety of contextual elements that involve how the figure is related to the broader story topic.

Analyses that attempt to capture latent content deal with the judgments, evaluations, and interpretations of content and its context. The study of latent content therefore assumes that the most important characteristics of communication may not be captured through sampling, however scientific, or statistical analysis of content categories, however sophisticated. Rather, the meaning of content is illuminated by the discernment of the researcher who brings the appropriate context to the communication as a whole and its social role. However, how tenable is the assumption that judgments made by researchers emerge from a context more appropriate to discern truth or more likely to be shared by a wider audience?

The study of latent content implicitly assumes that the researcher possesses one or both of two different, even contradictory, qualities. The first is that the researcher is an authoritative interpreter who can intuitively assess the meaning and effects of some communication for audiences. In other words, although human biases in selective exposure, perception, and recall exist in the naive perceiver, the researcher is somehow immune. For example, interpretations of the media's power to control the social construction of reality emerge from the assumed ability of the researcher—but not the media audience—to stand enough apart from such an effect to at least observe it.

A second, but contrary quality assumed for the researcher in analysis of latent content is that the researcher is himself or herself a kind of representative of the audience for a communication. If this is so, the observations or conclusions the researcher draws would be made by anyone. For example, studies of political bias may include categories in which media portrayals of candidates or groups are considered to be positive or negative. Even though these evaluations meet scientific criteria for reliability, their validity is always open to question. This is because the researcher, or more generally, the coders, cannot genuinely assume that they evaluate content the way others might. Again, who—apart from the researcher—might draw these inferences? Recall Tankard's (2001, p. 98) concern with the "rather subjective process" involved in the "lone-scholar" approach of early framing research described in chapter 1 (this volume).

In fact, this representative role of the researcher is implicitly assumed in the study of manifest, as well as latent, content. This assumption of researcher representativeness engages both the reliability and validity of a content analysis in terms of its broader social validity.

Reliability here deals with the actual utility of the content analysis protocol beyond its own research context. Whether content is simply counted or evaluated, it is unclear whether any broader audience could apply the definitions. Recall first that the standards of science for reliability are satisfied if others, trained to use the content analysis protocol, would classify content the same way as the coders. In fact, protocols are almost never tested in this way among a sufficiently large enough sample of coders taken from the natural audience of the content of interest.

The validity issue concerns the social meaningfulness of the analysis categories themselves. Specifically, how natural is that protocol classification system to the audience of that content? Seldom do content analysts have enough information about audiences to make judgments about content category meaning in that naturalistic setting.

A study by Fico et al. (1994) illustrates this problem. The study concerned prowar and antiwar advocacy during the 1991 Gulf War. The protocol explicitly defined criteria for categorizing prowar and antiwar sources quoted in stories, and the story as a whole was then categorized as prowar or antiwar based on such criteria as the amount of space and prominence given sources on each side. The problem concerned a small group of stories in which family members of soldiers in the Gulf were interviewed. These stories did not contain prowar or antiwar assertions but did deal with issues such as worry about the soldier's safety and hardship because of the soldier's absence. Clearly these stories had relevance to the debate over the war. Yet were they prowar or antiwar? Plausible interpretations could be made for either classification. Equally plausible, readers of these stories may not have been using that category for thinking about them. Absent fieldwork with readers of such stories, the appropriateness of a study's categories relating to judgment and interpretation remains unknown.

No easy solution to this problem exists if content analysis is used alone. Other research techniques must be applied to the study problem to develop useful theory. Obviously both manifest and latent approaches to content analysis can be profitably employed in the same research. Their combined application will enrich the research and extend its meaningfulness. Consider a published study on political officials that sought to illuminate any gender discrimination in portrayals of women. Silver (1986) took a sample of news stories and analyzed references to male and female legislators and administration officials. Silver counted references to the two genders and specifically recorded mentions of such manifest qualities as appearance and marital status. In addition to this analysis, Silver read sample stories dealing with specific issues engaging top male and female administration officials, gleaning from that reading inferences not apparent in the more systematic analysis.

## SUMMARY

The assumption of this text is that research should speak as truthfully as possible to as many as possible. This is the essence of the validity problem in content analysis as well as in other research.

Indeed, the parallels and perils for other research techniques are as serious. Survey researchers ask questions that assume implicitly a context and frame of reference that interviewees may not share. Experimenters achieve strong causal inference at the cost of so isolating phenomena that little may actually be learned about the broader world of interest.

However, validity as truth is what enquiry is all about. A variety of approaches and an openness to possibility are required.

# 8

# Data Analysis

Like most research methods, content analysis is comparable to detective work. Content analysts examine evidence to solve problems and answer questions. Of course, they try to limit their examinations only to relevant evidence. The research design, measurement, and sampling decisions we discussed in chapters 3, 4, and 5 (this volume) are, in effect, the content analyst's rules for determining what evidence is relevant and how to collect it, whereas the chapters on reliability and validity offer insights that can help the detective ensure that the evidence is of optimal quality. Ultimately, however, data collection ceases. After the evidence is collected, it must be reduced and summarized. Patterns within the evidence must be plumbed for meaning.

In quantitative content analysis, the process of data analysis typically involves statistical procedures, tools that summarize data so that patterns may be efficiently illuminated. In this chapter, we aim to help researchers think efficiently and logically about analyzing data quantitatively. The strategy is to illustrate the intuitively logical bases of several commonly used analysis techniques and provide guidance on applying them. These techniques are basic ones used most frequently in content analyses: descriptive measures such as means and proportions along with correlation and tests of statistical significance. We also introduce analysis of variance (ANOVA) and multiple regression. We present basic notions of probability to facilitate understanding of how and why particular statistics work. On the other hand, detailed discussion of these techniques or the mathematical basis of statistics is beyond the scope and goal of this text. Many excellent texts have delved more deeply into the mathematical basis of the statistics (Blalock, 1972; Hanushek & Jackson, 1977) or have focused more on underlying principles for a more general audience (Rowntree, 1981). Other sources have addressed the usefulness of computer statistical programs for exploring both basic and sophisticated statistical techniques (Riffe, 2003).

## AN INTRODUCTION TO ANALYZING CONTENT

Although a number of disciplines employ content analysis, mass communication researchers have been among the most persistent in exploiting the technique. An examination of studies (Riffe & Freitag, 1997) published in *Journalism & Mass Communication Quarterly* between 1971 and 1995 showed that about one fourth of all studies analyzed content.

The data analysis techniques we discuss in the following sections are those used most often by researchers who analyze content. An unpublished examination of the data tables and analysis sections of 239 studies in *Journalism & Mass Communication Quarterly* from 1986 through 1995 indicates that content analysts rely on several basic analysis techniques and a few more advanced ones. That is, a limited number of tools turn out to be useful for a variety of tasks. As in many kinds of work, knowing what tool will serve adequately for what job is essential knowledge.

Some of these analysis techniques are very simple indeed. Researchers who produced 28% of the 239 studies have been able to achieve their objectives using only means, proportions, or simple frequency counts. When other techniques have been used, they were often in combination with means and proportions. Techniques for finding relationships in collected data have included chi-square and Cramer's $V$ (used in 37% of studies) and Pearson's product–moment correlation (used in 15%). Techniques to assess differences between means or proportions of two samples were used in 17% of studies. More advanced techniques included ANOVA (used in 6% of the studies) and multiple regression (8% of the studies). Only 7% of the studies employed statistical techniques more sophisticated than these.

The purpose of this chapter, therefore, is not to break new statistical ground or to urge some particular type of analysis but rather to review these techniques and emphasize how they must relate to the particular content study's goals. In fact, analysis techniques should be carefully thought through in the context of study goals before any data are even collected. Decisions on data collection, measurement, and analysis are inextricably linked to one another, to the study's overall research design, and to the questions or hypotheses the study addresses.

# FUNDAMENTALS OF ANALYZING CONTENT

## Thinking About Data Analysis

The goal of a data analysis may be relatively simple: to describe characteristics of a sample or population. For example, researchers may be interested in learning the frequency of occurrence of some particular characteristic to assess what is typical or unusual. By contrast, the goal may be to go beyond such description to illuminate patterns or relationships in some sample or population. To describe relationships, researchers would focus on illuminating patterns of association between characteristics of one thing and characteristics of another.

As we noted in chapter 3 (this volume), good research design requires both familiarity with the relevant previous research and well-focused questions that facilitate data collection. Both of these aspects of good design are also crucial for good data analysis. Previous research and the thinking that goes into assessing its meaning are vital to focusing any data analysis. First, previous research provides guidance on what variables to examine and on how to collect data to measure them. Most important, earlier research provides direction for the formulation of hypotheses or research questions that themselves lend focus to both the data collection and data analysis. Finally, effective replication of studies and the building of a coherent body of research may require using identical measures and data analysis techniques for maximum comparability across studies.

## Hypotheses and Research Questions

A *hypothesis* is an explicit statement predicting that a state of one variable is associated with a state in another variable. A *research question* is more tentative, merely asking if such an association exists.

Quantitative content analysis is much more efficient when explicit hypotheses or research questions are posed than when a researcher collects data without either. The reasons, as we noted in chapter 3 (this volume), are straightforward. Hypotheses or questions mean research designs can focus on collecting only relevant data. Furthermore, an explicit hypothesis or research question permits the researcher to visualize the kind of analysis that addresses the hypothesis or question. Researchers can even prepare dummy tables to aid in visualization. In fact, the inability to visualize what the completed analysis tables "should look like" given the hypotheses or questions may well signal some problem in conceptualizing the study or in the collection and measurement of the data.

If a hypothesis predicts, for example, that locally produced news stories will be displayed more prominently than wire service copy in midsized daily newspapers, the simplest approach is to measure and record the source of news stories (local or wire service) and their position in the paper (e.g., front page, local front page, inside, etc.). Note that this hypothesis can be addressed with nominal-level data (as we discussed in chap. 4, this volume). The hypothesis obviously is supported if a greater proportion of local stories than wire service stories appear on front pages.

Now assume the study is only considering front pages, perhaps because of cost or other factors influencing the research. Despite what appears to be a simplification of the data collection, a more refined and detailed level of measurement, at the interval level, would be needed than the one using the simple front page, inside page distinction. Each front page story might instead be given a score computed by adding factors such as headline column width, above-the-fold placement, and story length. The higher a story's score, the more prominently the story has been placed. Averages or means for story placement of wire service and locally produced copy could then be compared to test the hypothesis. In this revised example, the hypothesis would be supported if the mean score for prominence of locally produced copy was larger than that for wire-service-produced copy.

## The Role of Inference

Although a researcher's specification of a hypothesis or research question affects the nature of data analysis, that analysis is also affected by whether the researcher plans to make inferences from the study data to a larger population. The goal of research is to describe a characteristic or find a relationship in collected data. However, the question may arise of whether a sample characteristic or a relationship in a sample of data really exists in the world from which the sample was drawn. On one hand, if all data from a population have been collected—for example, all the poems of an author or all the daily newspapers published in a city for a year—then that question is moot. The sample is the population. If only a small part of the known evidence or data can be used, how the data have been selected determines whether inferences about the parent population can be made.

Probability sampling enables the researcher to make valid inferences to some population of interest. Only probability sampling enables researchers to calculate sampling error, a measure of how much the sample may differ from the population. Specifically, it is possible to calculate the size of the error there might be between the frequency of some variable in a sample compared to that variable's actual frequency in the population. Then the researcher can compute a level of certainty or confidence indicating the likelihood that sampling error will be no more than what was calculated, referred to as the confidence level.

The term *sampling error* often appears in news stories about polls and surveys—especially in election years. A candidate is described as being preferred by a proportion of the polled voters within a certain margin of error and with a given level of confidence that the results are accurate. The notion of sampling error is exactly the same when a random sample of some population of content is taken. For example, consider instead a content analysis study that shows that a candidate is quoted in 47% of a random sample of 400 news stories on the election, with a sampling error of plus or minus 5%. That sampling error means that if a census of all relevant stories had been conducted instead of a sample, the candidate's actual news visibility would likely be somewhere between 42% and 52%—that is, within the range created by the sample proportion plus or minus the 5% sampling error. The level of confidence in a probability sample relates to the word *likely* in the preceding sentence. Results reported from every reputable probability sample are assumed to be at the 95% level of confidence unless otherwise noted. In such studies, the chances are 95 in 100 that the candidate's true news visibility will not exceed the range described by the sample proportion and sampling error. Of course, there is a 5 in 100 chance that even a properly drawn random sample may lead to a wrong conclusion, but a 95% chance of winning a bet is pretty good.

These concepts of error and confidence also play an important role in inference about relationships found in randomly sampled data. For example, if a candidate's name appears more frequently in stories about social issues, and the opponent's name is more often found in stories about economic issues, is this relationship of candidate and topic an artifact of the sampling, or are the two candidates actually addressing different agendas in their campaigns? To answer this question, tests of the "statistical significance" of the relationship are employed. Such tests tell researchers the likelihood of making an error by generalizing that a relationship found in the sample must actually exist in the population the sample came from.

## DESCRIBING AND SUMMARIZING FINDINGS

It should be clear by now how the probability sampling we introduced in chapter 5 (this volume) underlies, permits, and enhances certain types of data analysis. The researcher's choice among several types of analysis depends on the goals of the research, the level at which variables have been measured, and whether data have been randomly sampled from some population. The analysis techniques we describe in the following section proceed from relatively simple techniques used to describe data to more complex ones that illuminate relationships. Frequently, several different analysis approaches can achieve the same goals.

### Describing Data

Numbers are at the heart of quantitative content analysis. It should thus not be surprising that counting is at the heart of the analysis. What, however, may be surprising is how often very basic arithmetic, such as calculating a mean or proportion, suffices to clarify what is found.

*Counting.* Once data have been collected using the appropriate level of measurement, one of the simplest summarizing techniques is to display the results in terms of the frequencies with which the values of a variable occurred. The content analysis coding scheme provides the basic guidance, of course, for such a display. For instance, in a study of 200 television programs, the data on the number of African American characters can simply be described in terms of the raw numbers (e.g., 50 programs have African American characters and 150 do not). Or, in counting the number of African American characters, the total number of characters in the 50 programs can be displayed.

Displaying data in these ways, however, may not be illuminating because raw numbers do not provide a reference point for discerning the meaning of those numbers. Thus, summarizing tools such as proportions or means are used, depending on the level of measurement employed for the variables being analyzed.

*Means and Proportions.* A *mean* is simply the arithmetic average of a number of scores. It assumes an interval or ratio level of measurement. The mean is a sensitive measure because it is influenced by and reflects each individual score. A mean provides a reference point for what is most common or typical in a group. If the mean number of African American characters is 1, one expects that many of the programs in the sample have 1 African American character, although one also expects variability. Furthermore, the mean also has the advantage of being stable across samples. If several samples were taken from a population, the means would vary less than other measures of central tendency such as the *median* (the value that is a midpoint for the cases).

A *proportion* can be used with variables measured at the nominal as well as interval or ratio level of measurement. The proportion reflects the degree to which a particular category dominates the whole. A proportion is illuminating because it too provides a context for discerning the meaning of findings. If 55 movies out of 100 have graphic violence, that works out to 55%. Because the reference point is 100%, the importance of such a finding is easily grasped, and comparisons are possible across samples (e.g., 55% of 1980s movies versus 60% of 1990s movies).

Consider, as an example, a study of fairness in coverage of an abortion fight in Maryland that required that assertions of pro-life and pro-choice advocates be measured in each story (Fico & Soffin, 1995). It is clearly impossible to interpret the overall meaning of differences in length of such assertions story by story, and merely listing lengths of such assertions also might not be illuminating (even though only 24 stories were written on the fight). It is easy, however, to understand that the typical or mean story passage citing pro-life sources was 2.4 in. long, whereas the average pro-choice source passage was closer to 3.5 in. It was possible to list, story by story, whether one or both sides were cited; it was far easier to show that the proportion of all stories that were fair, at least to the extent of using both sides, was 82%.

A question necessarily occurs about what to do when variables have been measured at the ordinal level, for example, having coders assign favorability rankings to content. Although ordinal scales use numbers in much the same way interval or ratio scales do, an ordinal scale does not meet the mathematical assumptions of the higher levels. Furthermore, summary measures such as means used with ordinal scales merely "transfer" the underlying conceptual problem of what "more" of the concept means. In other words, if one does not really know how much more a favorability rating of 3 is compared to a favorability rating of 2, having an average favorability rating of 2.4 is not much additional help. The safe solution to analyzing data measured at the ordinal level is to report proportions for the separate values that make up the scale. Reporting means for ordinal scales makes sense when comparing two or more samples that have been coded using the same conceptual definitions for the variables. The emphasis, however, is not on discerning precise degrees of the measured concept present but rather on determining whether one sample has roughly more or less of it than the other.

## The Significance of Proportions and Means

Data from samples can be easily described using the basic tools we just presented. However, if the data are from a probability sample, the aim is not to describe the sample but to describe the population from which the data were drawn.

*Generalizing Sample Measures.*    Sampling error and level of confidence permit one to make inferences from a probability sample to a population. We introduced sampling error and level of confidence in chapter 5 (this volume). Recall that sampling error will vary with the size of the sample being used and with the level of confidence desired for the conclusions drawn from the analysis. However, for social science purposes, the conventional level of confidence is almost always frozen at the 95% or 99% confidence level. In other words, confidence level can be treated as a constant rather than as a variable.

Consider an example involving a content analysis of a random sample of 400 prime time television shows drawn from a population of such shows. The sample proportion of shows with Hispanic characters is 15%. Is this actually the proportion of such shows in the population of television programs? Might that population proportion actually be 20% or 10%? Sampling error will allow a range for the estimate at a given level of confidence.

Three ways are available to find sampling error for a sample of a given size. First, and simplest, error tables for given sample sizes are frequently included in many statistics books. Second, many data analysis computer programs include this in the output. Finally, hand computation is described in many statistics and research methods texts. The following are examples for computing sampling error for analyses using proportions and means.

Sampling error for a proportion is

$$SE_{(p)} = \sqrt{\frac{p \cdot q}{n}}$$

in which
  $p$ = the sample proportion in one category
  $q$ = the sample proportion in the other category
  and $n$ = the sample size

Sampling error for a mean is

$$SE_{(m)} = \frac{SD}{\sqrt{n-1}}$$

in which
  $SD$ = the standard deviation of the variable
  $n$ = the size of the sample

For a sample size of 400 at the 95% level of confidence, the sampling error for the proportion works out to nearly 5 percentage points. Therefore, in the population of relevant prime time television shows, the proportion of shows with Hispanic characters could be as low as 10% or climb to as high as 20%.

*The Significance of Differences.*   Describing findings from a random sample may be interesting, but frequently a research problem focuses on exploring possible differences in some characteristic in two or more such samples. In fact, hypotheses are often stated to emphasize the possibility of such a difference: "Newspaper stories will cite more sources of information than will television stories." A research question might emphasize such a possibility: "Do daily and weekly newspaper stories cite the same number of sources per story?" The analysis frequently goes beyond simply describing if two (or more) samples' means or proportions are different because an observed difference begs the question of why the difference occurs (e.g., differences in the news routines of daily or weekly newspapers). However, when random sampling has been used to obtain samples, the first possible answer that must be considered is that the difference does not really exist in the population the samples came from and that it is the artifact of sampling error. Tests of the statistical significance of differences in means or proportions address the likelihood that observed differences among samples can be explained that way.

Stated more specifically in terms of probability, tests for the significance of differences are used to assess the chance that an obtained difference in the means or proportions of two samples represents a real difference between two populations or a difference due to sampling error associated with the samples. In other words, using the previous example, are daily and weekly reporters so alike in their story sourcing methods that making a distinction between them based on type of publication is not worthwhile? A study may have described local daily stories as having a mean of 3.5 sources and local stories in a weekly newspaper as having a mean of 2.5. Does that difference reflect some systematic difference in information-gathering behaviors of daily and weekly reporters, or is the obtained difference merely an artifact of the sampling, and the behaviors in the two types of news organizations are really similar?

*Two-Sample Differences and the Null Hypothesis.*    The starting assumption of statistical inference is that the null hypothesis is true, for example, that there really is no population difference between apparently different groups. Each group can now be considered a subsample because each member of each group was still selected using probability sampling methods. Now the question comes down to determining whether the two samples belong to one common population or really represent two distinct populations as defined by the independent variable.

Probability samples reflect well the population from which they are drawn but not perfectly. For example, if the mean number of sexual references in the population of afternoon soap operas were subtracted from the mean number of sexual references in the population of programs in prime time, any difference would be a real one between the two populations. Samples from each population of shows, however, could turn up differences that are merely due to sampling variation. Do those differences reflect a real programming difference in the populations of interest or a sampling artifact?

A difference of means test or a difference of proportions test calculates how likely it is that the sample difference between two groups found in a probability sample could have occurred by chance. If the sample difference is so large that it is highly unlikely under the assumption of no real population difference, then the null hypothesis is rejected in favor of the hypothesis that the two groups in fact come from two different populations. Of course, the null hypothesis is rejected at a certain level of probability (usually set at the 95% level). There remains a 5% chance of making an error but a better 95% chance that the right choice is being made.

The statistical measures used in the difference of means and difference of proportions tests are called $z$ scores and $t$ scores. A $z$ score can be used with a difference of mean and a difference of proportion test, whereas $t$ only applies to small samples with variables measured at interval or ratio levels. The $z$ and $t$ score become equal at sizes larger than 30 or so. Again, standard computer analysis processing programs easily compute the statistics, but it is still possible to calculate them easily by hand using standard textbook formulas. Examples of these formulas applicable to analyses using means and proportions are the following:

Difference of proportions test is

$$Z = \frac{P_1 - P_2}{\sqrt{\dfrac{P_1(1 - P_1)}{n_1} + \dfrac{P_2(1 - P_2)}{n_2}}}$$

in which
$P_1$ = the proportion of the first sample
$n_1$ = sample size of the first sample
$P_2$ = the proportion of the second sample
$n_2$ = the sample size of the second sample

The denominator is the estimate for the standard error of the difference in the proportions.

Difference of means test is

$$t = \frac{\overline{X}_1 - \overline{X}_2}{S_{\overline{X}_1} - \overline{X}_2}$$

The denominator in the expression is the estimate of the standard error of the difference between sample means. In the case of equal variances in both samples, the denominator formula for $t$ is

$$S_{\overline{X}_1 - \overline{X}_2} = \sqrt{\frac{S_1}{n_1} + \frac{S_2}{n_2}}$$

In the case of unequal sample variances, the denominator formula for $t$ is

$$S_{\overline{X}_1 - \overline{X}_2} = \sqrt{\frac{(n_1 - 1)(S_1) + (n_2 - 1)(S_2)}{n_1 + n_2 - 2}} \bullet \left( \frac{n_1 + n_2}{n_1 n_2} \right)$$

in which
$\overline{X}_1$ = the mean of the first sample group
$\overline{X}_2$ = the mean of the second sample group
$S_1$ = the variance of the first group mean
$S_2$ = the variance of the second group mean
$n_1$ = the size of the first sample group
$n_2$ = the size of the second sample group

The result of the computation is a value for $z$ or $t$ that is compared to probability values in a table to find how likely the difference is due to sampling error or a real population difference. The values in the tables come from the normal distribution. A low probability value (.05 or less) means that the two sample means are so different that they very likely reflect a real population difference between the two. In other words, the chance of making a mistake in generalizing that a real difference exists is 5 in 100 or less. This is just the inverse of saying one's confidence in the decision to reject the null hypothesis is at the 95% level.

*Differences in Many Samples.*    A somewhat different approach is needed when the researcher is comparing the differences among three or more samples. As in the two-sample problem, the researcher wants to know if these samples all come from the same population. For example, the use of the term *abortion* in four Republican platforms in the last four presidential elections could be compared to see if this issue gained in importance during this period.

What is needed is a single, simultaneous test for the differences among the means. Why a single test and not simply a number of tests contrasting two pairs of means or proportions at a time? The reason is that if a great many comparisons are being made, some will turn up false differences due to random sampling alone. Recall that the 95% level of confidence is being used to reject the null hypothesis. That means that although true population differences are most likely to turn up, about 5% of the time an apparently significant difference will be obtained that does not truly represent any real difference in a population. Therefore, as the number of comparisons of sample differences becomes larger, it is more and more likely that at least one comparison will produce a false finding. Equally important, it is impossible to know which one is the false one. One possible way around this problem is to run a series of two-mean tests but with a more rigorous level of significance required, for example, 99% or 99.9%.

However, a single test that simultaneously compares mean differences is called an ANOVA. Unlike difference of proportions and difference of means tests, ANOVA uses not only the mean but also the variance in a sample. The variance is the standard deviation squared, and the standard deviation is a measure of how individual members of some group differ from the group mean.

ANOVA is a test that asks if the variability between the groups being compared is greater than the variability within each of the groups. Obviously, variability within each group is to be expected, and some individual scores in one group may overlap with scores in the other groups. If all the groups really come from one population, then the variability between groups will approximately equal that within any one of them.

Therefore, ANOVA computes an $F$ ratio that takes a summary measure of between-group variability and divides it by a summary measure of within-group variability:

$$F = \text{between group variability} / \text{within group variability}.$$

As in the case of a difference in means and a difference in proportions test, the null hypothesis predicts no difference; that is, all the groups come from the same population, and any difference is merely the result of random variation. If the null hypothesis is true, then the $F$ ratio is approximately unity or 1.

The empirically obtained ratio from the groups can then be assessed to determine whether the null hypothesis should be rejected. The larger the obtained $F$, the bigger the differences there are among the various groups. A computer analysis program will display a numeric value for the calculated $F$ along with a probability estimate that a difference this size could have occurred by chance under the null hypothesis of no difference in the population. The smaller that probability estimate, the more likely it is that the groups really do come from different populations.

Table 8.1 summarizes the various descriptive measures used with nominal, ordinal, interval, and ratio data.

## FINDING RELATIONSHIPS

Summary measures describing data and, where needed, their statistical significance, are obviously important. However, as we suggested in chapter 3 (this volume), measures describing relationships are the key to the development of social science. Specifically, these measures are useful and necessary when the state of knowledge in a social science generates hypotheses about the relationship of two (or more) things. Such hypotheses are frequently stated in terms of "the more of one, the more (or less) of the other." For example, "The higher the circulation of a newspaper, the more syndicated and wire service copy it will carry." Note that this hypothesis implies a higher level of measurement: circulation measured in thousands, for example, and amount of wire service copy that could range from zero to hundreds or thousands of square inches. A different way of stating the same hypothesis but relying on a lower level of measurement would be, "Bigger circulation newspapers

**TABLE 8.1**
**Common Data Descriptive Techniques in Content Analysis**

| Level of Measure | Summary Measure | Significance Test (If Needed) |
|---|---|---|
| Nominal | Frequency | — |
| | Proportion | Sample Error |
| | Difference of proportion | z test |
| Ordinal | Frequency | — |
| | Proportion | Sample Error |
| | Difference of proportion | z test |
| Interval | Frequency | — |
| | Mean and standard deviation | Sample Error |
| | Difference in means | z test, t test |
| | ANOVA | F test |
| Ratio | Frequency | — |
| | Mean and standard deviation | Sample Error |
| | Difference in mean | z test, t test |
| | ANOVA | F test |

*Note.* ANOVA = analysis of variance.

carry more wire service copy than smaller circulation newspapers." This statement suggests a classification of newspapers into two values of circulation, big and small (based on some determination), and more or less wire and syndicated material.

## The Idea of Relationships

Identifying how two variables covary or correlate is one of the key steps in identifying causal relationships, as we noted in chapter 3 (this volume). The assumption is that such covariance is causally produced by something, that it is systematic and therefore recurring and predictable. A contrary or null hypothesis is that the variables are not related at all, that any observed association is simply random or reflects the influence of some other unknown force acting on the variables of interest. In other words, if the observed association is purely random, what is observed on one occasion may be completely different than what is observed on some other occasion. Knowing just the state of one variable does not help predict the state of the other.

To restate one of the points we made in chapter 3 (this volume), covariation means that the presence or absence of one thing is observably associated with the presence or absence of another thing. Covariation can also be thought of as the way in which the increase or decrease in one thing is accompanied by the increase or decrease in another thing. These notions are straightforward and in fact, relate to many things observed in the daily lives of most people. (One of them, romance, makes this quite explicit. The lovestruck ones are "going together," and maybe later have a "parting of the ways.")

Although this notion of relationship is a simple one intuitively, it gets somewhat more complicated when what we want to know concerns the relative strength or degree of the relationship being observed.

First, what is meant by a relationship that is strong or weak? What does a relationship that is somewhere in the middle look like? On what basis, if any, is there confidence that a relationship of some type and strength exists? To put a point to that last question, how confident can one be in one's assumed knowledge of the particular relationship?

## Relationship Strength

Some observed relationships clearly are stronger than others. Think about that strength of a relationship in terms of degree of confidence. If, for instance, one had to bet on a prediction about a relationship, what knowledge about the relationship would maximize the chances of winning? Betting confidence should come from past observed reality (a social science approach) rather than subjectivity (e.g., "I feel lucky today"). Note that the question asked how to maximize the chances of winning rather than to "ensure winning."

Take a hypothetical example: Does the gender of a reporter predict the writing of stories about women's issues? If the traditional concept of news value guides reporters' selection of stories, then gender would be inconsequential to story selection: Men and women reporters would write about as frequently about women's issues. If the prediction were that women were more likely than men to write about women's issues, then gender should be systematically linked to observed story topic.

As straightforward as that seems, recall that the researcher begins with the assumption that gender and story topic are unrelated. Randomness, or the null hypothesis, governs any association between gender and story topic. In that case, knowing a reporter's gender would not help a researcher predict the topic of a reporter's stories. Given the assumption about gender (only two categories) and types of stories (only two categories in this example), the researcher would win bets only according to the overall proportion of women's issues stories written by the total population of reporters. If reporters at a news organization produced about 40% of their stories on women's issues, chances are that a typical story would be about some other topic. Given no relationship between gender and story topic, the researcher's best bet would be to predict that any single story would be topics other than those of interest to women, regardless of the reporter's gender. Therefore, given a sample of nine additional stories, always betting that the story concerned some topic not of interest to women would result in six wins and four losses.

Now assume a situation reflecting the strongest possible relationship: All women write only about women's issues, and no men do. In that case, knowing the gender of the reporter would enable the researcher to predict perfectly the topic of the reporter's stories.

Of course, seldom do such perfect relationships exist. Therefore, consider that one knows from past observations that women reporters write about 70% of their stories on women's issues and that men reporters write about 70% of their stories on other topics. Recall that 40% of all stories deal with women's issues. Knowing gender is not a perfect predictor, but knowing gender is better than not knowing it for the purpose of predicting story topic. When gender was unrelated to story topic, 60% of the predictions were correct based on the likelihood of the overall population of both men and women writing stories on various other topics. However, knowing now that gender is related to story topic, predicting that all women write on women's issues and that no men do results in winning 70% of the bets and losing only 30%.

What is needed is a number or statistic that neatly summarizes the strength observed in relationships. In fact, a variety of measures of association do exactly this and are employed depending on the level of measurement of the variables in the relationships being explored.

## Techniques for Finding Relationships

The measures of association we describe in the following section do something similar to the preceding protracted hypothetical example. Based on data from a population or a sample, a mathematical pattern of the association, if any, is calculated. The measures of association we discuss in the following set a perfect relationship at 1 and a nonrelationship at 0. A statistic closer to 1 thus describes a relationship with more substantive significance than a smaller one.

If the data used to generate the statistic measuring strength of association have been drawn from a probability sample, an additional problem exists. It is analogous to the problem in generalizing from a sample mean or proportion to a population mean or proportion. In this case, the statistical measure of association could merely be an artifact of randomness, a sample that turns out by chance to be different in important ways from the population from which it was drawn. Procedures of statistical inference exist to permit researchers to judge when a relationship in randomly sampled data most likely reflects a real relationship in the population.

*Chi-Square and Cramer's V.*   Chi-square indicates the statistical significance of the relationship between two variables measured at the nominal level. Cramer's *V* is one of a family of measures indexing the strength of that relationship. Cramer's *V* alone suffices when all population data have been used to generate the statistic. Both measures are needed when data have been randomly sampled from some population of interest.

Put another way, chi-square answers the key questions about the likelihood of the relationship being real in that population. Cramer's *V* answers the question about the strength the relationship has in that population.

The chi-square test of statistical significance is based on the assumption that the randomly sampled data have appropriately described, within sampling error, the population's proportions of cases falling into the categorical values of the variables being tested. For example, a random sample of 400 television drama shows might be categorized into two values of a violence variable: "contains physical violence" and "no physical violence." The same shows might also be categorized into two values of a sexuality variable: "contains sexual depictions" and "no sexual depictions." Four possible combinations of the variables could be visualized in terms of a dummy 2 × 2 table: violence with sexual depictions, violence without sexual depictions, no violence but with sexual depictions, and no violence and no sexual depictions.

A hypothesis linking the two variables might be that violent and sexual content are more likely to be present in shows together. If sample data seem to confirm this, how does chi-square put to rest the lingering anxiety that this may be a statistical artifact?

Chi-square starts with the assumption that there is in the population only random association between the two variables and that any sample finding to the contrary is merely a sampling artifact. What, in the example just cited, might a purely random association between such variables as violence and sexuality look like? As in the hypothetical example using gender and story topic, chi-square constructs such a null pattern based on the proportions of the values of the two variables being tested. Assume, for example, that 70% of all programs lack violence, and 30% have violent depictions. Furthermore, suppose that half of all programs have some form of sexual content. If knowing the violence content of a show was of no help in predicting its sexual content, then sexual content should be included in about half of both the violent and the nonviolent programs. However, if the two types of depictions are associated, one expects above average concentrations of sex in programs that also have violence.

For each cell in the table linking the two variables (violence, sex; violence, no sex; no violence, sex; no violence, no sex), chi-square calculates the theoretical expected proportions based on this null relationship. The empirically obtained data is then compared cell by cell with the expected null-relationship proportions. Specifically, the absolute value of the differences between the observed and expected values in each cell goes into the computation of the chi-square statistic. There-fore, the chi-square statistic is large when the differences between em-pirical and theoretical cell frequencies is large and small when the empirically obtained data more closely resemble the pattern of the null relationship. In fact, when the empirically obtained relationship is identical to the hypothetical null relationship, chi-square equals 0.

This chi-square statistic has known values that permit a researcher to reject the null hypothesis at the standard 95% and 99% levels of proba-bility. The computational work in computing a chi-square is still simple enough to do by hand (although tedious if the number of cells in a table is large). Again, statistical analysis computer programs produce chi-square readily. The formula for hand computation is

$$\text{Chi-square} = \sum \frac{(f_o - f_e)^2}{f_e}$$

in which

$f_o$ = the observed frequency for a cell
$f_e$ = the frequency expected for a cell under the null hypothesis

Knowing that a relationship is statistically significant or real in the population from which the sampled relationship has been obtained is important. Cramer's $V$ statistic can indicate how important, with val-ues ranging from 0 to a perfect 1.0. Based literally on the computed chi-square measure, $V$ also takes into account the number of cases in the sample and the number of values of the categorical variable being interrelated. Cramer's $V$ and chi-square make it possible to distinguish between a small but nonetheless real association between two vari-ables in a population and an association that is both significant and rel-atively more important. Statistical significance alone is not a discerning enough measure because a large enough sample will by it-self "sweep up" small but real relationships. Cramer's $V$ therefore per-mits an assessment of the actual importance of the relationship in the population of interest. A statistically significant relationship that is small in the population of interest will produce a small $V$. A significant relationship that is large in the population will produce a large $V$, with a 1.0 indicating a perfect relationship.

Cramer's *V* is produced by computer analysis programs, but is easily calculated by hand once chi-square has already been produced.

$$V = \sqrt{\frac{X^2}{n((\min(r-1)(c-1))}}$$

in which
$X^2$ = the calculated chi-square for the table
$n$ = the sample size, min is the lesser of the rows or columns
$(r-1)$ = the number of rows minus 1
$(c-1)$ = the number of columns minus 1

*Higher Level Correlation.*    Correlation techniques are also available for levels of measurement higher than the nominal. Spearman's rank order correlation, or rho, can be used with ordinal-level data and, as its name implies, is frequently used to determine how similarly two variables share common rankings. The computing formula for the statistic is as follows:

$$r_s = 1 - \frac{6 \, \Sigma \, D^2}{n(n^2 - 1)}$$

in which
$D$ = difference in each rank
$n$ = sample size

For example, a comparative study might rank the emphasis two newspapers give an array of topics. Using raw frequency of stories might be misleading if one is a larger newspaper, but converting frequencies to percentages makes the data comparable. Ranks can then be assigned to each paper's percentages to reflect topic emphasis; rank order correlation would show the papers' comparability. Another study (Fico, Atwater, & Wicks, 1985) looked at rankings of source use provided by newspaper and broadcast reporters. Spearman's rank order correlation made it possible to summarize the extent to which these reporters made similar valuations of the relative worth of particular kinds of sources.

Pearson's product–moment correlation is employed with data measured at the interval and ratio levels. Unlike the example just cited wherein newspaper topic emphasis was reduced to ranks, it employs the original measurement scales of the variables of interest, and because more information is provided by interval and ratio scales, Pearson's provides a more sensitive summary of any degree of association. In fact, because of this, Pearson's correlation is considered more powerful, able to turn up a significant association when the same data, analyzed using Spearman's correlation, could not. The formula for the Pearson product–moment correlation is

$$r = \frac{\Sigma(X - \overline{X})(Y - \overline{Y})}{\sqrt{\left[\Sigma(X - \overline{X})^2\right]\left[\Sigma(Y - \overline{Y})^2\right]}}$$

in which
$X$ = each case of the X variable
$\overline{X}$ = the mean of the X variable
$Y$ = each case of the Y variable
$\overline{Y}$ = the mean of the Y variable

It is worth mentioning, however, that the Pearson correlation makes an important assumption about what it measures, specifically, that any covariation is linear. What this means is that the increase or decrease in one variable is uniform across the values of the other. A curvilinear relationship would exist, for example, if one variable increased across part of the range of the other variable, then decreased across some further part of the range of that variable, then increased again. A relation would certainly exist but not a linear one and not one that could be well summarized by the Pearson measure. An easy way to envision a curvilinear relationship is to think about the relationship of coding experience and reliability in content analysis. As a coder becomes more practiced in using a content analysis system, reliability should increase; the relationship is steady and linear. However, after a time, fatigue occurs, and reliability curves or "tails off."

It is frequently recommended that a scatter diagram as shown in Fig. 8.1 be inspected if it is suspected that a linear relationship between the two variables of interest does not exist. In such a scatter diagram, each case relating the values of the two variables is plotted on a graph. If the two variables are highly related linearly, the dots representing the joint values will be tightly clustered and uniformly increasing or decreasing.

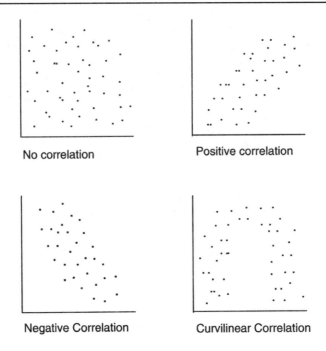

FIG. 8.1.   Scatter diagrams of correlations.

Both Spearman and Pearson correlation measures provide summary numbers for the strength of association between two variables. Both can range from a perfect −1 (negative) correlation to a perfect +1 (positive) correlation. In the case of a perfect negative correlation, for example, every instance in which one variable is high would find the variable in relation to it is correspondingly low. Because both variables are measured on scales using several or more points, the correlation measures are much more sensitive to small differences in the variables than would be the case for Cramer's *V*. Spearman's rank order correlation and Pearson's product–moment correlation are thus more powerful tests than those available for nominal-level data. If a relationship actually exists in the population of interest, Spearman's and Pearson's correlation will find it when Cramer's *V* might not.

Perfect relationships are rare in the world, of course, and a data set will have a number of inconsistencies that depress the size of the correlations. Statistics textbooks usually consider correlations of .7 or above to be strong, correlations of between .4 to .7 to be moderate, and correlations between .2 and the .4 level to be weak to moderate.

However, recall that $r$ is a measure of the strength of the linear relationship between two variables. It is not, by itself, the kind of tool that enables one to predict the value of one variable given knowledge of another variable. Rather, it is a kind of prelude to prediction. A very large $r$ means that it is worthwhile exploring the exact nature of one variable's influence on another. A small $r$ means that exploring the relation is relatively less worthwhile.

Another use of $r$, however, the $r$-square proportion, also helps a researcher assess more precisely how important one variable's influence on another is. $R$ square means the proportion of one variable's variation accounted for by the other. Thus, an $r$ of .7 produces an $r$ square of .49, meaning that just under half of one variable's variance is linearly related to another variable's variance. That is why $r$ must be relatively large to be meaningfully related causally to another variable.

*Correlation and Significance Testing.*   As just discussed in the context of chi-square and Cramer's $V$, the correlations from randomly sampled data require statistical tests of significance for valid generalization to the populations of content of interest. The null hypothesis, in this case, is that the true correlation equals 0. As in the case of chi-square and Cramer's $V$, the correlation coefficients also have mathematical properties that are well known. Therefore, the question about a correlation found in a random sample is whether it is large enough, given the size of the sample, that it cannot reasonably be due to chance. Is the size of the correlation so great that chances are it really exists within the population of interest?

The answer is provided by an $F$ test of statistical significance. The larger the $F$, the greater the chance that the obtained correlation reflects a real correlation in the population rather than a statistical artifact generated from random sampling. The computational process producing the $F$ is also accompanied by a probability value giving the probability that the relationship in the data was produced by chance.

It is also possible to put a confidence interval around a Pearson's correlation. With such an interval, the researcher can argue (at the 95% or higher confidence level) that the true population correlation is somewhere within the interval formed by the coefficient plus or minus the interval.

## Causal Modeling

Finding relationships through the measures of association just described is important. However, life is usually more complicated than two things varying together in isolation. For example, it may be interesting and important to find a relationship between reporter gender and news story topic. Gender alone, however, is hardly likely to explain everything about story topic. In fact, gender may be a relatively small component of the total package of factors influencing the presence or absence of topics about, for example, women in the news.

Furthermore, these factors may not directly influence the variable of interest. Factor A, for example, may influence Factor B, which then influences Factor Y, which is what one really wants to know about. More galling still, Factor D, thought to be important in influencing Y, may not be influential at all. Factors A and B may really be influencing Factor D, which then merely appears to influence Factor Y (this situation is called *spurious* correlation). What is needed in a model is a means of comprehending how all these factors influence each other and ultimately some variable of interest. How much do each of these factors influence that variable of interest, correcting for any mutual relationships?

The whole package of factors or variables directly or indirectly influencing the variation of some variable of interest can be assembled and tested in a causal model. Knowing what to include in the model and what to leave out is guided by theory, previous research, and logic. This is similarly the case when predicting which variables influence which other variables in the model, whether that influence is positive or negative, and the relative magnitude of those influences.

What is interesting and important in such a model is that it permits researchers to grasp a bigger, more complex piece of reality all tied into a conceptually neat package that is relatively easy to comprehend. Furthermore, each assumed influence in the model provides guidance to the whole community of researchers working on similar or related problems. The analysis technique that permits researchers to assess the influences going on within such a model is called *multiple regression*. However, first comes the model; seeing how well it actually fits data comes later. In fact, one of the easiest ways to think about a model of multiple causal influences is to draw a picture of it. Such models are easily drawn, as illustrated by Fig. 8.2, used to predict fair and balanced reporting as an outcome of economic and newsroom factors (Lacy, Fico, & Simon, 1989).

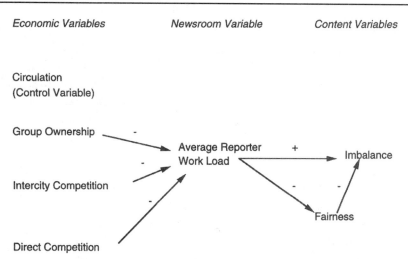

FIG. 8.2.   Hypothesized model showing relationships between economic, newsroom, and content variables.

Note first that each variable is named. Variables causally prior to others are on the left, with the "ultimate" dependent variable on the extreme right. The arrows indicate the assumed causal flows from one variable to the next.

The plus and minus signs indicate the expected positive or negative relationships. The arrows and signs are the symbolic representation of hypotheses presented explicitly in the study. Arrows that lack such signs would indicate research questions or simply lack of knowledge about what to expect. Note that in the example model, there are six arrows with signs that correspond to explicit study hypotheses.

The model is nonrecursive, which means the causal relationship flows in one direction. Models can be recursive, which involves two variables influencing each other. Mutual influence between variables can occur in two ways. First, the influence between two variables occurs either simultaneously or so quickly that a time lag cannot be measured. Second, the influence between two variables is cyclical with a lag that can be measured. In the latter situation, models can be drawn that incorporate time into a cyclical relationship.

As noted, such a model gives guidance to future research, and it undergoes change. This change occurs both theoretically and empirically. First, the model grows as variables outside the current model are brought into it. For example, new variables causally prior to all the other variables in the model may be added. In addition, new variables may be added that intervene between two already included in the model.

Second, such models change as they undergo empirical tests. Specifically, each arrow linking two variables in the model can be tested against data to determine the validity of the relationship. Furthermore, the whole model can be tested all at once to determine the validity of all its separate parts and its overall usefulness as a model describing social reality. Multiple regression is a tool for providing the assessment of the validity of such a model. When regression is used with such causal models, it is called *path analysis*. The arrows represent causal paths that are tested empirically.

The theoretical model in the fairness study was subjected to this analysis, with the results shown in Fig. 8.3. Note the dropping of some of the arrows, the addition of new variables and lines of influence, and the correspondence of some predicted signs to empirically obtained ones.

## Multiple Regression

Multiple regression permits assessment of the nature of the linear relationship between two or more variables and some dependent variable of interest. Correlation can only indicate when two things are strongly (or weakly) related to each other. Multiple regression can indicate how, for

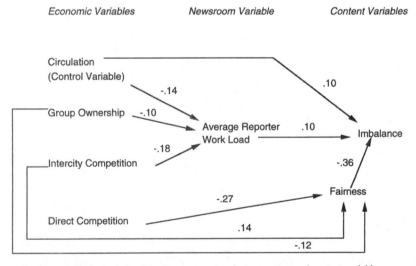

FIG. 8.3.   Empirical relationships between economic, newsroom, and content variables.

every unit increase in some independent variable, the dependent variable will have a specified change in its unit of measure.

Multiple regression requires that the dependent variable be interval or ratio level, although the independent variables can be dichotomous in nature (called *dummy variables*). When all independent variables are dummy variables, multiple regression is equivalent to ANOVA. One recommendation is that quasi-interval measures, such as political leaning, have at least five measurement points.

The technique also assumes that each of these variables is normally distributed around its mean. Whether the data set meets this requirement can be assessed by examining each variable's measures of skewness or departure from a normal distribution. Because small samples are likely to be more skewed, the technique is also sensitive to the overall number of cases providing data for the analysis. The usual standard is that at least 20 cases be available for each variable in the model.

Multiple regression assesses the nature of the way variables vary together, but it does so controlling for all the ways other variables in the model are varying as well. Think of it this way: Multiple regression correlates each independent variable with the dependent variable at each measurement level of all the other variables.

Regression analysis creates an equation that allows the best prediction of the dependent variable based on the data set. The equation takes the following form:

$$y = a + b_1X_1 + b_2X_2 + \ldots b_nX_n + e.$$

In the equation, $y$ is the value of the dependent variable when various values of the independent variables ($X_1$, $X_2$ ... $X_n$) have been placed in the equation. The letter $a$ represents an intercept point and would be the value of $y$ when all the Xs equal zero. The $e$ represents the error term, which is the variation in $y$ not explained by all the Xs. The error term is usually dropped, but it is important to remember all statistical analysis has error.

Each independent variable has a regression coefficient, which is represented by $b_1$, $b_2$, ... $b_n$. This coefficient equals the amount by which the X values are multiplied to figure out the $y$ value. The coefficient specifies how much the dependent variable changes for a given change in each independent variable.

Interpreting these regression coefficients is relatively straightforward; that is, the proportion of stories dealing with political issues will increase 1% with each increase of 1,000 in the circulation size of the daily newspapers in which they appear. However, different ways of measuring the variables in the models can produce more complication in the interpretation of importance. What researchers are most frequently interested in is assessing how each variable, relative to the others, contributes to the variation in the dependent variable.

Regression coefficients are expressed in the original units of the variables, and because of this, they can be difficult to compare. To compare the contribution of independent variables, the regression coefficients can be standardized. Standardization of coefficients is similar to standardization of exam scores, or putting the scores on a curve. Standardization places the coefficients on a normal curve by subtracting each score from the variable mean and dividing by the standard deviation. The standardized, or beta, coefficients are most useful for within-model comparisons of the relative importance of each independent variable's influence on the dependent variable. The numbers in the model for the previous fairness study are beta coefficients.

Multiple regression computes a beta for each independent variable. The beta varies according to each variable's standard deviation. The interpretation is that for each change of 1 $SD$ in the independent variable, the dependent variable changes by some part of its standard deviation as indicated by the beta coefficient. For example, if the beta relating circulation size to proportion of political news was .42, that means that for each increase of 1 $SD$ in average circulation size, the proportion of political news would increase by .42 of its standard deviation. If a third variable, staff size, had a beta of .22, it is easy to see that it is less influential because its variation produces relatively less variation on political news than does circulation size.

An additional statistic, used along with multiple regression, is the $r$-squared statistic. The $r$-square statistic is the proportion of the dependent variable's variance that is accounted for by all of the variation of the independent variables in the model. In other words, a large $r$ squared produced by a model means that the variables included are indeed substantively important in illuminating the social processes being investigated. A smaller $r$-squared means that independent variables outside the model are important and in need of investigation.

Finally, if the data were drawn from a random sample, a test of statistical significance is necessary to determine whether the coefficients found in the regression analysis are really zero or reflect some actual relationship in the population. Regression analysis also generates significance tests to permit the assessment of each coefficient and of the entire set of variables in the regression analysis as a whole.

Table 8.2 summarizes various measures of association used with nominal, ordinal, interval, and ratio data.

## STATISTICAL ASSUMPTIONS

These procedures were presented in a manner designed to be intuitively easy to grasp; however, one runs the risk of oversimplifying. In particular, statistical procedures carry certain assumptions about the data being analyzed. If the data differ to a great degree from the assumed conditions (e.g., a few extreme values or outliers with regression analysis), the analysis will lack validity. Researchers always should test data for these assumptions. For example, Weber (1990) pointed out that content analysts should be particularly careful in this regard when transforming frequencies, time, and space measures into percentages to control for length of a document. Percentages have a limited range, and the distribution is not linear; means and variances for percentages are not independent; and content analysis data are often not normally distributed. Linearity, independence of mean and variance, and normal distribution are assumptions for commonly used statistical procedures. When transforming content measures to percentages and using sophisticated statistical analysis, data should be checked to see if they fit assumptions.

Statistical procedures vary in how sensitive they are to violations of assumptions. With some procedures, minor violations will not result in invalid conclusions. However, researchers will have more confidence in their conclusions if data are consistent with statistical assumptions.

### TABLE 8.2
### Common Data Association Techniques in Content Analysis

| Level of Measure | Summary Measure | Significance Test (If Needed) |
|---|---|---|
| Nominal | Cramer's $V$ | Chi square |
|  | Phi |  |
| Ordinal | Spearman's rho | $z$ test |
| Interval | Pearson's $r$ | $F$ test |
|  | Regression | $F$ test |
| Ratio | Pearson's $r$ | $F$ test |
|  | Regression | $F$ test |

Readers should consult statistics books to help them evaluate assumptions about data (Blalock, 1972; Tabachnick & Fidell, 1996).

## SUMMARY

Data analysis is exploration and interpretation, the process of finding meaning in what has been observed. Whatever the numbers turned up through statistical techniques, deriving meaning from them is the goal. Statistical analysis can help people understand data patterns only when the analysis is conducted in ways consistent with standard practices. This chapter is a very brief survey of some often-used statistics. Which statistics are appropriate to a particular study depends on the hypotheses or research questions, the level of measurement of variables, and the nature of the sample. Like any good tool, statistics must be appropriate to the project. One size does not fit all.

Used properly, statistical techniques are valuable ways of expanding one's understanding. Yet, they can generate puzzles and questions not thought of before. It is the rare study that does not contain a sentence beginning, "Further research is needed to ...." For most researchers, that sentence is less an acknowledgment of the study's limitations and more of an invitation to join the exploration.

# 9

## Computers

The use of computers in content analysis has grown greatly in importance during the past 20 years. Content analysts have moved from inputting data into large mainframe computers with punch cards to using personal computers for a variety of research tasks. As "number-crunching" devices, computers will calculate all the statistics we discussed in chapter 8 (this volume) and many more using standard statistical programs such as Statistical Package for the Social Sciences. Once data are entered, these programs allow for fast and flexible manipulation of these data. However, the ability to crunch numbers in multiple ways has little to do with the quality of the research. As Riffe (2003) concluded, "Ultimately, the success of the research enterprise depends less on the sophistication of the data analysis or the impenetrability of the statistical procedure used than it does on the clarity of the research questions or hypotheses and the effectiveness of the research design" (pp. 207–208).

Increasingly, researchers have used computers as a content analysis aid in several other ways. Using computers to identify content, access content, and even to code content has increased as database creation has become easier and software development continues. Despite this rapid growth, however, all three uses have advantages and limitations that merit special note.

### USING COMPUTERS TO FIND AND ACCESS CONTENT

Computers allow scholars to tap into databases through libraries, online services, and the Internet and to broaden the base of content available for study. Although several indexes of text content are available, databases increasingly include both an index and the content itself. Large

U.S. newspapers, such as the *New York Times* and *Washington Post,* are indexed, and these indexes allow scholars easy access to stories about particular topics. However, the number of indexed newspapers is a small proportion of all dailies in the country.

Researchers content analyzing television news often turn to the Vanderbilt Television News Archives. The archives include videotapes for a price but have a free indexed collection of abstracts from network television newscasts dating from 1968. These abstracts can be very useful in locating stories about given topics, but some researchers have used the abstracts in lieu of TV news content (Iyengar & Simon, 1993; Kuklinski & Sigelman, 1992; Ragsdale & Cook, 1987).

Althaus, Edy, and Phalen (2002) studied the use of abstracts as surrogates for full transcripts and/or videotape. Althaus et al. (2002) issued strong warnings about such use for content analysis and concluded

> Our quantitative analysis confirms that abstract data can accurately reflect some dimensions of full-text transcripts, but it also sounds a warning about leaning too heavily on proxy measures of news content. While the abstracts do a good job of reproducing the aggregate distribution of news sources and topics, they provide, at best, imprecise representations of the evaluative tone of policy statements. At worst, they can produce decidedly inaccurate and misleading portrayals of what many sources actually say in the news. (p. 488)

Any researcher thinking of using abstracts from the Vanderbilt Television News Archives should consult the Althaus et al. (2002) article and be prepared to provide strong justification for not using transcripts that are ready available.

A variety of databases that include a range of media content are available for researchers, usually at a price. Some of the more popular (Hansen, 2003) include Dialog (http://www.dialog.com), which provides access to newspapers as well as government and business documents; Factiva (http://www.factiva.com/products), formerly Dow Jones Interactive, which contains millions of articles from 9,000 sources; BurrellesLuce (http://www.burrellesluce.com), which offers transcripts from more than 160 networks and cable stations; and NewsLibrary (http://www.newslibrary.com or http://nl.newsbank.com), which offers access to more than 80 newspapers.

Perhaps the most often used database of media content is Lexis-Nexis (http://www.Lexis.com), which incorporates content from hundreds of publications and television programs. Both journalists and scholars use it to access content. Dyer, Miller, and Boone (1991) downloaded stories from *Associated Press Wire* and the *Business Wire* using Nexis to study coverage of the 1989 Exxon Valdez oil spill in Alaska. Dyer et al. then used computer coding to analyze terms used in the articles.

A complete index may allow a researcher to identify the population of relevant items under study, in this case all stories about the Exxon Valdez; without indexes, researchers must examine all the editions or programs being considered just to identify relevant items. If the population of electronically located items is large, random sampling can then be applied. If the population is small, the entire collection of units might be examined.

Kim (2003) studied the congruency between press coverage of U.S. cigarette export policy with Korea and Taiwan and U.S. government foreign policy objectives during the 1980s. Using a key word search, 51 articles during 1985 to 1988 from eight daily U.S. newspapers were found in the Lexis-Nexis database.

Although using computers to find material has advantages, content analysts should be careful. Dependence on indexes can result in the failure to consider content not indexed electronically. The study of journalism in the United States often becomes the study of the major network newscasts and a few indexed national and regional newspapers. Although it is legitimate to study these media institutions, they are not representative of the majority of news organizations in the United States. They have influence, but researchers should be careful of overgeneralizing from content that is collected because it is convenient.

The nature of the database can affect the kinds of operationalizations a researcher can use. Some databases may be searched using descriptors—topic words assigned or tagged to particular stories. A story may be tagged with descriptors such as "women's issues," "international trade," and so forth. On the other hand, researchers may search an entire text looking for key words that are within the text, not tagged to it. Neuzil (1994) examined 9 months of three daily newspapers' databases using multiple operations. Neuzil searched the content from these papers using full-text search, descriptor search, and printed index search. The best results came from using full-text search with key words. The other two forms failed to identify all the articles within a topic area. Used carefully, computer identification using descriptors or key words is very useful. However, researchers should not assume this process alone will identify all content relevant to the study.

Although computers can identify appropriate content, they can also allow researchers access more easily than contacting providers directly. Indeed, many databases permit downloading of material, allowing more efficient acquisition of information. For example, in the study of wire service coverage of the Valdez accident, the researchers might have approached a local newspaper to gain access to Associated Press wire material. However, this would have been time consuming and expensive. Using Nexis to identify and download the material was convenient and took less time.

Tankard, Hendrickson, and Lee (1994) studied use of Lexis-Nexis to access content and listed advantages and disadvantages of such databases. Advantages included

1. Researchers have an easier time getting larger and perhaps more representative samples than without databases.
2. Databases process large amounts of data quickly.
3. Database searchers are particularly good at locating rare types of content.

However, disadvantages included:

1. The universe being sampled in such studies is not clear.
2. Content not of interest is sometimes identified by computers.
3. Typical databases may omit information; for example, most cannot report other, accompanying measures of prominence such as photographs, pull quotes, the position on the page, and headline information about type, size, and style.
4. Database searches can be expensive, although libraries are increasingly acquiring and updating CD-ROM databases to complement more expensive online services.

The second problem—misidentifying irrelevant content—can be a serious problem because of multiple meanings of key words. For example, a search using the key words "Bush" and "White House" could include a story about George Bush's presidency or one about planting new shrubbery around a house painted white. One means of overcoming this problem is to develop very particular key word descriptions. This, however, raises another risk, that of eliminating content that might be applicable but not meeting the particular description.

Fan (1988) used a series of "filtration runs" to identify text specific to the issues he was studying. In each of a series of steps, Fan applied a simple set of rules for inclusion of text. This reduced the need for a complex set or rules that would be applied in a single computer run. Fan (1988) found a number of advantages to this filtration method, including "the disambiguation accomplished. In the study, the word 'neglect' typically implied support of more military spending. Without the filtration steps to focus on paragraphs specifically discussing defense spending, it would not have been possible to give 'neglect' this very special meaning" (p. 47). Fan's filtration process allowed him to control for the context by eliminating content at each step that did not relate directly to his topic of study.

A content analyst considering easy-to-use databases to locate or access content must think carefully about the keywords and descriptors being programmed into the search. More than a quarter of a century ago, Kerlinger (1973) warned

> The electronic computer is utterly stupid: it will do exactly what a programmer tells it to do. If a programmer solves a problem brilliantly, the machine will perform "brilliantly." If the programmer programs incorrectly, the machine will faithfully and obediently make the errors the programmer has told it to make. (p. 706)

Hansen (2003) listed three major problems with using databases for content analysis. First, Hansen warned that electronic searches can be inconsistent and imprecise because searches can take a variety of forms. As a result, different searchers end up with very different lists of the content of interest. Second, Hansen said online records of printed content do not necessarily correspond with the printed version of the content. What a reader sees in a newspaper is rarely what the same reader would see in a database, and policies about placing newspaper content in databases vary from newspaper to newspaper. This problem is important particularly if one is trying to infer to the factors that influenced creation of the content in a print version or the impact of the print version on readers. Third, creating databases from electronic versions of print content is a labor-intensive process that often introduces errors and inaccuracies in the databases. Hansen (2003) summarized simply by writing "The watchword is 'database content analysts beware' " (p. 229).

## COMPUTER CONTENT ANALYSIS

In addition to finding or accessing content, some content analysis projects save time and money with programs that actually categorize content, doing work traditionally done by human coders. Use of these programs has grown, but computer content analysis is not new, nor should it be used with all projects.

## Types of Computer Content Analysis

Computerized content analysis can take a variety of forms, but most seem to fall into seven categories: word counts, key-word-in-context (KWIC) and concordances, dictionaries, language structure, readability, artificial intelligence, and dynamic content analysis (J. Bryant, personal communication, May 27, 1997; Franzosi, 1995; Holsti, 1969; Krippendorff, 2004a; Weber, 1990).

The simplest form of computer content analysis involves counting words. A computer identifies all the words used in a collection of text and calculates how many times each is used. The result is often a list that orders words by the frequency of appearance. Comparison of lists allows inference about the creators of the content. Weber (1990), for example, compared word lists from the Democratic and Republican platforms in 1976 and 1980 to examine the parties' concerns. Military and defense ranked higher in the 1980 Republican platform.

Word count content analysis is quick and might yield inferences about the content creators, but it removes words from their context and can affect meaning attached to the words. KWIC and concordances can help improve the validity of content analysis by identifying the words of interest and surrounding words that give context.

Weber (1990) argued that this information is useful because it draws attention to variations in the use of a word in context, and the lists "provide structured information that is helpful in determining whether the meaning of particular words is dependent on their use in certain phrases or idioms" (p. 44).

KWIC programs are similar to concordances used in literary studies. A concordance lists virtually every word in a text with its context and the page on which the word appeared. Concordances and KWIC are not what purists would see as content analyses because a computer can only highlight word usage; it does not categorize the words for meaning.

A third use of computers in performing content analysis moves beyond highlighting words and context to categorization. These dictionary programs assign words to groups according to some categorization system, and several standard dictionaries, for example, the *Harvard*

*Psychological Dictionary* (Holsti, 1969), have been developed. Krippendorff (1980) differentiated between thesaurus and dictionary approaches. A thesaurus approach uses programs that place words within predetermined categories that represent shared meanings to reduce the text to more manageable data. This approach has been criticized because groups of synonyms may be no easier to interpret than lists of ungrouped words and because these groupings may have no theoretical basis connected to the study's purpose.

Dictionary programs, on the other hand, classify words based on meaning groupings particular to the research objective. Studies of psychological bases for word selection in personal letters might use dictionaries created with an eye to basic psychological processes. Examination of political writing would involve dictionaries based on an understanding of political communication.

In a study of horoscope columns in Australian newspapers, Svensen and White (1995) created a computer dictionary. Svensen and White concluded that the writing in horoscopes was designed to make readers be dependent, helpless, and obedient to the instructions of the columns.

An early application of dictionary content analysis that continues is the General Inquirer system (Stone, Dunphy, Smith, & Ogilvie, 1966). Developed at Harvard, the General Inquirer is a collection of computer programs designed to

> (a) identify systematically, within text, instances of words and phrases that belong to categories specified by the investigator; (b) count occurrences and specified co-occurrences of these categories; (c) print and graph tabulations; (d) perform statistical tests; and (e) sort and regroup sentences according to whether they contain instances of a particular category or combination of categories. (Stone et al., 1966, p. 68)

The General Inquirer, later updated (Kelly & Stone, 1975), uses a dictionary designed to connect empirical results with theory. These dictionaries use "tags" that are assigned to words. These tags can be applied at several levels, providing different word groups. The *Harvard III Psychosociological Dictionary* had 55 first-order tags in 13 headings. For example, these included persons (self, selves, others), roles (male role, female role, neuter role, job role), and so on. The 28 second-order tags concern more connotative meaning and included tags such as institutional context (academic, artistic, community, economic, family, legal, medical military, political, recreational, religious, technological, and so on). Holsti (1969) wrote, "For example, *teacher* is tagged with three meanings: job role, higher status, and academic—one first-order tag followed by two second-order tags" (p. 158).

Over time, a variety of dictionaries have been developed and validated for use in categorizing verbal and written communication. For example, Schnurr, Rosenberg, and Oxman (1992) used an adaptation of the General Inquirer system with the *Harvard III Psychosociological Dictionary* to explore whether verbal communication can be used to differentiate individuals along dimensions of personality, affect, and interpersonal style. Schnurr et al. (1992) found that such prediction worked better with computer content analysis of Thematic Apperception Test responses than with the analysis of free speech responses to open-ended questions.

Other computer programs have been developed to use dictionaries for classification. Jacob, Mudersbach, and van der Ploeg (1996) used a computer program called RELATEX/RELATAN to classify ill people correctly by examining their verbal communication. Tuberculosis patients used concepts and themes differently than cancer patients and healthy people. However, the sample was small, with only 17 cancer and 11 tuberculosis patients.

A similar approach uses a computer to classify terms by topic or issue rather than meaning. For example, Dyer et al. (1991) studied wire services stories about the Exxon Valdez crisis. Dyer et al. used terms associated with legal, economic, and environmental issues to classify articles. If any of the terms were present, the computer classified the story as having that issue in its text.

In a study of network television news content, Hamilton (2004) used the DICTION program, which was originally developed to study the language of politics, to analyze a week of network news from November 1999. DICTION includes about 10,000 words that are classified into 33 categories that are further reduced to five summary measures of content. Hamilton associated the classifications of terms with either hard news or soft news and then correlated these measures with ratings and advertising rates. The study is interesting and suggests a potentially fruitful use of computer content analysis, but an obvious limitation comes from the assumption that relationships found with content from a week in November generalize to the other 51 weeks. This means, of course, that replication with a more representative sample would be warranted.

Dictionaries seem to have the advantage of high reliability because computers categorize only on the basis of their programs without human biases. However, Weber (1984) pointed out that the ambiguity of word meanings can create validity problems. Many words have more than one meaning and may fit multiple categories. Some words within categories are stronger representatives of that category than other words. These problems must be resolved by researchers on a study-by-study basis.

The Hamilton (2004) study might also suffer validity problems because of variations in word usage by television journalists. The content analysis classified as soft news "human interest" terms, which included personal pronouns, family terms (wife and grandchild), and terms of friendship. The assumption that these terms are used primarily with soft news should be tested empirically. Television often uses human interest elements in hard news reports. These elements include individual examples that make difficult concepts more "human" and therefore easier to understand (Zillmann, 2002). In other words, the use of human interest-related terms is not exclusive to soft news. The dictionary approach for analyzing television news has promise, but the validity of the assumptions underlying the content classifications would benefit from comparison with human coding for hard and soft news.

The fourth form of computer content analysis examines language structure. These programs move beyond individual word groups and counts to examine the grammar and syntax of larger language units, such as sentences. Franzosi (1990) developed a "semantic text grammar" based on structural relationships among types of words. For example, words are divided into accepted language groupings (e.g., subject, action words, objects of action, and modifiers). These word groupings are further classified by relations among the types of words. For example, the subject of the sentence includes an actor, which is a type of person, and all actor modifiers. The action element of a sentence is made up of an action phrase (e.g., a verb) and action modifiers. A computer can be used to restructure the text and organize it by these grammatical categories. Franzosi (1995) advocated this approach to studying textual material in publications, such as newspapers, as a form of sociohistorical research. This approach provides groupings of text, but the computer cannot evaluate the meaning of the text per se. A researcher uses the computer restructuring and organization of the text to analyze its meaning.

Use of content analysis for studying structure need not be limited to language. Simonton (1994) studied the first six notes in 15,618 themes by 479 classical composers using a computer. The structure of these melodies allowed successful classification of composers and provided insight into a variety of topics such as melodic originality across time and the relationship between melodic originality and music popularity.

A fifth form of computer content analysis is the application of readability formulas to text. With the spread of microcomputers, this form of content analysis has become available to millions of computer users. Most sophisticated word-processing software includes one or more formulas for measuring readability. A variety of readability formulas are available, such as the Flesch Reading Ease formula (1974) and Gunning Fog Index (1952), and although they all measure the difficulty of reading text, they also vary in their basic computational logic. The Flesch formula is based on the average sentence length and syllables per 100 words, whereas Gunning's index is based on average sentence length and number of words of three or more syllables in a collection of text. Researchers using these formulas need to be aware of their underlying logic.

An examination of readability formulas is beyond the scope of this text, and a variety of books and articles are available on the subject (Flesch, 1974; Gunning, 1952; Zakaluk & Samuels, 1988). However, such formulas have been used in studies of commercially produced text. Danielson et al. (1992) studied the comparative readability of reading newspapers and novels from 1885 to 1990. Gillman (1994) examined readability of newspaper news and sports leads, and Bodle (1996) used readability formulas to help compare quality of student and professional newspapers.

Although it represents a small subset of content analysis, readability computer analysis plays an important role in the examination of commercially prepared text because readability affects access to the text's meaning. Complex writing reduces the number of people who can understand the content and affects its impact on individuals and society. Perhaps the continuing decline in newspaper circulation is due partially to the increasing difficulty in reading newspapers found by Danielson et al. (1992).

In a sixth form of computer content analysis, artificial intelligence attempts to mimic the cognitive processes of humans. People use a "fuzzy logic" that allows associations among objects and ideas that cannot be anticipated by computers. Artificial intelligence also involves a computer learning from previous decisions as humans do.

Use of content analysis incorporating this artificial intelligence extends beyond scholarly application. For example, Gottschalk (1994) applied artificial intelligence software to the analysis of verbal measures to identify cognitive and intellectual problems caused by age, alcohol, drugs, and insanity. However, the application of artificial intelligence to content analysis as a scholarly method remains underdeveloped.

Currently, artificially intelligent computers are extremely expensive because of the need for huge memory capacity, and they are limited to a particular function. The "Deep Blue" computer at IBM became proficient at playing chess, beating world champion Gary Karpov in 1997. Although Deep Blue has helped IBM continue to develop artificial intelligence, such computers typically are limited in the numbers of functions they can perform. Nevertheless, artificial intelligence technology holds promise for content analysis as it becomes less costly, but the promise may be years in coming.

The final form of computer content analysis is known as dynamic content analysis because it allows content analysis of video data in real time. Bryant and Evans are exploring this process at the University of Alabama (B. Evans, personal communication, September 9, 2004). Coders can simultaneously input data for up to 32 attributes, as they watch video. For example, this approach was used to analyze television mysteries. Coders recorded data about which characters revealed which clues when, whether other characters were present, and who victimized whom with what effect. Its real-time property permits recording how long each of these processes occurred and which ones overlapped with others, dimensions that are difficult to match with traditional analysis techniques. The result allows the researcher to examine the structure of the mystery program and the relationship among the characters.

Dynamic content analysis holds potential for use with computer programs that study audience preferences and reactions. In such preference studies, a group of participants may be exposed to content while providing continuous feedback to a computer about their impressions and attitudes toward the content. The feedback usually involves rating the content on a scale. By using dynamic content analysis with audience preference data, researchers can connect particular content to audience reaction while controlling for audience demographics.

One approach is to view dynamic content analysis as a combination of experimental design and content analysis. As experimental design, the content viewed becomes the stimulus, and the reaction of the audience is the response. One might argue that dynamic content analysis is not truly content analysis because a protocol is not used. However, if an audience that is involved in real time content analysis is sampled randomly, the reactions can be used to infer to the population from which the audience was selected. This holds the potential for measuring the connotations the population members apply to one or more symbols. The connotations of a large group would have variance, but the central tendency and dispersion could be measured.

For example, if a researcher wanted to study connotations typically associated with cultural symbols, a pilot study could narrow down the range of possible affective connotations. A representative sample of people could be exposed to the symbols through a PowerPoint® or video and asked to react to the symbols by selecting among the connotations presented. Of course, to control for presentations, the cultural symbols, such as a flag or religious artifact, would be presented in various contexts.

## When to Use Computers for Content Analysis

Despite its flexibility and potential, computer content analysis may not be appropriate to all research projects. Holsti (1969) suggested when computer content analysis was particularly useful:

1. When the unit of analysis is the symbol or word, and analysis concerns number of times a symbol or word is used. For example, use of the image of the Cold War for political gain could be studied by counting the number of times communism, or a variation thereof, appeared in political speeches during the 1950s.

2. When the analysis is extremely complex, for example, using a large number of categories with a large number of recording units such as when inference is to be based on the co-occurrence of two or more terms in the same sentence. The extent of a journalist's bias might be identified by the occurrence of a politician's name and an evaluative modifier in the same sentence.

3. When the analysis involves examining the data in multiple ways. Some studies use complex semantic grammar to analyze text material, such as magazines and newspapers, (Franzosi, 1990), and computers allow the complicated manipulations that allow a better understanding of these language data.

4. When the data come from documents that are of basic importance to a variety of disciplines, researchers, and lines of inquiry and might be used in multiple studies. The expense of computer analysis can, in effect, be "spread out" over the studies. Holsti cited the example of a database built from computer analysis of texts of all major political party platforms since 1844. It seems likely that researchers will continue to generate hypotheses that can be tested against such data sets.

The first two reasons are still appropriate more than 35 years after Holsti's advice was published, but the third and fourth seem less relevant today because the cost of computer content analysis has declined drastically and because of the widespread availability of large-capacity, high-speed personal computers. On the other hand, a new reason could be added to Holsti's list: when the type of computer analysis is appropriate to material that is available or made readily available in electronic form. After all, the biggest cost in computer content analysis is the labor cost for data input. Electronic scanning can reduce input costs when the text is legible to a computer.

Holsti (1969) also specified situations when computer content analysis would not be appropriate:

1. When the research involves a single study of specialized information, and computer analysis might be too expensive. The development of cheap scanner technology has made this rule less applicable today than in 1969.

2. When the number of documents is large, but the information from each is limited. If a researcher studied only the first two paragraphs of newspaper stories from 200 dailies, and they were not available electronically, the cost of data input and clearing up scanner material might be more time consuming and expensive than doing the coding without computers.

3. When the research calls for measures of space and time. Video timers and rulers work better for measuring these variables. However, computers attached to VCRs can measure time if instructed when to begin and end that timing process.

4. When thematic analysis is being used. In this instance, researchers should compare using computer analysis with individual analysis. Thematic analysis involves the relation among words that may or may not be measurable by a computer program.

In an effort to better understand the strengths and weaknesses of computer content analysis, a 1991 study (Nacos et al., 1991) compared the same content analyzed by computer and by people. Using two sets of content, Nacos et al. classified newspaper treatment of the Grenada invasion and the Three Mile Island accident. Nacos et al. found high correlations between the computer and human categorizations with one but not the other set. Nacos et al. concluded that computer content analysis has promise but offered warnings for those who use computers. Nacos et al.'s concerns were related to issues of topic complexity and the ability of a computer to categorize beyond its programmed rules. As topics being content analyzed increase in political and social complexity, computer content analysts should be careful about the categorization rules and the content units being examined. At minimum, the categorization procedure should be pretested before programming into the computer. These warnings from Holsti (1969) and Nacos et al. also pertain to textual analysis for which a variety of computer programs are already available.

The computer analysis of visual content—video, photograph, and graphics—is much less developed. Although not specifically aimed at traditional academic content analysis, some computer programs that can aid in coding of video are available. Several programs produced by Noldus Information Technology (http://www.noldus.com/site/nav10000) do not code video for a researcher but allow enhanced control over images being analyzed. They were developed as ways to help researchers code human and animal behavior from videotape. However, it could be adapted to content analysis in projects analyzing behavior portrayed in commercial video.

A project at the University of Mannheim started in 1994 with the aim of developing computer content analysis for video and audio material that would work in a way similar to computer analysis used with text. The aim is to be able to code and count elements of video (brightness, motion, scenes) and audio (audio cuts and loudness) in much the same way computers count words and sentences in text. Information about the project can be found at http://www.informatik.uni-mannheim.de/pi4/projects/MoCA/

The issue of whether a technology can be adapted, of course, raises obvious questions about whether it, or any technology, should be used. Ultimately, the decision to use or not use a computer for coding content depends on answers to three questions:

1. Will it yield valid measures?
2. Will it cut the cost of the study?
3. Will it improve the reliability?

The answer to the first question is pivotal. A computer program must yield measures appropriate to a study. If the variable being measured is number of seconds devoted to particular news topics on television, a computer program might not be available that will do this. It also would be inappropriate to substitute a dictionary program when physical space is the variable.

If a computer and human coding both yield equally valid measures, the second and third questions become important. If a computer program will cut cost while maintaining or increasing reliability of coding, then it should be used. If a computer program will increase reliability of coding with the equivalent cost of human coding, then it should be used. The difficult decisions come when researchers have a program that will increase cost but improve reliability or reduce costs at the expense of reliability. The response to the former decision depends on budget, but the response to the second dilemma is to avoid sacrificing reliability for money. The goal of scholarship is to produce valid conclusions, not to save money.

Cost savings are related to the form of content available. Electronically stored data and text that can be easily scanned into electronic form usually produce cost savings with computers. However, text that must be keyboarded by someone can increase costs.

## Finding Computer Programs to Use

The growth of the computer hardware and software industries has made finding computer programs fairly simple, and the Internet is useful in identifying such programs and downloading them. The use of a search engine will provide the locations of content analysis software. The sophistication and cost of these programs vary. For example, a program called VBPro uses a keyword approach. It was created by Mark Miller (http://mmmiller.com/vbpro/vbpro.html) and has been used in several articles (Andsager, 2000; Dyer et al., 1991; Miller, Andsager, & Riechert, 1998). The program prepares text for analysis, creates list of words and their frequency, finds and tags words in content, codes content units defined by researcher for presence, and maps terms in multidimensional space for co-occurrence.

Other programs available on the Web in 2004 include CATPAC (http://www.galileoco.com), which produces word counts, co-occurrence counts (frequency with which words appear together), cluster analysis (groupings of words associated with each other), and perceptual maps (clusters of words displayed on dimensional grids). The program costs about $600 for academics, and a student version costs $49. A content analysis program called INTEXT will perform a variety of analyses on both German and English text. Information about the program is available at http://www.intext.de Now in the public domain, its analysis tools include list words, KWIC, readability, and a variety of other content analysis processes. Researchers interested in advances in video content analysis should read Ngo, Pong, and Zhang (2001).

All computer content analysis programs assume certain characteristics of the hardware, such as platform (DOS, Windows, Apple) and processing memory size. Prices and discounts available for academics also vary. As with any investment, content analysts should use comparison shopping and check with people who have used programs if possible. This could start with Web sites devoted to content analysis, and several such sites are available. A short list of interesting sites available in 2004 includes

http://www.car.ua.edu
http://academic.csuohio.edu/kneuendorf/content/
http://www.content-analysis.de
http://www.temple.edu/mmc/reliability/

## SUMMARY

Computers play a variety of roles in content analysis. In almost all quantitative content analysis, computers are used to analyze data. Computers help analysts locate and access content efficiently, and computers code content. However, the use of computer content analysis with large data sets of mass media content remains limited. Several coding programs are available, and they vary in price from free to several hundred dollars.

Although computers can be extremely useful and efficient in finding and coding content, researchers must be careful in their application. Computers are appropriate for some studies but not for others. The comprehensiveness of databases and the type of search determine how well databases provide relevant content. The nature of the variables being created, availability of appropriate programs, and the impact on expenses determine whether computers should be used for coding.

# References

Abelman, R. (1994). News on The 700 Club: The cycle of religious activism. *Journalism Quarterly, 71,* 887–892.

Abelman, R., & Neuendorf, K. (1985). How religious is religious television programming? *Journal of Communication, 35*(1), 98–110.

Adams, W. C. (1980). Local television news coverage and the central city. *Journal of Broadcasting, 24,* 253–265.

Allport, G. W. (Ed.). (1965). *Letters from Jenny.* New York: Harcourt, Brace and World.

Althaus, S. L., Edy, J. A., & Phalen, P. F. (2002). Using the Vanderbilt Television Abstracts to Track Broadcast News Content: Possibilities and Pitfalls. *Journal of Broadcasting & Electronic Media, 46*(3), 473–492.

Altschull, J. H. (1984). *Agents of power.* New York: Longman.

Andsager, J. L. (2000). How interest groups attempt to shape public opinion with competing news frames. *Journalism & Mass Communication Quarterly, 77,* 577–592.

Armstrong, C. L. (2004). The influence of reporter gender on source selection in newspaper stories. *Journalism & Mass Communication Quarterly, 81,* 139–154.

Babbie, E. (1995). *The practice of social research* (7th ed.). Belmont, CA: Wadsworth.

Bantz, C. R., McCorkle, S., & Baade, R. C. (1997). The news factory. In D. Berkowitz (Ed.), *Social meanings of news: A text reader* (pp. 269–285). Thousand Oaks, CA: Sage.

Barnhurst, K. G., & Mutz, D. (1997). American journalism and the decline in event-centered reporting. *Journal of Communication, 47*(4), 27–53.

Bauer, R. A. (1964). The obstinate audience: The influence process from the point of view of social communication. *The American Psychologist, 19,* 319–328.

Baxter, R. L., DeRiemer, C., Landini, N., Leslie, L., & Singletary, M. W. (1985). A content analysis of music videos. *Journal of Broadcasting & Electronic Media, 29,* 333–340.

Beam, R. A. (2003). Content differences between daily newspapers with strong and weak market orientations. *Journalism & Mass Communication Quarterly, 80,* 368–390.

Berelson, B. R. (1952). *Content analysis in communication research.* New York: Free Press.

Berelson, B. R. (1954). Content analysis. In G. Lindzey (Ed.), *Handbook of social psychology* (Vol. 1, pp. 488–518). Reading, MA: Addison-Wesley.

Bernstein, C., & Woodward, B. (1974). *All the president's men.* New York: Simon & Schuster.

Blalock, H. M., Jr. (1972). *Social statistics* (2nd ed.). New York: McGraw-Hill.

Bodle, J. V. (1996). Assessing news quality: A comparison between community and student daily newspapers. *Journalism & Mass Communication Quarterly, 73,* 672–686.

Bowers, J. W. (1989). Introduction. In J. Bradac (Ed.), *Message effects in communication science* (pp. 10–23). Newbury Park, CA: Sage.

Bradac, J. (Ed.). (1989). *Message effects in communication science.* Newbury Park, CA: Sage.

Brown, J. D., & Campbell, K. (1986). Race and gender in music videos: The same beat but a different drummer. *Journal of Communication, 36*(1), 94–106.

Bryant, J. (1989). Message features and entertainment effects. In J. Bradac (Ed.), *Message effects in communication science* (pp. 231–262). Newbury Park, CA: Sage.

Budd, R. W., Thorp, R. K., & Donohew, L. (1967). *Content analysis of communication.* New York: Macmillan.

Campbell, D. T., & Stanley, J. C. (1963). *Experimental and quasi-experimental designs for research.* Chicago: Rand McNally.

Cantril, H., Gaudet, H., & Hertzog, H. (1940). *The invasion from Mars.* Princeton, NJ: Princeton University Press.

Carroll, R. L. (1989). Market size and TV news values. *Journalism Quarterly, 66,* 49–56.

Chaffee, S. H., & Hochheimer, J. L. (1985). The beginnings of political communication research in the United States: Origins of the "limited effects" model. In M. Gurevitch & M. R. Levy (Eds.), *Mass communication yearbook 5* (pp. 75–104). Beverly Hills, CA: Sage.

Cohen, J. A. (1960). Coefficient of agreement for nominal scales. *Educational and Psychological Measurement, 20,* 37–46.

Cohen, J. A. (1968). Weighted kappa: Nominal scale agreement with a provision for scaled disagreement or partial credit. *Psychological Bulletin, 70,* 213–220.

Cohen, S., & Young, J. (Eds.). (1973). *The manufacture of news.* London: Constable.

Craft, S. H., & Wanta, W. (2004). Women in the newsroom: Influences of female editors and reporters on the news agenda. *Journalism & Mass Communication Quarterly, 81,* 124–138.

Craig, S. R. (1992). The effect of television day part on gender portrayals in television commercials: A content analysis. *Sex Roles, 26,* 197–211.

Culbertson, H. M. (1975, May 14). Veiled news sources—who and what are they? *ANPA News Research Bulletin,* No. 3.

Culbertson, H. M. (1978). Veiled attribution—an element of style? *Journalism Quarterly, 55,* 456–465.

Culbertson, H. M. (2003). Applied public relations research. In G. H. Stempel III, D. H. Weaver, & G. C. Wilhoit (Eds.), *Mass communication research and theory* (pp. 53–75). Boston, MA: Allyn & Bacon.

Culbertson, H. M., & Somerick, N. (1976, May 19). Cloaked attribution—what does it mean to readers? *ANPA News Research Bulletin,* No. 1.

Culbertson, H. M., & Somerick, N. (1977). Variables affect how persons view unnamed news sources. *Journalism Quarterly, 54,* 58–69.

Danielson, W. A., & Adams, J. B. (1961). Completeness of press coverage of the 1960 campaign. *Journalism Quarterly, 38,* 441–452.

Danielson, W. A., Lasorsa, D. L., & Im, D. S. (1992). Journalists and novelists: A study of diverging styles. *Journalism Quarterly, 69,* 436–446.

Davis, J., & Turner, L. W. (1951). Sample efficiency in quantitative newspaper content analysis. *Public Opinion Quarterly, 15,* 762–763.

Deese, J. (1969). Conceptual categories in the study of content. In G. Gerbner, O. R. Holsti, K. Krippendorff, W. J. Paisley, & P. J. Stone (Eds.), *The analysis of communication content* (pp. 39–56). New York: Wiley.

de sola Pool, I., & Shulman, I. (1959). Newsmen's fantasies, audiences, and newswriting. *Public Opinion Quarterly, 23,* 145–158.

de Vreese, C. H. (2004). The effects of frames in political television news on issue interpretation and frame salience. *Journalism & Mass Communication Quarterly, 81,* 36–52.

Dick, S. J. (1993). *Forum talk: An analysis of interaction in telecomputing systems.* Unpublished doctoral dissertation, Michigan State University, East Lansing, MI.

Dietz, P. E., & Evans, B. (1982). Pornographic imagery and prevalence of paraphilia. *American Journal of Psychiatry, 139,* 1493–1495.

Dillon, D. R., O'Brien, D. G., Hopkins, C. J., Baumann, J. F., Humphrey, J. W., Pickle, J. M., Ridgeway, V. R., Wyatt, M., Wilkinson, C., Murray, B., & Pauler, S. (1992). Article content and authorship trends in *The Reading Teacher* 1948–1991. *The Reading Teacher, 45,* 362–368.

Dominick, J. R. (1999). Who do you think you are? Personal home pages and self presentation on the World Wide Web. *Journalism & Mass Communication Quarterly, 77,* 646–658.

Douglas, W., & Olson, B. M. (1995). Beyond family structure: The family in domestic comedy. *Journal of Broadcasting & Electronic Media, 39,* 236–261.

Duncan, D. F. (1989). Trends in gay pornographic magazines: 1960–1984. *Sociology and Social Research, 73,* 95–98.

Duncan, D. F. (1990). Health education and health psychology: A comparison through content analysis. *Psychological Reports, 66,* 1057–1058.

Duncan, D. F. (1991). Health psychology and clinical psychology: A comparison through content analysis. *Psychological Reports, 68,* 585–586.

Dyer, S. C., Jr., Miller, M. M., & Boone, J. (1991). Wire service coverage of the Exxon Valdez crisis. *Public Relations Review, 17*(1), 27–36.

Ekstrand, V. T. (2002). Online news: User agreements and implications for readers. *Journalism & Mass Communication Quarterly, 79,* 602–618.

Ellis, L., Miller, C., & Widmayer, A. (1988). Content analysis of biological approaches in psychology. *Sociology and Social Research, 72,* 145–150.

Emery, E., & Emery, M. (1978). *The press and America: An interpretative history of the mass media* (4th ed.). Englewood Cliffs, NJ: Prentice Hall.

Entman, R. F. (1993). Framing: Toward clarification of a fractured paradigm. *Journal of Communication, 43*(4), 51–58.

Evans, W., Krippendorff, M., Yoon, J., Posluszny, P., & Thomas, S. (1990). Science in the prestige and national tabloid presses. *Social Science Quarterly, 71,* 105–117.

Evarts, D. R., & Stempel, G. H., III. (1974). Coverage of the 1972 campaign by TV, newsmagazines and major newspapers. *Journalism Quarterly, 53,* 645–648, 676.

Fan, D. P. (1988). *Prediction of public opinion from the mass media: Computer content analysis and mathematical modeling*. New York: Greenwood.

Fico, F. (1984). News coverage of part-time and full-time legislatures. *Newspaper Research Journal, 6*(1), 49–57.

Fico, F. (1985). The search for the statehouse spokesman. *Journalism Quarterly, 62,* 74–80.

Fico, F., Atwater, T., & Wicks, R. (1985). The similarity of broadcast and newspaper reporters covering two state capitals. *Mass Communication Review, 12,* 29–32.

Fico, F., & Cote, W. (1997). Fairness and balance in election reporting. *Newspaper Research Journal, 71,*(3–4), 124–137.

Fico, F., & Cote, W. (1999). Fairness and balance in the structural characteristics of stories in newspaper coverage of the 1996 presidential election. *Journalism & Mass Communication Quarterly, 76,* 123–137.

Fico, F., & Drager, M. (2001). Partisan and structural balance in news stories about conflict generally balanced. *Newspaper Research Journal, 22*(1), 2–11.

Fico, F., Ku, L., & Soffin, S. (1994). Fairness, balance of newspaper coverage of U.S. in Gulf War. *Newspaper Research Journal, 15*(1), 30–43.

Fico, F., Richardson, J., & Edwards, S. (2004). Influence of story structure on perceived story bias and news organization credibility. *Mass Communication and Society, 7,* 301–318.

Fico, F., & Soffin, S. (1994). Covering local conflict: Fairness in reporting a public policy issue. *Newspaper Research Journal, 15,* 64–76.

Fico, F., & Soffin, S. (1995). Fairness and balance of selected newspaper coverage of controversial national, state and local issues. *Journalism & Mass Communication Quarterly, 72,* 621–633.

Flesch, R. (1974). *The art of readable writing*. New York: Harper & Row.

Foote, J. S., & Saunders, A. C. (1990). Graphic forms in network television. *Journalism Quarterly, 67,* 501–507.

Franzosi, R. (1990). Computer-assisted coding of textual data. *Sociological Methods and Research, 19,* 225–257.

Franzosi, R. (1995). Computer-assisted content analysis of newspapers: Can we make an expensive research tool more efficient? *Quality & Quantity, 29,* 157–172.

Freud, S. (1911). Psychoanalytical notes upon an autobiographical account of a case of paranoia (Dementia Paranoids). *Standard Edition, 14,* 73–102.

Garramone, G. (1984). Voter response to negative political advertising. *Journalism Quarterly, 61,* 250–259.

Garramone, G. (1985). Effects of negative political advertising: The roles of sponsor and rebuttal. *Journal of Broadcasting and Electronic Media, 29,* 147–159.

Garramone, G. (1988). Appeals and strategies of negative political advertising. *Journal of Broadcasting and Electronic Media, 32,* 415–427.

Garramone, G., Atkin, C. K., Pinkleton, B. E., & Cole, R. T. (1990). Effects of negative political advertising on the political process. *Journal of Broadcasting and Electronic Media, 34,* 299–311.

Gerbner, G., Gross, L., Morgan, M., & Signorielli, N. (1994). Growing up with television: The cultivation perspective. In J. Bryant & D. Zillmann (Eds.), *Media effects: Advances in theory and research* (pp. 17–41). Hillsdale, NJ: Lawrence Erlbaum Associates, Inc.

Gerbner, G., Signorielli, N., & Morgan, M. (1995). Violence on television: The Cultural Indicators Project. *Journal of Broadcasting and Electronic Media, 39,* 278–283.

Gillman, T. (1994). The problem of long leads in news and sports stories. *Newspaper Research Journal, 15*(4), 29–39.

Gitlin, T. (1980). *The whole world is watching: Mass media in the making and unmaking of the new left.* Berkeley: University of California Press.

Golan, G., & Wanta, W. (2001). Second-level agenda setting in the New Hampshire primary: A comparison of coverage in three newspaper and public perceptions of candidates. *Journalism & Mass Communication Quarterly, 78,* 247–259.

Gottschalk, L. A. (1994). The development, validation, and application of a computerized measurement of cognitive impairment from the content analysis of verbal behavior. *Journal of Clinical Psychology, 50,* 349–361.

Grabe, M. E. (1996). The South African Broadcasting Corporation's coverage of the 1987 and 1989 elections: The matter of visual bias. *Journal of Broadcasting & Electronic Media, 40,* 153–179.

Greenberg, B. S., & Brand, J. E. (1994). Minorities and the mass media: 1970s to 1990s. In J. Bryant & D. Zillmann (Eds.), *Media effects: Advances in theory and research* (pp. 273–314). Hillsdale, NJ: Lawrence Erlbaum Associates.

Greenberg, B. S., & Schweitzer, J. C. (1989). "Mass communication scholars" revisited and revised. *Journalism Quarterly, 66,* 473–475.

Greenberg, B., Sherry, J., Busselle, R., Rampoldi-Hnilo, L., & Smith, S. (1997). Daytime television talk shows. *Journal of Broadcasting & Electronic Media, 41,* 412–426.

Gunning, R. (1952). *The technique of clear writing.* New York: McGraw-Hill.

Hamilton, J. T. (2004). *All the news that's fit to sell.* Princeton, NJ: Princeton University Press.

Haney, W. V. (1973). *Communication and organizational behavior: Text and cases.* Homewood, IL: Irwin.

Hanson, C. T. (1983, May/June). Gunsmoke and sleeping dogs: The prez's press at midterm. *Columbia Journalism Review, 22,* 27–35.

Hansen, K. A. (2003). Using databases for content analysis. In G. H. Stempel III, D. H. Weaver, & G. C. Wilhoit (Eds.), *Mass communication research and theory* (pp. 220–230). Boston: Allyn & Bacon.

Hansen, K. A., Ward, J., Conners, J. L., & Neuzil, M. (1994). Local breaking news: Sources, technology and news routines. *Journalism Quarterly, 71,* 561–572.

Hanushek, E. A., & Jackson, J. E. (1977). *Statistical methods for social scientists.* New York: Academic.

Harmon, M. (1989, Spring). Market size and local television news judgment. *Journal of Media Economics, 2*(1), 31–40.

Harvey, T. (1991, October 20). Cuba rejects opportunity to initiate basic reforms. *The Birmingham News,* p. 15–A.

Holsti, O. R. (1969). *Content analysis for the social sciences and humanities.* Reading, MA: Addison-Wesley.

Hovland, C. I. (1959). Reconciling conflicting results derived from experimental and survey studies of attitude change. *The American Psychologist, 14,* 8–17.

Hunter, J. E., & Gerbing, D. W. (1982). Unidimensional measurement, second order factor analysis and causal models. *Research in Organizational Behavior, 4,* 267–320.

Husselbee, L. P., & Elliott, L. (2002). Looking beyond hate: How national and regional newspapers framed hate crimes in Jasper, Texas, and Laramie, Wyoming. *Journalism & Mass Communication Quarterly, 79,* 833–852.

Husselbee, L. P., & Stempel, G. H., III. (1997). Contrast in U.S. media coverage of two major Canadian elections. *Journalism & Mass Communication Quarterly, 74,* 591–601.

Iyengar, S., & Simon, A. F. (1993). News coverage of the Gulf crisis and public opinion: A study of agenda-setting, priming, and framing. *Communication Research, 20,* 365–383.

Jacob, W., Mudersbach, K., & van der Ploeg, H. M. (1996). Diagnostic classification through the study of linguistic dimensions. *Psychology Reports, 79,* 951–959.

Jolliffe, L., & Catlett, T. (1994). Women editors at the "seven sisters" magazines, 1965–1985: Did they make a difference? *Journalism Quarterly, 71,* 800–808.

Jones, R. L., & Carter, R. E., Jr. (1959). Some procedures for estimating "news hole" in content analysis. *Public Opinion Quarterly, 23,* 399–403.

Jones, S. (1994) Unlicensed broadcasting: Content and conformity. *Journalism Quarterly, 71,* 395–402.

Jung, J. (2002). How magazines covered media companies' mergers: The case of the evolution of Time Inc. *Journalism & Mass Communication Quarterly, 79,* 681–696.

Kaid, L. L., & Wadsworth, A. J. (1989). Content analysis. In P. Emmert & L. L. Barker (Eds.) *Measurement of communication behavior* (pp. 197–217). New York: Longman.

Kamhawi, R., & Weaver, D. (2003). Mass communication research trends from 1980 to 1999. *Journalism & Mass Communication Quarterly, 80,* 7–27.

Kelly, E. F., & Stone, P. J. (1975). *Computer recognition of English word senses.* Amsterdam: North-Holland.

Kenney, K., & Simpson, C. (1993). Was coverage of the 1988 presidential race by Washington's two dailies biased? *Journalism Quarterly, 70,* 345–355.

Kensicki, L. J. (2004). No cure for what ails us: The media-constructed disconnect between societal problems and possible solutions. *Journalism & Mass Communication Quarterly, 81,* 53–73.

Kerlinger, F. N. (1973). *Foundations of behavioral research* (2nd ed.). New York: Holt, Rinehart & Winston.

Kerr, P. A., & Moy, P. (2002). Newspaper coverage of fundamentalist Christians. *Journalism & Mass Communication Quarterly, 79,* 54–72.

Kim, K. K. (2003). It's all about trade: United States press coverage of cigarette export talks and policy. *Mass Communication & Society, 6*(1), 75–97.

Klapper, J. T. (1960). *The effects of mass communication.* New York: Free Press.

Krippendorff, K. (1980). *Content analysis: An introduction to its methodology.* Beverly Hills, CA: Sage.

Krippendorff, K. (2004a). *Content analysis: An introduction to its methodology.* Thousand Oaks, CA: Sage.

Krippendorff, K. (2004b). Reliability in content analysis: Some common misconceptions and recommendations. *Human Communication Research, 30,* 411–433.

Kuklinski, J. H., & Sigelman, L. (1992). When objectivity is not objective: Network television news coverage of U.S. senators and the "paradox of objectivity." *Journal of Politics, 54,* 810–833.

Kurpius, D. D. (2002). Sources and civic journalism: Changing patterns of reporting? *Journalism & Mass Communication Quarterly, 79,* 853–866.

Kurpius, D. D., & Mendelson, A. (2002). A case study of deliberative democracy on television: Civic dialogue on C-SPAN call-in shows. *Journalism & Mass Communication Quarterly, 79,* 587–601.

Lacy, S. (1987). The effects of intracity competition on daily newspaper content. *Journalism Quarterly, 64,* 281–290.

Lacy, S. (1988). The impact of intercity competition on daily newspaper content. *Journalism Quarterly, 65,* 399–406.

Lacy, S. (1992). The financial commitment approach to news media competition. *Journal of Media Economics, 59*(2), 5–22.

Lacy, S., & Fico, F. (1991). The link between newspaper content quality and circulation. *Newspaper Research Journal, 12*(2), 46–57.

Lacy, S., Fico, F., & Simon, T. F. (1989). The relationships among economic, newsroom and content variables: A path model. *Journal of Media Economics, 2*(2), 51–66.

Lacy, S., Fico, F., & Simon, T. F. (1991). Fairness and balance in the prestige press. *Journalism Quarterly, 68,* 363–370.

Lacy, S., & Ramsey, K. A. (1994). The advertising content of African-American newspapers. *Journalism Quarterly, 71,* 521–530.

Lacy, S., & Riffe, D. (1993). Sins of omission and commission in mass communication quantitative research. *Journalism Quarterly, 70,* 126–132.

Lacy, S., & Riffe, D. (1996). Sampling error and selecting intercoder reliability samples for nominal content categories. *Journalism & Mass Communication Quarterly, 73,* 963–973.

Lacy, S., Riffe, D., & Randle, Q. (1998). Sample size in multi-year content analyses of monthly consumer magazines. *Journalism & Mass Communication Quarterly, 75,* 408–417.

Lacy, S., Riffe, D., Stoddard, S., Martin, H., & Chang, K. K. (2000). Sample size for newspaper content analysis in multi-year studies. *Journalism & Mass Communication Quarterly, 78,* 836–845.

Lacy, S., Robinson, K., & Riffe, D. (1995). Sample size in content analysis of weekly newspapers. *Journalism & Mass Communication Quarterly, 72,* 336–345.

Lasswell, H. D. (1927). *Propaganda technique in the World War.* New York: Peter Smith.

Lasswell, H. D., Lerner, D., & de sola Pool, I. (1952). *The comparative study of symbols.* Stanford, CA: Stanford University Press.

Law, C., & Labre, M. P. (2002). Cultural standards of attractiveness: A thirty-year look at changes in male images in magazines. *Journalism & Mass Communication Quarterly, 79,* 697–711.

Lee, S. K., & Hoon, T. H. (1993). Rhetorical vision of men and women managers in Singapore. *Human Relations, 46,* 527–543.

Leslie, M. (1995). Slow fade to ?: Advertising in Ebony Magazine, 1957–1989. *Journalism & Mass Communication Quarterly, 72,* 426–435.

Lester, P., & Smith, R. (1990). African-American photo coverage in *Life, Newsweek,* and *Time,* 1937–1988. *Journalism Quarterly, 67,* 128–136.

Liebler, C. M., & Bendix, J. (1996). Old-growth forest on network news: News sources and the framing of an environmental controversy. *Journalism & Mass Communication Quarterly, 73,* 53–65.

Lombard, M., Snyder-Duch, J., & Bracken, C. C. (2002). Content analysis in mass communication: Assessment and reporting of intercoder reliability. *Human Communication Research, 28,* 587–604.

Lombard, M., Snyder-Duch, J., & Bracken, C. C. (2004). A call for standardization in content analysis reliability. *Human Communication Research, 30,* 434–437.

Lowery, S. A., & DeFleur, M. (1988). *Milestones in mass communication research* (2nd ed.). White Plains, NY: Longman.

Malamuth, N. M., & Spinner, B. (1980). A longitudinal content analysis of sexual violence in the best-selling erotic magazines. *The Journal of Sex Research, 16,* 226–237.

Massey, B. L., & Haas, T. (2002). Does making journalism more public make a difference? A critical review of evaluative research on public journalism. *Journalism & Mass Communication Quarterly, 79,* 559–586.

Matera, F. R., & Salwen, M. B. (1996). Unwieldy question? Circuitous answers? Journalists as panelists in presidential election debates. *Journal of Broadcasting & Electronic Media, 40,* 309–317.

McCombs, M. E. (1972). Mass media in the marketplace. *Journalism Monographs, 24.*

McCombs, M. E., & Shaw, D. L. (1972). The agenda-setting function of mass media. *Public Opinion Quarterly, 36,* 176–187.

McCombs, M. E., & Reynolds, A. (2002). News influence on our pictures of the world. In J. Bryant & D. Zillmann (Eds.), *Media effects: Advances in theory and research* (2nd ed., pp. 1–18). Mahwah, NJ: Lawrence Erlbaum Associates.

McLeod, D. M., Kosicki, G. M., & McLeod, J. M. (2002). Resurveying the boundaries of political communication effects. In J. Bryant & D. Zillmann (Eds.), *Media effects: Advances in theory and research* (2nd ed., pp. 215–267). Mahwah, NJ: Lawrence Erlbaum Associates.

McLeod, D. M., & Tichenor, P. J. (2003). The logic of social and behavioral sciences. In G. H. Stempel III, D. H. Weaver, & G. C. Wilhoit (Eds.), *Mass communication research and theory* (pp. 91–110). Boston, MA: Allyn & Bacon.

McLoughlin, M., & Noe, F. P. (1988). Changing coverage of leisure in *Harper's, Atlantic Monthly,* and *Reader's Digest:* 1960–1985. *Sociology and Social Research, 72,* 224–228.

McMillan, S. J. (2000). The microscope and the moving target: The challenge of applying content analysis to the World Wide Web. *Journalism & Mass Communication Quarterly, 77,* 80–98.

Merrill, J. C. (1965). How *Time* stereotyped three U.S. presidents. *Journalism Quarterly, 42,* 563–570.

Miller, D. C. (1977). *Handbook of research design and social measurement* (3rd ed.). New York: McKay.

Miller, M. M., Andsager, J. L., & Riechert, B. P. (1998). Framing the candidates in presidential primaries: Issues and images in press releases and news coverage. *Journalism & Mass Communication Quarterly, 75,* 312–324.

Mintz, A. (1949). The feasibility of the use of samples in content analysis. In H. D. Lasswell, N. Leites, R. Fadner, J. M. Goldsen, A. Gray, I. L. Janis, A. Kaplan, D. Kaplan, A. Mintz, I. de sola Pool, & S. Yakobson (Eds.), *Language of politics* (pp. 127–152). New York: George W. Stewart, Publishers, Inc.

Moen, M. C. (1990). Ronald Reagan and the social issues: Rhetorical support for the Christian Right. *The Social Science Journal, 27,* 199–207.

Morris, M., & Ogan, C. (1995). Why communication researchers should study the internet: A dialogue. *Journal of Communication, 46*(1), 39–50.

Moser, C. A., & Kalton, G. (1972). *Survey methods in social investigation* (2nd ed.). New York: Basic Books.

Nacos, B. L., Shapiro, R. Y., Young, J. T., Fan, D. P., Kjellstrand, T., & McCaa, C. (1991). Content analysis of news reports: Comparing human coding and a computer-assisted method. *Communication, 12,* 111–128.

Neuzil, M. (1994). Gambling with databases: A comparison of electronic searches and printed indices. *Newspaper Research Journal, 15*(1), 44–54.

Ngo, C., Pong, T., & Zhang, H. (2001). Recent advances in content-based video analysis. *International Journal of Images and Graphics, 1,* 445–468.

Niven, D. (2003). Objective evidence of media bias: Newspaper coverage of congressional party switchers. *Journalism & Mass Communication Quarterly, 80,* 311–326.

O'Dell, J. W., & Weideman, D. (1993). Computer content analysis of the Schreber case. *Journal of Clinical Psychology, 49,* 120–125.

Oliver, M. B. (2002). Individual differences in media effects. In J. Bryant & D. Zillmann (Eds.), *Media effects: Advances in theory and research* (2nd ed., pp. 507–524). Mahwah, NJ: Lawrence Erlbaum Associates.

Olson, B. (1994). Sex and soap operas: A comparative content analysis of health issues. *Journalism Quarterly, 71,* 840–850.

Osgood, C. E., Suci, G. J., & Tannenbaum, P. H. (1957). *The measurement of meaning.* Urbana: University of Illinois Press.

Osgood, C. E., & Walker, E. G. (1959). Motivation and language behavior: Content analysis of suicide notes. *Journal of Abnormal Social Psychology, 59,* 58–67.

Oxford University. (1979). Newton, Isaac. In *The Oxford Dictionary of Quotations* (3rd ed., p. 362). New York: Oxford University Press.

Papacharissi, Z. (2002). The presentation of self in virtual life: Characteristics of personal home pages. *Journalism & Mass Communication Quarterly, 79,* 643–660.

Paul, M. J. (2001). Interactive disaster communication on the Internet: A content analysis of sixty-four disaster relief home pages. *Journalism & Mass Communication Quarterly, 78,* 739–753.

Perse, E. M., & Rubin, A. M. (1988). Audience activity and satisfaction with favorite television soap opera. *Journalism Quarterly, 65,* 368–375.

Peter, J., & Lauf, E. (2002). Reliability in cross-national content analysis. *Journalism & Mass Communication Quarterly, 79,* 815–832.

Peterzell, J. (1982, July/August). The government shuts up. *Columbia Journalism Review, 21,* 31–37.

Pfau, M., Haigh, M., Gettle, M., Donnelly, M., Scott, G., Warr, D., & Wittenberg, E. (2004). Embedding journalists in military combat units: Impact on newspaper story frames and tone. *Journalism & Mass Communication Quarterly, 81,* 74–88.

Potter, W. J., Vaughan, M. W., Warren, R., & Howley, K. (1995). How real is the portrayal of aggression in television entertainment programming? *Journal of Broadcasting & Electronic Media, 39,* 496–516.

Pratt, C. A., & Pratt, C. B. (1995). Comparative content analysis of food and nutrition advertisements in *Ebony, Essence,* and *Ladies' Home Journal. Journal of Nutrition Education, 27,* 11–18.

Project for Excellence in Journalism. (2002). *Local TV news project.* Retrieved August 15, 2004, from http://www.journalism.org/rsources/research/reports/localTV/default.asp

228

REFERENCES

Ragsdale, L., & Cook, T. E. (1987). Representatives' actions and challengers' reactions: Limits to candidate connections in the House. *American Journal of Political Science, 31,* 45–81.

Ramaprasad, J. (1993). Content, geography, concentration and consonance in foreign news coverage of ABC, NBC and CBS. *International Communication Bulletin, 28,* 10–14.

Rapoport, A. (1969). A system-theoretic view of content analysis. In G. Gerbner, O. Holsti, K. Krippendorff, W. J. Paisley, & P. J. Stone (Eds.), *The analysis of communication content* (pp. 17–38). New York: Wiley.

Reese, S. D., Gandy, O. H., Jr., & Grant, A. E. (Eds.). (2001). *Framing public life: Understanding of the social world.* Mahwah, NJ: Lawrence Erlbaum Associates.

Reid, L. N., King, K. W., & Kreshel, P. J. (1994). Black and white models and their activities in modern cigarette and alcohol ads. *Journalism Quarterly, 71,* 873–886.

Reynolds, A., & Barnett, B. (2003). This just in … How national TV news handled the breaking "live" coverage of September 11. *Journalism & Mass Communication Quarterly, 80,* 689–703.

Reynolds, P. D. (1971). *A primer in theory construction.* Indianapolis, IN: Bobbs-Merrill.

Riffe, D. (1984). International news borrowing: A trend analysis. *Journalism Quarterly, 61,* 142–148.

Riffe, D. (1991). A case study of the effect of expulsion of U.S. correspondents on *New York Times'* coverage of Iran during the hostage crisis. *International Communication Bulletin, 26,* 1–2, 11–15.

Riffe, D. (2003). Data analysis and SPSS programs for basic statistics. In G. H. Stempel III, D. H. Weaver, & G. C. Wilhoit (Eds.), *Mass communication research and theory* (pp. 182–208). Boston: Allyn & Bacon.

Riffe, D., Aust, C. F., & Lacy, S. R. (1993). The effectiveness of random, consecutive day and constructed week samples in newspaper content analysis. *Journalism Quarterly, 70,* 133–139.

Riffe, D., Ellis, B., Rogers, M. K., Ommeren, R. L., & Woodman, K. A. (1986). Gatekeeping and the network news mix. *Journalism Quarterly, 63,* 315–321.

Riffe, D., & Freitag, A. (1997). A content analysis of content analyses: 25 years of *Journalism Quarterly. Journalism & Mass Communication Quarterly, 74,* 873–882.

Riffe, D., Goldson, H., Saxton, K., & Yu, Y. (1989). Females and minorities in children's Saturday morning television commercials: 1987. *Journalism Quarterly, 66,* 129–136.

Riffe, D., Hedgepeth, J. K., & Ziesenis, E. B. (1992). The influence of journals on curriculum and instruction. *Journalism Educator, 47*(3), 54–60.

Riffe, D., & Johnson, G. (1995, August). *Unnamed sources in White House coverage.* Paper presented at the annual convention, Association for Education in Journalism and Mass Communication, Washington, DC.

Riffe, D., Lacy, S., & Drager, M. (1996). Sample size in content analysis of weekly news magazines. *Journalism & Mass Communication Quarterly, 73,* 635–644.

Riffe, D., Lacy, S., Nagovan, J., & Burkum, L. (1996). The effectiveness of simple random and stratified random sampling in broadcast news content analysis. *Journalism & Mass Communication Quarterly, 73,* 159–168.

Riffe, D., Place, P., & Mayo, C. (1993). Game time, soap time, and prime time TV ads: Treatment of women in Sunday and rest-of-week commercials. *Journalism Quarterly, 70,* 437–446.

Riffe, D., & Shaw, E. F. (1982). Conflict and consonance: Coverage of the third world in two U.S. papers. *Journalism Quarterly, 59,* 617–626.

Rowntree, D. (1981). *Statistics without tears: A primer for non-mathematicians.* New York: Scribner's.

Sapolsky, B. S., Molitor, F., & Luque, S. (2003). Sex and violence in slasher movies: Re-examining the assumptions. *Journalism & Mass Communication Quarterly, 8,* 28–38.

Schnurr, P. P., Rosenberg, S. D., & Oxman, T. E. (1992). Comparison of TAT and free speech techniques for eliciting source material in computerized content analysis. *Journal of Personality Assessment, 58,* 311–325.

Schreber, D. (1955). *Memoirs of my nervous illness.* I. Macalpine & R. Hunter (Trans.). London: W. Dawson & Sons. (Original work published 1903)

Schutz, W. C. (1952). Reliability, ambiguity and content analysis. *Psychological Review, 59,* 119–129.

Schweitzer, J. C. (1988). Research article productivity by mass communication scholars. *Journalism Quarterly, 65,* 479–484.

Scott, W. A. (1955). Reliability of content analysis: The case of nominal scale coding. *Public Opinion Quarterly, 19,* 321–325.

Scott, D. K., & Gobetz, R. H. (1992). Hard news/soft news content of national broadcast networks. *Journalism Quarterly, 69,* 406–412.

Severin, W. J., & Tankard, J. W., Jr. (1992). *Communication theories: Origins, methods, and uses in the mass media* (3rd ed.). White Plains, NY: Longman.

Shils, E. A., & Janowitz, M. (1948). Cohesion and disintegration in the Wehrmacht in World War II. *Public Opinion Quarterly, 12,* 300–306, 308–315.

Shimanoff, S. (1985). Expressing emotions in words: Verbal patterns of interaction. *Journal of Communication, 35*(3), 16–31.

Shoemaker, P. J., & Reese, S. D. (1990). Exposure to what? Integrating media content and effects studies. *Journalism Quarterly, 67,* 649–652.

Shoemaker, P. J, & Reese, S. D. (1996). *Mediating the message: Theories of influence on mass media content* (2nd ed.). White Plains, NY: Longman.

Silver, D. (1986). A comparison of coverage of male and female officials in Michigan. *Journalism Quarterly, 63,* 144–149.

Simmons, B., & Lowry, D. (1990). Terrorists in the news, as reflected in three news magazines, 1980–1988. *Journalism Quarterly, 67,* 692–696.

Simon, T. F., Fico, F., & Lacy, S. (1989). Covering conflict and controversy: Measuring balance, fairness and defamation in local news stories. *Journalism Quarterly, 66,* 427–434.

Simonton, D. K. (1990). Lexical choices and aesthetic success: A computer content analysis of 154 Shakespeare sonnets. *Computers and the Humanities, 24,* 251–265.

Simonton, D. K. (1994). Computer content analysis of melodic structure: Classical composers and their compositions. *Psychology of Music, 22,* 31–43.

Slattery, K. L., & Hakanen, E. A. (1994). Sensationalism versus public affairs content of local TV news: Pennsylvania revisited. *Journal of Broadcasting & Electronic Media, 38,* 205–216.

Stamm, K. R. (2003). Measurement decisions. In G. H. Stempel III, D. H. Weaver, & G. C. Wilhoit (Eds.), *Mass communication research and theory* (pp. 129–146). Boston: Allyn & Bacon.

Stavitsky, A. G., & Gleason, T. W. (1994). Alternative things considered: A comparison of National Public radio and Pacifica Radio news coverage. *Journalism Quarterly, 71,* 775–786.

Stegner, W. (1949). The radio priest and his flock. In I. Leighton (Ed.), *The aspirin age: 1919–1941* (pp. 232–257). New York: Simon & Schuster.

Stempel, G. H., III. (1952). Sample size for classifying subject matter in dailies. *Journalism Quarterly, 29,* 333–334.

Stempel, G. H., III. (1985). Gatekeeping: The mix of topics and the selection of stories. *Journalism Quarterly, 62,* 791–796, 815.

Stempel, G. H., III. (2003). Content analysis. In G. H. Stempel III, D. H. Weaver, & G. C. Wilhoit (Eds.), *Mass communication research and theory* (pp. 209–219). Boston: Allyn & Bacon.

Stempel, G. H., III, & Stewart, R. K. (2000). The Internet provides both opportunities and challenges for mass communication researchers. *Journalism & Mass Communication Quarterly, 77,* 541–548.

Stone, D. B. (1993). Faculty hiring: Diversity trends in AEJMC News ads. *Mass Communication Review, 20,* 192–201.

Stone, P. J., Dunphy, D. C., Smith, M. S., & Ogilvie, D. M. (1966). *The General Inquirer: A computer approach to content analysis in the behavioral sciences.* Cambridge, MA: MIT Press.

Stouffer, S. A. (1977). Some observations on study design. In D. C. Miller (Ed.), *Handbook of research design and social measurement* (3rd ed., pp. 27–31). New York: McKay.

Strodthoff, G. G., Hawkins, R. P., & Schoenfeld, A. C. (1985). Media roles in a social movement. *Journal of Communication, 35*(2), 134–153.

Sumpter, R. S., & Braddock, M. A. (2002). Source use in a "news disaster" account: A content analysis of voter news service stories. *Journalism & Mass Communication Quarterly, 79,* 539–558.

Svensen, S., & White, K. (1995). A content analysis of horoscopes. *Genetic, Social and General Psychology Monographs, 121*(1), 7–23.

Tabachnick, B. G., & Fidell, L. S. (1996). *Using multivariate statistics* (3rd ed.). New York: HarperCollins.

Tankard, J. (2001). The empirical approach to the study of framing. In S. D. Reese, O. H. Gandy, & A. E. Grant (Eds.), *Framing public life: Perspectives on media and our understanding of the social world* (pp. 95–106). Mahwah, NJ: Lawrence Erlbaum Associates.

Tankard, J. W., Jr., Hendrickson, L. J., & Lee, D. G. (1994, August). *Using Lexis/Nexis and other databases for content analysis: Opportunities and risk.* Paper presented to the annual convention of the Association for Education in Journalism and Mass Communication, Atlanta, GA.

Thorson, E. (1989). Television commercials as mass media messages. In J. Bradac (Ed.), *Message effects in communication science* (pp. 195–230). Newbury Park, CA: Sage.

Tichenor, P. (1981). The logic of social and behavioral science. In G. H. Stempel III & B. H. Westley (Eds.), *Research methods in mass communication* (pp. 10–28). Englewood Cliffs, NJ: Prentice Hall.

Tomasello, T. (2001). The status of Internet-based research in five leading communication journals, 1994–1999. *Journalism & Mass Communication Quarterly, 78,* 659–674.

Tremayne, M. (2004). The Web of context: Applying network theory to use of hyperlinks in journalism on the Web. *Journalism & Mass Communication Quarterly, 81,* 237–253.

Trumbo, C. (2004). Research methods in mass communication research: A census of eight journals 1990–2000. *Journalism & Mass Communication Quarterly, 81,* 417–436.

Vincent, R. C., Davis, D. K., & Boruszkowski, L. A. (1987). Sexism on MTV: The portrayal of women in rock videos. *Journalism Quarterly, 64,* 750–755, 941.

Vogt, W. P. (1999). *Dictionary of statistics & methodology: A nontechnical guide for the social sciences* (2nd ed.). Thousand Oaks, CA: Sage.

Wanta, W., Golan, G., & Lee, C. (2004). Agenda setting and international news: Media influence on public perceptions of foreign nations. *Journalism & Mass Communication Quarterly, 81,* 364–377.

Washburn, P. C. (1995). Top of the hour newscast and public interest. *Journal of Broadcasting & Electronic Media, 39,* 73–91.

Weaver, D. H. (2003). Basic statistical tools. In G. H. Stempel III, D. H. Weaver, & G. C. Wilhoit (Eds.), *Mass communication research and theory* (pp. 147–181). Boston: Allyn & Bacon.

Weaver, J. B., Porter, C. J., & Evans, M. E. (1984). Patterns of foreign news coverage on U.S. network TV: A 10-year analysis. *Journalism Quarterly, 61,* 356–363.

Weber, R. P. (1984). Computer-aided content analysis: A short primer. *Qualitative Sociology, 7,* 126–147.

Weber, R. P. (1990). *Basic content analysis* (2nd ed.). Newbury Park, CA: Sage.

Weiss, A. J., & Wilson, B. J. (1996). Emotional portrayals in family television series that are popular among children. *Journal of Broadcasting & Electronic Media, 40,* 1–29.

Wells, R. A., & King, E. G. (1994). Prestige newspaper coverage of foreign affairs in the 1990 congressional campaign. *Journalism Quarterly, 71,* 652–664.

Westley, B. H., Higbie, C. E., Burke, T., Lippert, D. J., Maurer, L., & Stone, V. A. (1963). The news magazines and the 1960 convention. *Journalism Quarterly, 40,* 525–531, 647.

Westley, B. H., & MacLean, M. S., Jr. (1957). A conceptual model for communication research. *Journalism Quarterly, 34,* 31–38.

Whaples, R. (1991). A quantitative history of *The Journal of Economic History* and the cliometric revolution. *The Journal of Economic History, 51,* 289–301.

Whitney, D. C. (1981). Information overload in the newsroom. *Journalism Quarterly, 58,* 69–76, 161.

Wicks, R. H., & Souley, B. (2003). Going negative: Candidate usage of Internet Web sites during the 2000 presidential campaign. *Journalism & Mass Communication Quarterly, 80,* 128–144.

Wimmer, R. D., & Dominick, J. R. (1991). *Mass media research: An introduction* (3rd ed.). Belmont, CA: Wadsworth.

Wimmer, R. D., & Dominick, J. R. (1997). *Mass media research: An introduction* (5th ed.). Belmont, CA: Wadsworth.

Wimmer, R. D., & Dominick, J. R. (2003). *Mass media research: An introduction* (7th ed.). Belmont, CA: Wadsworth.

Windhauser, J. W., & Stempel, G. H., III. (1979). Reliability of six techniques for content analysis of local coverage. *Journalism Quarterly, 56,* 148–152.

Winfield, B. H., & Friedman, B. (2003). Gender politics: News coverage of the candidates' wives in campaign 2000. *Journalism & Mass Communication Quarterly, 80,* 548–566.

Wrightsman, L. S. (1981). Personal documents as data in conceptualizing adult personality development. *Personality and Social Psychology Bulletin, 7,* 367–385.

Yu, Y., & Riffe, D. (1989). Chiang and Mao in U.S. newsmagazines. *Journalism Quarterly, 66,* 913–919.

Zakaluk, B. L., & Samuels, S. J. (Eds.). (1988). *Readability: Its past, present, and future.* Newark, DE: International Reading Association.

Zillmann, D. (2002). Exemplification theory of media influence. In J. Bryant & D. Zillmann (Eds.), *Media effects: Advances in theory and research* (2nd ed., pp. 19–41). Mahwah, NJ. Lawrence Erlbaum Associates.

Zullow, H. M., Oettingen, G., Peterson, C., & Seligman, M. E. P. (1988). Pessimistic explanatory style in the historical record: CAVing LBJ, presidential candidates, and East versus West Berlin. *The American Psychologist, 43,* 673–682.

# Author Index

# Subject Index